2024 교원임용시험 전공영어 대비

Build Up *New*

박현수 영어교육론 Ⅳ 문제은행

박현수·송은우 공저

박문각 임용 동영상강의 www.pmg.co.kr

Guideline for Pre-service Teachers

토픽별 문항정리
임용시험 최적화 훈련

박문각

친애하는 예비 교사 여러분, 여러분을 열렬히 응원하는 박현수입니다.

Build-up IV의 시작에서 제가 삶에서 중요한 지표로 삼고 있는 글귀를 나누고자 합니다. 다음의 글귀는 제가 가고자 하는 길에서 저에게 무한한 용기와 인내를 갖게 해주는 마법의 한마디입니다. 그 마법이 여러분에게도, 여러분의 삶에도 녹아내리기 바랍니다.

좋은 마침이 있어야 새로운 시작이 있습니다.
There have to be good endings for there to be new beginnings.

늘 우리는 새로운 시작을 꿈꿉니다. 하지만 우리가 꿈꾸는 새로운 시작은 지금 여러분이 서 있는 그 자리에 좋은 마침이 있어야 가능합니다. 좋은 마침을 위해 여러분은 오늘도 당당하게 자신을 마주하며 또박또박 하루 속으로 걸어가시기 바랍니다. 좋은 하루의 마침은 또 다른 좋은 하루의 시작으로 이어져 여러분의 꿈으로 열릴 것입니다.

너무 힘들어 여기까지인가 그만 등 돌리고 싶을 때, 힘든 게 아니라 간절하지 않은 것입니다.
When I feel that's enough, it's not too hard, and want to turn back, it' not that it's hard, it's that I'm not in earnest.

끝날 것 같지 않은 임용을 준비하면서 이미 여러분 중 누군가는 겪었을 테고, 어느 누군가는 겪고 있을 테고, 다른 누군가는 겪을 슬럼프라는 늪에서 여러분이 가고자 하는 그 길에 대한 간절함을 생각해 보십시오.

그 간절함이 끝없어 보이는 그 슬럼프로부터 여러분을 구할 것입니다. 우리는 사실 삶의 최종 목적지에서 지금을 바라본다면 현재의 고통과 어려움은 신비한 계획 속의 어느 지점을 통과하고 있는 것인지 모릅니다. 또한, 여러분이 겪는 현재의 고통과 어려움은 여러분의 뿌리 속 자양분이 되어 훗날 제자들 앞에서 보다 당당한 모습의 여러분을 만들어 줄 것이며, 지혜가 가득한 성숙한 어른의 모습으로, 그들의 신뢰가 가득한 멘토로, 그 자체가 될 것이라 자신합니다.

여러분이 지금 지나는 이 길을 좀 더 당당하고 기쁘게 마주하실 수 있도록, 그리고 여러분의 간절한 꿈을 반드시 지켜내실 수 있도록 오늘도 여러분과 함께 합니다.

2023년 또 다른 달, 7월
박현수

안녕하세요. 임용고시 수험생 여러분 송은우입니다.
벌써 여름입니다~! 상반기 기본 강의가 모두 끝나고 곧 문제 풀이 강의가 시작되네요.

시험까지 이제 겨우 4~5개월 남았다니 떨리기도 하고 아쉽기도 하고 여러분의 마음이 복잡할 거라고 생각됩니다. 저 역시 금방 다가올 2024년도 임용시험을 생각하니 마음이 두근거립니다. 그런 복잡한 마음을 잊기에 딱 좋은 강의가 바로 "문제 풀이" 강의입니다. :) 상반기에 공부한 내용을 머릿속으로 정리하며 하루하루 바쁘게 문제를 풀다 보면 어느새 8월이 다 가고 9월 실전 모의고사가 시작되기 때문입니다. 그렇다면 우리가 문제 풀이 강의에서 목표로 해야 할 것은 무엇일까요? 많은 문제를 풀면서 임용 문항에 익숙해지는 것? 상반기에 놓치고 학습하지 못한 개념을 다시 정립하는 것? 답안 쓰는 연습을 하는 것? 정답은 여러분 개인마다 목표가 다를 수 있다는 것입니다. 상반기 공부의 완성도에 따라 각자에게 적합한 목표는 다를 것입니다. 나에게 맞는 목표를 설정하고 반드시 성취하여 9월 실전 모의고사를 탄탄히 준비하시기를 바랍니다.

올해 빌드업 4는 기출 수준 혹은 그 이상의 난이도를 가진 문제들로 구성하였습니다. 긴 지문이 부담스럽지만 의외로 해설이 간단한 문항, 지문은 짧지만 깊이 있는 답안을 요구하는 문항, 답안에 포함해야 할 정보가 많은 까다로운 문항, 기본 이론의 이해를 확인하는 문항 등 다양한 문항을 수록하여 초수부터 재수, 삼수 이상의 학생들까지 모두에게 충분한 challenge가 되도록 구성하였습니다. 다양한 문항을 접해보면서 여러분 각자가 가지고 있는 strong points & weak points를 찾아보시기 바랍니다. 내가 더 잘하는 부분을 통해서 자신감을 얻고 수정 · 보완해야 할 부분을 찾아서 빠르게 고쳐나감으로써 합격에 한 걸음 더 가까워지시기 바랍니다.

8월 문제 풀이 강의는 여러분의 예습 정도에 따라 쉽고 재미있는 강의가 될 수도 있고 어렵고 좌절감이 밀려오는 강의가 될 수도 있습니다. 그래서!!! 강의 전 여러분들에게 부탁드릴 것이 있습니다. 5~6월 기출문제 풀이 때와 마찬가지로 각 문항을 가장 적합한 전략을 기반으로 미리 풀어보자는 것입니다. 한 문항을 10분 이상 작성하는 것은 문제 풀이 수업에 매우 부적절한 전략입니다. 해당 문항을 빠르고 정확하게 파악하기 위한 전략은 무엇일지 먼저 생각한 후 문제를 풀고 답안을 작성해 보시기 바랍니다. 그리고 강의를 들으면서 저와 함께 각 문항을 푸는 데 가장 좋은 전략은 무엇일지, 내가 작성한 답안에서 보완할 점은 무엇일지, 주어진 data 안에서 유의미한 부분은 어디인지 함께 확인하는 시간을 갖도록 하겠습니다.

여러분과 더 유익하고 알찬 강의로 만나게 될 생각을 하니 8월이 굉장히 기다려집니다. 여러분도 부디 열정과 에너지를 가득 갖고 수업에 오시기를 바라면서 여러분을 위한 한 문장을 남기고 마무리하겠습니다.

A little more persistence, a little more effort, and what seemed hopeless failure may turn to glorious success.

영어교육론
송은우

2023학년도 기출분석 및 2024학년도 대비 영어교육론 시험 전략

2023년 대비 중등 임용시험에서 영어교육론은 2022년 중등 임용시험보다 1문항이 더 출제되어 11문항 (총 23문항 총 40점)으로, 역대 최대 출제 영역이 되었다. 이것은 중등 임용시험의 정체성에 따라 영어교 사의 필수 자질인 how to teach에 대한 자필평가의 중요성이 반영된 것으로 판단된다. 전체적인 출제 항 목을 보면 2022년 개정 교육과정의 주요 개념들이 반영되어 보다 생동감 있고 학생 중심의 수업으로 진행하기 위한 교사의 역량 강화가 가장 큰 특징으로 분석된다. 따라서 각 출제 항목 안에서 교사의 역량 에 따른 학생들의 자율성이 극대화되는 실제적인 교실 수업 data가 주를 이루고 있으며, 또한 디지털 리터러시 역량을 키우고자 하는 교실 수업 방향에 맞춰 교실 내 수업활동 뿐 아니라 평가에 적용하는 사례로 computerized adaptive testing이 출제되었다.

― A형 문항 유형

A형 문항들의 출제 항목을 중심으로 살펴보자면, 기입형으로 언어 습득 과정(U-shaped learning) 중 교 실 수업에서 흔히 보이는 과잉일반화 오류에 대한 현상으로 backsliding과 대규모의 교실 수업에서 학생 개개인에 맞춰 평가를 진행할 수 있는 computerized adaptive testing 등 2문항이 출제되었다. 서술형 으로는 textbook adaptation의 사례와 group work에서 개인의 역할 및 reading comprehension을 보 다 효과적으로 이해하는 도구인 graphic organizer에 대한 문항, 학생들의 언어 발달 상황에 따른 학습 자 언어의 구체적 특징에 관한 문항, 그리고 문화 지도와 병행된 언어 지도에 대한 원리 및 분석 등 총 6 문항이 출제되었다.

― B형 문항 유형

B형의 문항들을 분석해보자면, 교실 지도에서 교사의 역량 강화 및 학습자 중심 수업과 관련된 내용이 문항의 공통적인 특징이며, 그 예로 기입형 1문항으로 action research, 서술형 문항으로 classroom observation(reflective teaching)와 사지선다형 문제 개발과 관련된 문항 등 2문항이 교사의 역량 강 화를 위한 문항으로 출제되었으며, 학습 과정 및 평가에 관련된 서술형 문항들로는 writing 첨삭으로 content와 organization에 대한 1문항, 어휘 지도에서 concordancer를 사용하여 진행되는 수업 과정 1문항이 출제되어 총 5문항이 출제되었다.

― 2024학년도 대비 중등 임용 영어교육론의 방향

A형과 B형의 문항 유형에서 살펴봤듯이, 2023년 기출은 현재 진행되는 교실 수업 방향을 가늠할 수 있는 주요 교육론 개념들을 실제 교실 지도와 연결하여 구체적이고 다각적인 임용 지원자들의 how to teach에 대한 역량을 간접적으로 측정하기 위한 의도가 명확히 보인다. 따라서, 2024년 중등 임용의 방향 역시 현 재 진행되는 교실 지도 중심으로 national curriculum의 개정인 2022년 개정 교육과정의 주요 과제에 따른 교실 지도에 대한 whole picture를 그려보고 그 안에서의 주요 교육론 개념들에 대한 정리가 반드시 이루어져야 할 것이다.

2023학년도 기출 전공A 기입형 ❶

Read the conversation and follow the directions. [2 points]

(Ms. Kim, a new teacher, and Mr. Song, a head teacher, are discussing Ms. Kim's concerns about her student's writing performance.)

T1: Ms. Kim, did the process-oriented evaluation in your writing class go well this semester?
T2: I'm still making comments to students, but there is something I'm worried about.
T1: What is it?
T2: I'm afraid that one of my students is making more errors now than he was at the beginning of the semester.
T1: He got worse as the semester went on?
T2: Yes. He turned in the writing assignment. However, there were so many errors in his writing.
T1: What kinds of errors?
T2: Unlike the beginning of the semester, now he has problems with irregular verbs.
T1: Can you give me an example?
T2: When the semester began, he wrote words like "drank," "wore," and "heard" without errors. Now I am seeing errors like "drinked," "weared," and "heared." He is suddenly treating irregular verbs like regular verbs.
T1: Hmm. Now that I think about it, he is probably progressing!
T2: What are you talking about?
T1: Well, according to U-shaped course of development, he is starting to understand the rules of the past tense.
T2: Oh, I see.

Note: T1 = Mr. Song, T2 = Ms. Kim

Fill in the blank with the ONE most appropriate word.

In the above conversation, Ms. Kim's student seems to regress, making errors with irregular verbs that he used to use correctly, due to overgeneralization. This phenomenon is commonly called _____, in which the learner seems to have grasped a rule or principle but then moves from a correct form to an incorrect form.

모범답안 Backsliding

2023학년도 기출 전공A 기입형 ❹

Read the passage and follow the directions. [2 points]

A test taker is sitting in front of a computer, examining some sample items, and quickly learns how to take computer-based tests. Meanwhile, a computer program begins to 'guess' his ability level, and keeps trying to 'match' the test with his current language ability. This is how this technique works.

The computer program usually begins by showing an item of moderate difficulty, for example, an item that the test taker has a fifty percent chance of getting right. If he gets this item right, the computer program reestimates his ability level in real time and shows either an item of equal difficulty or a slightly more challenging item. If the test taker gets his first item wrong, however, the computer program will show either an item of equal or slightly lesser difficulty. The test taker keeps taking the test until, for instance, he gets several items wrong in a row. To put it another way, the computer program repeats its matching work until it collects enough information to determine the test taker's current English ability level.

Fill in the blank with the THREE most appropriate word.

> The testing procedure described above enables us to make more individualized and educationally useful tests. It can also provide test takers with a better test-taking experience with fewer items, and with increased precision. This testing procedure is commonly referred to as _____.

모범답안 computer adaptive testing / computerized adaptive testing

---

2023학년도 기출 전공A 서술형 ❽

Read the passages in <A> and <B>, and follow the directions. [4 points]

A

> There are always sound reasons for adapting materials in order to make them as accessible and useful to learners as possible. When adapting materials, having clear objectives is a necessary starting point. The objectives a teacher may hope to achieve by adapting classroom materials can be listed as follows:
>
> - To cater to learners' language proficiency levels: The teacher can modify the difficulty of language features such as grammar and vocabulary in the materials.
> - To reinforce learner autonomy: Through materials adaptation, the teacher can give students opportunities to focus on their own learning processes to become more independent learners.
> - To enhance higher-level cognitive skills: The teacher can adapt materials in such a way as to require students to hypothesize, predict, or infer.
> - To encourage learners to tap into their own lives: Through materials adaptation, the teacher can increase the relevance of the contents or activities in relation to the students' experiences.

B

> Ms. Lee is teaching first-year high school students, and she is preparing for her English reading class next semester. Based on the results of a needs analysis, she has decided to adapt two chapters of the textbook materials to meet her students' needs. For Lesson 2, which is about career paths, she will use magazine pictures of various jobs like engineer, baker, and fashion designer, along with some pictures related to jobs in the textbook. She will use these pictures as a springboard to get students in groups to share their dream jobs. She thinks this adaptation will help students think about more varied jobs in the real world. For Lesson 5, there is a reading passage about Simon's adventure in Kenya in the textbook. However, she worries that there are only simple activities to check students' understanding of the story. So, she will edit the story, intentionally deleting a few sentences at the end. This will challenge the students to think about the story's structure and look ahead to possible endings, using the storyline.

Based on <A>, identify the ONE objective that Ms. Lee wants to achieve through adaptation in Lesson 2 and the ONE objective in Lesson 5. Then, explain your answers with evidence from <A> and <B>.

모범답안 Lesson 2 encourages learners to tap into their own lives while Lesson 5 enhances higher-level cognitive skills. The former leads students to share their dream jobs based on magazine pictures of real-world jobs for the relevance of content related to students' experiences. The latter challenges students to predict or infer the intentionally deleted endings of a story.

2023학년도 기출 | **전공A 서술형 9**

Read the worksheet in <A> and the class observation note in <B>, and follow the directions. [4 points]

A

Worksheet

Family History

Group Name: _____
Student Number & Name: _____

Role	Assignment	Student Assigned
Discussion Leader	Keeping the conversation going if it falters	
Passage Chooser	Choosing three passages that are important to the story to discuss	
Word Master	Showing the meanings of new words	
Grammar Checker	Using syntactic clues to interpret the meanings of sentences	
Story Summarizer	Summing up the story briefly	
Online Manager	Posting the activity outcome to the web or social network service	

- **Before Reading**
Can you guess who will mention the following statements? Match the pictures of the characters in the story with their corresponding statements.

· **While Reading**

Based on the text about the Brown and the Garcia families, complete the following figure.

Family History

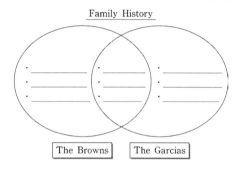

The Browns   The Garcias

· **After Reading**

What do you think about the characters in the story? Complete the sentences.

1. I feel sorry for _____ because _____.
2. I think _____ is a nice person, but _____.

B

Mr. Han's Class Observation Note

2. How did the teacher use teaching aids?	I set up a Reader's Club using a metaverse platform. While doing the reading activity in an online environment, each student took a specific role. I checked students' comprehension of the passage using the worksheet.
3. Did all the students participate actively?	The students looked absorbed in reading the three paragraphs of the text. After the reading activity, they actively participated in the discussion, carrying out their assigned roles. S1 managed the discussion and controlled each student's speaking time. S2 used an online dictionary when one student asked the meaning of a word, 'crane', and shared a picture of a crane with its meaning. S3 selected one linguistically complex sentence and explained its structure to the other students. S4 uploaded the summary that S5 wrote to the cloud and posted it on the class blog. Lastly, S6 selected another three paragraphs that they would read in the next class.
4. Did the students use suitable reading strategies?	During the discussion, students used various reading strategies such as activating schema, allocating attention, previewing, skimming, scanning, and criticizing. My students were pretty good at making guesses based on the pictures. I also noticed that using a graphic organizer helped students comprehend the story. By comparing and contrasting the two families, they extracted information from the text. My students understood the text very well based on the figure.

Note: S = student

Identify the role that S2 performed in the group activity with the TWO most appropriate words from <A>, and identify the tool that Mr. Han used at the 'While Reading' stage in <A> with the TWO most appropriate words from <B>. Then, explain your answers, respectively, with evidence from <A> and <B>. Do NOT copy more than FOUR consecutive words from <A> and <B>.

모범답안 As a group role, S2 performs a word master who shows the meaning of the new word 'crane' with its picture. In the 'While Reading' stage, Mr. Han uses a graphic organizer in which students complete the figure by comparing/contrasting the extracted information about the two families.

2023학년도 기출 전공A 서술형 ⑩

Read the passage in <A> and the conversation in <B>, and follow the directions. [4 points]

A

Second language learners pass through a predictable sequence of development. Since the early 1990's, some research has investigated the acquisition of pragmatic abilities in the L2. 'Requesting' is one of the pragmatic features that has received attention. In a review of studies on the acquisition of requests in English, six stages of development were suggested.

Stage	Characteristics	Example
1	Using body language or gestures	*Sir (pointing to the pencil). Teacher (holding the paper).*
2	Using verbless expressions	*A paper. / More time.*
3	Using imperative verbs	*Give me. / Give me a paper.*
4	Using 'Can I have _____?' as a formulaic expression	*Can I have some candy?*
5	Using 'can' with a range of verbs, not just with 'have'	*Can you pass me the book?*
6	Using indirect requests	*I want more cookies.*

B

(Students are doing a problem-solving task in groups. S1 plays the role of moderator in the activity.)

S1: We have to find some ways to make the environment more sustainable. Suhee, what's your opinion?
S2: I'm sorry, but nothing comes to mind now. I need more time to think.
S1: Okay. Tell us if you're ready. Minho, how about you? Can you share your ideas with us?
S3: We should use one-time products as less as possible.
S1: Hold on, Minho. What does 'one-time products' mean? Can I have some examples?
S3: Well, paper cups, plastic bags...
S2: Ah, I see. You mean 'disposable products', right?
S3: Yes.
S1: Minho, I like your idea.
S2: I'm ready. Driving electronic cars reduces air pollution.
S3: Sounds great.

S1: Now I think we have enough opinions for the presentation. Suhee, can you speak for us in the presentation session?
S2: I'm afraid not. Minho can do better than me.
S3: Umm. Okay. I'll take the speaker role. I'll do my best.
S2: Thanks, Minho. I'll write the presentation script for you.
S1: Wow, thank you.

Note: S = student

Based on <A>, identify the developmental stages where S1 and S2 are, respectively. Then, explain your answers with evidence from <B>.

모범답안 While S1 belongs to Stage 5, S2 is in Stage 6 as the developmental stage. S1 uses 'can' with various verbs such as 'share' or 'speak' for requests. On the other hand, S2 uses indirect requests like "I need more time to think". (or "Minho can do better than me.").

2023학년도 기출 전공A 서술형 ⑫

Read the passage in <A> and the lesson plan in <B>, and follow the directions. [4 points]

A

In designing activities for cultural instruction, it is important to consider the purpose of the activity, as well as its usefulness for teaching language and culture in an integrative fashion. The most basic issue in cross-cultural education is increasing the degree to which language and culture are integrated. Several suggestions for dealing with this issue are as follows:

1. Use cultural information when teaching vocabulary. Teach students about the cultural connotations of new words.
2. Present cultural topics in conjunction with closely related grammatical features whenever possible. Use cultural contexts for language-practice activities, including those that focus on particular grammatical forms.
3. Make good use of textbook illustrations or photos. Use probing questions to help students describe the cultural features of the illustrations or photos.
4. In group activities, use communication techniques for cultural instruction, such as discussions and role-plays.
5. Teach culture while involving the integration of the four language skills. Do not limit cultural instruction to lecture or anecdotal formats..

B

Lesson 4. World-famous Holidays	
Objectives	Students will be able to 1. introduce world-famous holidays using –er *than* and 2. perform activities related to the holidays to deepen their understanding of diverse cultures.

Development	Step 1	• T asks Ss to speak out about anything related to the pictures in the textbook on p. 78. • T asks Ss some questions to elicit their ideas about what cultural features they see in the pictures of world-famous holidays. • Ss tell each other about the cultural differences among the holidays based on the pictures.
	Step 2	• T tells Ss about the origins of the world-famous holidays in detail. • T explains the cultural characteristics of those holidays. • T shares his experiences related to the holidays, and Ss listen to T's stories.
	Step 3	• T has Ss listen to a story about the world-famous holidays, and underline the expressions of comparative forms in the story on p. 79. • T talks with Ss about the meanings and functions of the expressions based on the cultural characteristics of the holidays. • T asks Ss, in pairs, to search the Internet for more information about cultural differences among the holidays and to describe the differences using comparative forms.
	Step 4	• T introduces new words in the story on the screen. • T explains the meanings of the words (*traditional, adapting, polite*, etc.), comparing them with their synonyms and/or antonyms. • Ss note the words and memorize them using mnemonic devices.
	Step 5	• T has Ss sit in groups of four, and choose one distinct aspect of the world-famous holidays, such as costume, food, and festivals. • Ss write a culture capsule in groups about the differences. • T gives preparation time, and each group performs a role-play based on the culture capsule in front of their classmates.

Note: T = teacher, Ss = students

Identify the TWO steps from <B> that do NOT correspond to the suggestions in <A>. Then, support your answers, respectively, with evidence from <A> and <B>.

모범답안 Steps 2 and 4 do not follow suggestions 5 and 1, respectively. In step 2 the teacher asks students to just listen to his experiences (anecdotes) and explanation (lecture) about world-famous holidays, not facilitating integrated skills. Also, in Step 4, without mentioning the cultural connotations of new words, the teacher just explains their meanings with synonyms and/or antonyms.

2023학년도 기출 | 전공B 기입형 ❶

Read the teacher log and follow the directions. [2 points]

Teacher Log

Skill-integration is considered more and more important in modern language learning, but I found that at any one time I was almost always teaching just one skill in isolation. As part of my development as a teacher, I wanted to integrate multiple language skills and pursue a more real-life style of communication.

To do this, I first investigated my own class practices. I video-recorded eight lessons. After reviewing the video files, I found that in six lessons I taught only one skill. In the other two, I was only able to integrate listening and speaking but never reading or writing. I drew up a plan to integrate language skills more often. What I did was implement the project-based learning approach so that students could collaborate in groups to advance their projects. I conducted the experiments over the second half of the semester and gathered the data. Then, I video-recorded another eight lessons toward the end of the semester to test the effectiveness of the measure I had implemented. After I analyzed the videos and the data, the results were as follows: two of the lessons showed the integration of speaking and reading skills, two other lessons integrated reading and writing skills, and one lesson integrated all four skills! Based on these results, I feel the approach really improved my teaching practice and my ability to teach students with the four skills in an integrated fashion.

Fill in the blank with the TWO most appropriate words.

The log above describes how the teacher addresses a problem in the classroom and resolves it through a systematic process of inquiry. Sometimes referred to as teacher research or classroom research, _____ is considered an important part of self-reflective teacher development. It usually involves four steps: planning, acting, observing, and reflecting. Its major goal is to improve both student learning and teaching effectiveness.

모범답안 action research

2023학년도 기출 전공B 서술형 ❻

Read the passage in <A> and the email in <B>, and follow the directions. [4 points]

─────────────── A ───────────────

Ms. Hong, a new English teacher, had a hard time getting her students to talk in her English speaking class. She investigated the issue and found a checklist related to the problems that hinder the students' active engagement in speaking. The checklist consisted of seven categories with descriptions: no preparation time, uneven participation, poor listening ability, lack of speaking strategy use, mother-tongue use, nothing to say, and inhibition. Based on her observations, she evaluated how often her students struggled with the problems in the checklist during her English speaking class.

Class Observation Checklist

Descriptions	Scale		
	1	2	3
1. Students need some quiet time before they are engaged in a speaking activity.		✔	
2. In group activities, some of the students free-ride without contributing to the discussion.		✔	
3. Students have listening difficulties when engaged in speaking activities.	✔		
4. Students are not aware of speaking strategies and need to develop their own.			✔
5. When students speak the same mother tongue, they tend to use it in group work, especially when the teacher is far away.			✔
6. Students complain that they cannot think of anything to say.		✔	

7. Students are often inhibited from trying to say things in English in the speaking class.			✓

Note: 1 = seldom, 2 = sometimes, 3 = often

　Ms. Hong gave careful thought to six, out of the seven problems, that she checked as "sometimes" or "often" in the checklist. She came up with satisfactory solutions to four of the problems; but for the other two, she decided to ask for help. She sent an email about the two problems to Mr. Park, a head teacher, in order to seek some advice. He replied as in <B>.

B

From ∨ parkminsu5827@school.korea
To ∘ Ms. Hong (Teacher)
Subject Re: Asking for advice

Dear Ms. Hong,

I am sorry to reply to your email so late. I have thought about the two problems you mentioned in your email, and my suggestions for the problems are, in brief, as follows:

The first problem arises quite often in speaking classes. If the task you want to do in class is based on group work, I think you need to choose a task such as jigsaw that we talked about the other day. When I included that activity in my English speaking class, the students' participation increased significantly overall while they were pooling all their information in groups.

The second problem is another one that happens frequently in English speaking classes. Why don't you appoint one of the group members as monitor? I think the very awareness that someone is monitoring helps the students put more effort into using the target language.

I hope these suggestions work well in your class. If you have any more questions or problems, please feel free to talk to me.

Best regards,

Park, Min-su

Based on <A> and <B>, identify the TWO problems Ms. Hong asked for Mr. Park's advice about. Then, explain why he made the suggestions for her two problems, respectively. Do NOT copy more than FOUR consecutive words from <A> and <B>.

모범답안 Ms. Hong asks for Mr. Park's advice about two problems, 'uneven participation' and 'mother-tongue use.' Thus, he is convinced that a jigsaw significantly increases overall students' participation. Also, he thinks that the very awareness that someone is monitoring pushes students to use the target language, instead of their mother tongue.

Guide

가이드

2023학년도 기출 | 전공B 서술형 ❼

Read the conversation in <A> and the two writing drafts in <B>, and follow the directions. [4 points]

A

(Mr. Min, a middle school English teacher, is talking with his student, Jinhee, about her writing.)

T : Jinhee, I think you put a lot of effort into this first draft.

S : Yeah. But I think I made many mistakes.

T : Don't worry. I'll give you some comments on the categories you need to improve so that you can revise your draft. Can you do that?

S : Yes.

T : Great. Let's begin with content. I like your story, but it'll be better if you add more details here. Do you remember that we discussed how to use supporting details last week?

S : Yes, I do.

T : Good. I also saw that you had problems with organization.

S : You're right. Many events are popping up in my mind, but I can't put them logically.

T : One way to solve the problem is to use linking words such as *and, so, but, however, then, thus*, and so on, in order to show a logical sequence of events.

S : I see.

T : Two more categories are vocabulary and grammar. These two expressions here need to be changed. Look up the appropriate expressions in a dictionary. In addition, *swimed* here and *very not much* here are not correct. Think about how you can correct them.

S : Okay.

T : If you have any questions, just let me know. I'm looking forward to reading your second draft.

S : Thank you.

Note: T = teacher, S = student

B

<First draft>

I went to a game park with my family last weekend. When we arrived, we ate delicious snacks. I swimed in the pool. My father did not swim. My mother did it very not much. We went on the rides. It was very funny and smily. We were very tired. We took a taxi to come home.

<Second draft>

I went to a game park with my family last weekend. When we arrived, we ate delicious snacks. Both my brother and I love sweets. My brother got three cups of ice cream and I got strawberry cake. I swimed in the pool, but my father did not swim. My mother did it very not much. Then, we went on the rides. It was very funny and smily. We were very tired, so we took a taxi to come home.

Identify the TWO categories Jinhee revised in the second draft based on Mr. Min's comments in <A>. Then, explain how she revised the categories, respectively, with evidence from <B>.

모범답안 ☞ Jinhee revises the second draft in terms of content and organization. First, she provides supporting details about who gets which snacks. Also, she puts a logical sequence of events by linking words such as 'but', 'then', and 'so' between sentences.

Read the passage in <A> and the teaching procedures in <B>, and follow the directions. [4 points]

_____ A _____

　The basic aspects the students need to know about a lexical item are its written and spoken forms, and its denotational meaning. However, there are additional aspects which also need to be learned, as are described in the following table.

Aspects	Descriptions
Grammar	A grammatical structure may be lexically bound, and lexical items also have grammatical features.
Collocation	Collocation refers to the way words tend to co-occur with other words or expressions.
Connotation	The connotations of a word are the emotional or positive-negative associations that it implies.
Appropriateness	Students need to know if a particular lexical item is usually used in writing or in speech; or in formal or informal discourse.
Word formation	Words can be broken down into morphemes. Exactly how these components are put together is another piece of useful information.

_____ B _____

Teaching Procedure 1

1. Present the following expressions in the table. Ask students to choose which expressions are possible.

do my homework	(O/X)	make my homework	(O/X)
do some coffee	(O/X)	make some coffee	(O/X)
do the laundry	(O/X)	make the laundry	(O/X)

2. Ask students to find more examples using do and make, referencing an online concordancer.

Teaching Procedure 2

1. Ask students to identify countable and uncountable nouns.

advice	employee	equipment	facility
information	money	proposal	result

2. Tell students to choose the expression of quantity that does NOT fit with the noun in each sentence.

　(a) The researchers found [*a significant proportion of / some of / most of*] the results were not corroborated by other sources.

Identify ONE aspect in <A> that each teaching procedure in <B> focuses on, respectively. Then, explain your answers with evidence from <B>.

모범답안
Teaching procedures 1 and 2 focus on collocation and grammar, respectively. The former presents some words which co-occur with 'do', and 'make'. On the other hand, the latter asks students to identify countable and uncountable nouns and choose expressions of their quantity.

2023학년도 기출 전공B 서술형 ⑪

Read the passages in <A> and <B>, and follow the directions. [4 points]

_____ **A** _____

A high school English teacher, Mr. Choi, wanted to learn how to write selected-response items (e.g., multiple-choice items) more efficiently. He wrote several items before the workshop began, and found some of them were flawed according to the guidelines he learned during the workshop. The following are some of the guidelines along with examples of flawed items.

General Guidelines for Writing Selected-response Items

① Make certain that there is only one, clearly correct answer.
② State both the stem and the options as simply and directly as possible.
③ Present a single clearly formulated problem to avoid mixed content.
④ Avoid negative wording whenever possible. If it is absolutely necessary to use a negative stem, highlight the negative word.

Item 1

My forehead itches every day during the summer. Using sunscreen hasn't helped much. I think I'd better go to the ___ to get my skin checked.

    a. dentist
    b. optometrist
    c. pediatrician
→ d. dermatologist

Item 2

Where did Henry go after the party last night?

    a. Yes, he did.
    b. Because he was tired.
→ c. To Kate's place for another party.
 ? d. He went home around eleven o'clock.

Item 3

I never knew where _____.

    a. had the boys gone
→ b. the boys had gone
    c. the boys have gone
    d. have the boys gone

Item 4

According to the passage, which of the following is not true?

    a. My sister likes outdoor sports.

    b. My brother is busy with his plans.

→ c. My sister and I often do everything together.

    d. My brother is more energetic and outgoing than I.

Note: '→' indicates the key; '?' indicates a possible answer.

B

    After the workshop, to improve the quality of the items, the teacher revised some items according to the guidelines. The following are the revised items.

Item 1

I think I'd better go to the _____ to get my skin checked.

    a. dentist

    b. optometrist

    c. pediatrician

→ d. dermatologist

Item 2

Where did Henry go after the party last night?

    a. Yes, he did.

    b. Because he was tired.

    c. It was about eleven o'clock.

→ d. To Kate's place for another party.

Item 3

I never knew _____.

    a. where had the boys gone

→ b. where the boys had gone

    c. the boys where had gone

    d. the boys had gone where

Item 4

According to the passage, which of the following is NOT true?

    a. My sister likes outdoor sports.

    b. My brother is busy with his plans.

→ c. My sister and I often do everything together.

    d. My brother is more energetic and outgoing than I.

Based on <A>, identify the ONE most appropriately revised item in <B> according to guideline ②, and the ONE most appropriately revised item according to guideline ③. Then, explain each of the items with evidence from <A> and <B>.

> 모범답안 Item 1 in <B> is appropriately revised based on guideline ② in that the original complicated stem is changed into a simple and direct one sentence. Also, following guideline ③, Item 3 in <B> presents a clear single problem about an 'indirect question' by changing tenses in the original options into the same past perfect 'had gone'.

Contents

Build Up New

박현수 영어교육론 Ⅳ

Second Language Acquisition

기입형

서술형

Chapter
01 Second Language Acquisition

🔒 정답 및 모범 답안 p. 2

✅ 기입형

01   Read the passage and follow the directions.

As part of a speaking test, Ms. Kim and her student, Bomin, are talking about her favorite sports. Below is an excerpt of the conversation.

Ms. Kim : Bomin, what's your favorite sport?
Bomin : I, favorite, soccer!
Ms. Kim : Your favorite sport is soccer?
Bomin : Oh, yes. My favorite sport is soccer.

Ms. Kim's Note

During the speaking lesson, I evaluated students' oral proficiency by asking them about their favorite sports. Bomin, one of my students, seemed a little bit nervous because of speaking test. So, she made an error saying "I, favorite, soccer" instead of "my favorite sport is soccer". However, soon after I gave feedback as a signal for her to try again, she noticed the incorrect previous erroneous utterance and corrected it by saying "My favorite sport is soccer."

Complete the comments by filling in the blank with the appropriate words.

In the conversation above, the teacher reformulates Bomin's incorrect utterance, saying "Your favorite sport is soccer". Such corrective feedback helps Bomin focus on the gaps between her own linguistic knowledge and the correct usage of language. Also, it enables her to produce grammatically correct and sociolinguistically appropriate utterance, which is called _____ (TWO words) suggested by Swain.

Your Answer _____

02 Read the passage and follow the direction.

Mr. Park's Note

Today, I participated in Teacher's seminar about how to help students learn effectively from a socio-cultural perspective. The following shows part of the reading material from the seminar. It deals with diverse supporting strategies that a teacher can provide for students in class depending on their proficiency levels.

For beginners

- **Use visuals**: connect keywords with visuals.
- **Use repetition**: develop familiarity with the words by having students repeat them.
- **Provide word banks**: provide students with new words including keywords of the day.
- **Incorporate a student's home language**: let students process content in their native language.

For intermediate-level students

- **Modified texts**: provide a text that contains the same content but with modified language.
- **Guiding questions**: offer questions before processing a text.
- **Sentence starters**: help students begin their thinking with sentence starters.
- **Sentence frames**: support students by helping them connect ideas together.

Complete the comments by filling in the blank with ONE word.

Based on a sociocultural perspective, _____ occurred within the zone of proximal development is the key to managing the level-differentiated instruction. However, this pedagogical concept can be successful only when teachers know how to properly apply it according to their students' levels. That is, as seen in Mr. Park's note, teachers should correctly choose the supporting strategies according to students' proficiency levels before lessons and appropriately provide students with them during the lessons.

Your Answer

03   Read the passage and follow the directions.

Ms. Kim's Teaching Note

Today I participated in a teacher's seminar talking about common phenomenons of students found in early cognitive development. Before attending the seminar, I was deeply worried about the frequent errors from my low intermediate-level students. For example, in the first step of learning, they seemed to use the target rule correctly. However, in the next step, even after learning some grammar rules clearly and practicing repeatedly, they show incorrect usage of the rule by especially overgeneralizing them. Thus, I really wanted to know what was wrong with my grammar lessons. Thanks to the seminar, I realized that I need to wait until my students have recovered from the regression rather than considering it as a problem. Below is part of the article I have read from the teacher's seminar.

The _____ course of development

Michael Long perhaps says it best when speaking of the trajectory of a language learner's progress: "Progress is not linear; backsliding is common, giving rise to so-called _____ behavior observed in first and second language acquisition". _____ behavior or a "_____ course of development" as Ellis refers to it, describes situations in L2 acquisition when a learner's proficiency suddenly but temporarily drops off only to return once again to their usual level. According to Ellis, "It is clear that this occurs because learners reorganize their existing knowledge to accommodate new knowledge". The reorganization of prior knowledge is often referred to as restructuring. Language instructors whose students regress upon learning about and attempting to practice a new linguistic form should understand that their students are actually advancing, even when, early on, they already seemed to have "acquired" the form. In second language acquisition and teaching, patience is indeed a virtue. Below is the graph showing the _____ course of development.

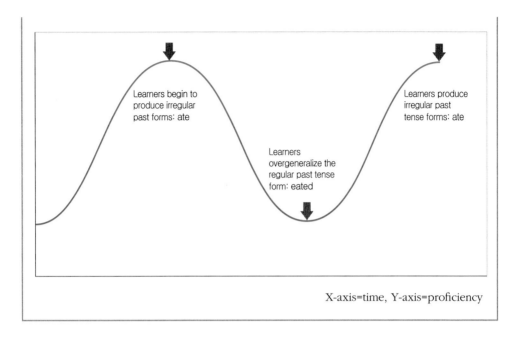

Learners begin to produce irregular past forms: ate

Learners overgeneralize the regular past tense form: eated

Learners produce irregular past tense forms: ate

X-axis=time, Y-axis=proficiency

Fill in the blanks with the ONE most appropriate word in common.

Your Answer

04 Read the passage and follow the directions.

> ### Teacher's Note
>
> After having several times of reading lessons, my students were accustomed to using reading strategies such as skimming, scanning, and reading for details. Thus, at this time, I'd like to help them to examine their own way to read and learn best. Until now, I gave directions on which strategies they need to use to read a text properly. However, from the next lesson, I will train them to choose some reading strategies by themselves. In other words, they need to plan, monitor, and evaluate their reading process on their own. By controlling their own reading, I believe, they can be active learners who learn more deeply. Thus, I will prepare lessons including the following strategies.
>
> - Identifying what you already know.
> - Monitoring and clarifying your comprehension. (Think-aloud)
> - Summarizing the text.
> - Visualizing the meaning from the text.
> - Writing a reading journal.

Complete the comments on the Teacher's Note above by filling in the blank with ONE word.

> For reading lessons, the teacher tries to teach various kinds of _____ strategies to help students understand the way they learn.

Your Answer _____

05 Read the teaching log in <A> and concordancers in <B>, and follow the directions.

| A |

Ms. Kim's Teaching Log

In order to minimize the students' lexical errors in writing, dialog, and exams, I designed my lessons based on the lexical approach. I believed that mechanically memorizing many words itself does not guarantee the right use of the words, so I wanted them to learn words in context and the relation among words. After several English lessons, I realized that many of my students used unacceptable combinations of words such as "look a novel" or "eat medicine," influenced by their native language, in particular Korean meaning system. Hence, I decide to introduce a specific type of concordancer in class to help the students to use words properly.

| B |

Concordancer 1		
Isle of Man investors to	get	payout.
took the piss out of it to	get	through.
I tried to	get	the trade unions into a form.
Right,	get	on with it.
So high you can't	get	over it.
She must	get	the bike before the car returned.
If you can't	get	a replacement, lift the gutter.

Results when searched for "get". The length of sentences were edited.

Concordancer 2		
Count	%	Word
97	0.4612%	take
91	0.4333%	you
78	0.3984%	other
77	0.3395%	make
68	0.2709%	choice
60	0.2459%	our
55	0.2201%	great
49	0.2134%	time

Results when searched for words (e.g., take, you, other...) with news articles.

Complete the following comments by filling in the blanks in appropriate words.

According to Ms. Kim's teaching log, she wanted students to focus on some words to co-occur in English. Of two types Concordancer 1 is more appropriate for her students. That is, it provides (1) _____ (ONE word) of the word 'get' so that students can figure out which words can go together with 'get'. Besides, with this activity students can develop their awareness to the proper use of words in given context as well as refrain from using some unacceptable word combinations such as "look a novel" or "eat medicine," which are caused by (2) _____ (ONE word) of Korean language.

Your Answer (1) _____

(2) _____

06 Read the passage and fill in the blank with THREE words from the passage.

Below is part of a conversation between two English teachers.

T1 : What are you reading?

T2 : I'm reading an article about teaching pronunciation.

T1 : Interesting. What is it talking about? Stress and intonation?

T2 : Yes, they are part of it but I am looking for the best method to help them acquire clear pronunciation for specific sounds.

T1 : You mean, segmental units?

T2 : Right. Most of my students are fluent in speaking English. But sometimes when they speak fast, they mispronounce vowels like /ɜː/ into /ɑː/ and /ʌ/ into /ɜː/.

T1 : Hmm, they need a lot of practice for the vowel sounds. Did you try to provide such confusing words in pairs?

T2 : In pairs?

T1 : Yes. For example, you prepare pairs of words that have minimal phonetic difference.

T2 : Oh, yes I did. Actually, the article is talking about the same method as a solution.

T1 : Then, just do it. What's the matter?

T2 : There is one big difference between the method I used and what the article suggests.

T1 : Big difference? What is it?

T2 : The article suggests _____.

T1 : Can you explain more about it?

T2 : So, I used to give the list of words in pairs without context such as 'heard – hard', and 'firm and farm'. But, the article says I should provide them in a more contextualized manner. For example, I should give the pairs within example sentences describing the event in a *firm* and a *farm*. If needed, I can also add pictures to sentences. So, they can naturally pick up the sound difference within context.

T1 : Oh, yes, I see what you mean. Context is one of the most important reference points for meaning or form. So, teaching language items with context allows students to clearly understand the difference in meaning or form.

T2 : You can say that again.

T=teacher

Your Answer

07 **Read the passages and follow the directions.**

---| **A** |---

T   : Joo-hyun, what did you do for summer vacation?

Joo-hyun : Well, I visit my cousin's house in Yang-yang.

T   : You visit?

Joo-hyun : Oh, I visited my cousin's house.

T   : Oh yeah? What did you do there?

Joo-hyun : I go surfing.

T   : You go?

Joo-hyun : Ah! I went surfing!

T   : Great! That must be a lot of fun.

Joo-hyun : Yes, it is fun.

T   : It is?

Joo-hyun : Oh my, okay. It was fun!

---| **B** |---

T   : Eun-ji, you did a good job! You get grade 'A' in your writing test.

Eun-ji : Oh, don't say that.

T   : Sorry?

Eun-ji : I mean, I did my best and . . . I think 'A' is undeserved.

T   : Oh, I get it. You tried to show modesty. That's the way the Koreans say. In American culture, you just show your appreciation.

Eun-ji : Oh, I see! Thank you for giving me a good grade.

T   : It sounds better! Well, I evaluated the test based on objective criteria. So, you deserve 'A'.

T=teacher

Referring to <A> and <B>, fill in each blank with a suitable term.

In the conversation <A>, the teacher uses (1) _____ (ONE word) that prompts the student to self-correct. On the other hand, in the conversation <B>, the teacher uses a clarification request which gives signals to the student that there is an error in her utterance and invites the student to reformulate it. Through giving feedback on the errors, the teacher pushes his students, Joo-hyun and Eun-ji, to use the grammatically and sociolinguistically correct utterances, which is called (2) _____ (TWO words).

Your Answer (1) _____

(2) _____

08 **Read the passage and follow the directions.**

Before the teacher starts his lesson in a middle school English class, he asks students questions to warm up, starting with Kang-min.

T : What did you do last weekend, Kang-min?
S : I visit my grandma in the hospital.
T : Ah, you visited your grandma in the hospital?
S : Yes, I visit her.
T : I see. Did you do anything else?
S : Yeah, Um, I see a movie with my best friend, Dong-hee.
T : See?
S : Sorry! I saw a movie with Dong-hee.
T : Great! What movie did you see?
S : I saw the movie "The Giant".

T=teacher, S=student

Based on the classroom talk above, complete comments by filling in the blanks using ONE word in common.

This classroom talk reveals different types of student responses to the teacher's corrective feedback. _____ is defined in their work as "a student's utterance that immediately follows the teachers' feedback and that constitutes a reaction in some way to the teachers' intention to draw attention to some aspect of the student's initial utterance." Put another way, this shows that the student tries to do with the teacher's feedback. Two types of student _____ appear in this talk: one that produces an utterance still needing repair and the other that produces a repair of the error on which the teacher's feedback focused.

Your Answer _____

09 Read the following CALL material in <A> and its comments. Answer the question.

───────┤ **A** ├───────

Not all CALL materials provide clear feedback for learners, but teachers can find CALL software for grammar that does. Teachers can look for software that provides grammar assessment and feedback about correctness both before and after instruction. Take a look at the grammar section below. It begins with two assessments: Diagnosing Your Grammar Errors and Grammar test. This shows the learner the results for the grammar test. Color is used to show correctness—blue for correct, red for incorrect, and green for corrected. By clicking on "Feedback" at the bottom right on the screen, the learner is informed of the type of mistakes made, and directed to go to the textbook or grammar software program for more work in the problem areas—in this case, articles, the passive, and count/noncount nouns.

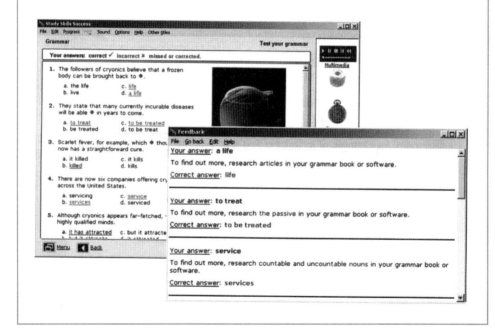

Complete the comments on the diagnostic grammar test in <A> by filling in the blank with THREE words.

B

Most researchers argue that explicit feedback for learners about why their responses were correct or incorrect produced the best results for grammar learning, compared to feedback that simply pointed out the location of learners' errors. That is when they receive explicit feedback on their performance, they have the opportunity to _____ between their knowledge and correct grammar.

Your Answer _____

10 Read the interaction between Ms. Park, an English teacher, and Jinsu, a 1st-year middle school student and follow directions.

She tries to continue to communicate in English with Jinsu, who is a somewhat fluent Korean speaker of English for his age, after showing a video clip on animals in Africa.

T : Jinsu, what did you watch on the video clip?

S : A man was hunting for some animals.

T : Did he succeed in catching an animal?

S : Yes, he did. He catched a hyena.

T : And why did he try to catch an animal?

S : I think he catched an animal for pleasure, not for food.

(In the next lesson a week later)

T : Tell me what happened to you last week.

S : I visited my grandmother in Busan.

T : Were you happy with the visit?

S : No, I was not. But I felt it bored to be with her. She was too talkative for me.

T : (*Laughing*) Your grandmother seemed to feel alienated from you. Was not there anything interesting there?

S : I experienced one interesting event. It was to go with my cousins to the river for catching fish.

T : How many fish did you catch? .

S : We catched a lot of fish. We cooked and ate them very deliciously.

T=teacher, S=student

Complete the comments on the above interaction by filling in the blank with ONE word.

L2 learners usually go through some stages of learner language development. At times, certain erroneous linguistic features, as seen in Jinsu's utterances above, may establish themselves as 'acceptable' rules in the cognitive structure of even learners who have already achieved fluency in a second language; in the end, they utter ungrammatical sentences in some expressions. This phenomenon is referred to as _____. When Ms. Park tries only to communicate in English without appropriate feedback, either affective or cognitive, it is likely enough that Jinsu's English competence fails to reach completion—she is expected to feel frustrated by Jinsu's utterances 'catched,' instead of 'caught,' in the next lesson. Put another way, he may stay at a stage of incomplete second language acquisition.

Your Answer _____

11   Read the conversation below, and follow the directions.

In a class, a teacher and students are talking about their favorite movies.

Jin   : My favorite movie is "Titanic" because I love Leonardo DiCaprio who is impossibly handsome. I watched its 3-D version, too.

Hoyoung : Hmm . . . But that's too old one. I recently have watched a movie titled "The detective" which was released last week. I could not help sobbing because of Christopher's acting. He is a new talent but his acting is super.

T   : 'Talent' is a wrong word. You need to say, 'Christopher is a new actor.'

Hoyoung : Okay. Christopher is a new actor.

T   : Good. Go ahead.

Hoyoung : Anyway . . . After watching it, I go back home and search the reviews of the movie, which were high praise overall.

T   : Oh, you went back home and searched the reviews?

Hoyoung : Yes. I search them on the Internet at that day.

T=teacher

Fill in each blank with ONE word.

The conversation above demonstrates how the teacher provides Hoyoung with feedback fundamental to second language acquisition. Two types of feedback were used. First, in the first underlined feedback the teacher provides the (1) _____ evidence of the target language to inform the learner of the incorrectness of his utterance. On the other hand, the teacher's second underlined feedback is the (2) _____ evidence of the target language which exposes the learner to the well-formed target language.

Your Answer   (1) _____

                  (2) _____

12   Review the classroom conversation and follow the directions.

Two students, Jinho and Miran, are talking about their hobbies and an excerpt of the conversation is shown below.

Jinho : What is your hobby?

Miran : I'm attending a cooking academy these days. It's very interesting.

Jinho : Wow! What kinds of food did you learn cooking recently?

Miran : So many things. Korean-style pizza. I also cooked Bibimbap yesterday.

Jinho : How was it?

Miran : I failed it because of <u>lice</u>.

Jinho : lice?

Miran : When I cooked lice, I burned it up. I also burned up the pot.

Jinho : Ah, you meant rice!

Miran : Yes! But when I saw the Bibimbap the teacher made as an example for us, it was so . . . so . . . um . . . y'know . . . 전문가<u>tic</u>.

Jinho : Haha. I'm sure your cooking will get better soon.

Fill in each blank with ONE word.

The Cross-Linguistic Influence (CLI) recognizes the effect of one's native language on a second as well as the second language influencing the first. In other words, all learned languages influence each other in various ways. The classroom conversation demonstrated above illustrates such cases. When Miran wants to pronounce *rice* [raɪs], she produces *lice* [laɪs] due to the (1) _____ of her native language, Korean, which does not have a [r] sound. Besides, Miran is using a strategy called (2) _____ when saying '전문가tic.' She uses a Korean word 전문가 by adjusting it to English morphology (adding an English suffix '-*tic*').

Your Answer   (1) _____

                    (2) _____

13 Read the passage in <A> and a teacher's note in <B>, and follow the directions.

┤ **A** ├

   Michael Long proposed a/an (1) _____ approach that the learner must be aware of the meaning and use of the language features before the form is brought to their attention. This occurs when a learner has a communication problem, and so is likely to understand the meaning or function of the new form. These are the conditions most researchers would consider optimal for learning. In this regard, they suggest one best way to teach problematic grammar forms within a communicative framework, which is a/an (2) _____ activity. It aims to focus learners' attention quite explicitly on the form of the grammar structure while stimulating meaningful L2 communication and creating a purposeful context for language use.

┤ **B** ├

Teacher's Note

   After reading an article about effective pedagogical ways to teach grammar forms, I designed the following task aimed at directing learners' attention to some specific linguistic form when they process both the input (listening to a script) and the output.

Lead-in (2-5 minutes)：To set lesson context and engage student

- T tells Ss that they'll do dictation and explains how it is going to happen.

Exposure (3-5 minutes)：To provide a model of production expected in coming tasks

- T writes on the board the sentence: 'What time do you have breakfast?' and highlights 'what' 'do' 'have' in the sentence.
- Then T asks Ss whether these words help reconstruct the question or not.
- T asks about the remaining ones 'time', 'breakfast' and tells Ss that these are helpful because these are the keywords.

> Receptive task(s) (8-10 minutes)：Provide students with a grammar dictation activity

- T asks Ss to put pens down and listen carefully.
- T reads the 1st time and Ss listen only. Then T gives Ss 2 minutes to write keywords. T reads one more time and Ss listen only. Then T gives Ss 2 minutes for them to add to their notes.
- At this stage, Ss work individually and they should not consult with their peers.

> Productive Task(s) (13-18 minutes)：To provide an opportunity to practice target productive skills

- T puts Ss in pairs and asks them to look at their notes and try to build up the text. The pair will have one strong and one weak students.
- T then asks in each pair to join another pair and form a group of four and compare their texts, discuss and make improvements to their final versions.

> Feedback and Error Correction (3-5 minutes)：To provide feedback on students' production

- T hands out copies of the original text and asks Ss to read both and compare content and accuracy.

> Controlled practice (4-6 minutes)：To check whether students included all relevant information as in the original text

- T asks Ss some questions about the information in the original text to see whether Ss have included all relevant information.

> Language focus (4-6 minutes)：Clarify grammar and revise the indefinite article

- T asks Ss to underline the indefinite articles in the original text and compare it to the ones in their versions. T then quickly explains how the indefinite article works and clarifies any mistakes Ss might have made in their texts.

T=teacher, Ss=students

Based on the information in <A> and <B>, fill in each blank in <A> with the ONE most appropriate term. Write the answers in order.

Your Answer　(1) _____

(2) _____

14 Read the passages and follow the directions.

Teacher's Note

At a teacher's conference, I read an article about the attention-processing model. It introduces the concepts of controlled and automatic processing which are described as a brand new skill and more accomplished skills of students, respectively. So far, I have focused on teaching new forms as many as possible rather than helping students to use them naturally and unconsciously. After reading this article, I decided to prepare my lesson in a different way. So, I came up with the following lesson procedure, hoping to help students practice the target forms in context and then use them smoothly and naturally.

1. T introduces some useful English expressions commonly used in daily conversations.

1	Thanks so much + for + [noun] / [-ing verb].
2	I really appreciate + [noun].
3	My pleasure / No worries / No problem / Anytime
4	I'm sorry for + [noun] / [-ing verb].
5	How does that sound?
6	Anything is fine / I am okay with both / It doesn't matter.

2. T reads aloud the expressions several times and Ss repeat after T.

3. T puts Ss in pairs and provides the worksheet below to practice the expressions in the limited conversation.

※ *Below is an excerpt from a conversation between friends. A is inviting B for dinner. Let's practice the conversation with your partner. Take turns to play A and B.*

A : **Thanks so much for your help! I really appreciate** it.
B : **My pleasure. I'm sorry for** my late reply.
A : It's totally okay. Have you seen my message? Dinner together? **How does that sound?**
B : Fantastic!
A : Do you prefer red or white wine?
B : Oh, either. **It doesn't matter.**

---

4. When Ss become familiar with the expressions, T provides the new worksheet below to practice the expressions with less attention to the forms during a conversation. Ss monitor each other's utterance. When Ss finish, T nominates several pairs and asks to present the conversation they have completed in their own words.

> ※ *Fill in the blanks in your own words and practice the conversation with your partner. After each turn of practice, talk about any incorrect expressions if needed.*
>
> A : I am sorry for _____.
> B : _____.
> A : _____. How does that sound?
> B : _____.
> A : Thank you for _____. I really appreciate
>   _____.
> B : _____.
> A : Do you prefer _____?
> B : _____.

5. T puts Ss in groups of four and asks them to have a free conversation using the expressions they have learned as many as possible.

T=teacher, Ss=students

Fill in each blank with the ONE most appropriate word from the passage. write the answers in order.

According to the attention-processing model, the lesson procedure facilitates the gradual acquisition of target expressions as (1) _____ processing initially predominate and then become (2) _____. After practising target forms in the limited conversation, students complete a conversation with their own words, and then attain the stage of having a free conversation with target expressions.

Your Answer (1) _____

(2) _____

✎ 서술형

01 Review the lesson procedure and follow the directions.

┤ **A** ├

Types of Errors

1. Overgeneralization: This is the use of one form or construction in one context and extending its application to other contexts where it should not apply.

2. Hypercorrection: Sometimes too much effort from teachers in correcting their students' errors induces the students to make errors in otherwise correct forms. Students make mistakes in grammar, punctuation, or pronunciation that result from trying too hard to be correct.

3. Fossilization: Some errors, especially errors in pronunciation, persist for long periods and become quite difficult to get rid of.

4. Avoidance: Some syntactic structures are difficult to be produced by some learners. Consequently, these learners avoid these structures and use instead simpler structures.

┤ **B** ├

Below is part of the conversation between a teacher and students.

T : Juwan, how was your trip to Jeju Island ['aɪlənd]?

Juwan : Jeju Island [**áislənd**] was beautiful! My grandparents also came with us!

T : They came to Jeju Island ['aɪlənd] with your family?

Juwan : Yes, on Jeju Island [**áislənd**], there are so many fresh seafood dishes!

T : You must have a good time in Jeju!

Juwan : Indeed!

T : How about Minju? Did you have a good weekend?

Minju : Yes, I did. I went to Seoul Zoo. It's Right [**laɪt**] next to my house.

T   : Minju. Repeat after me, *(T emphasizes the /r/ sound.)* Right. [**raɪt**]
        Right. [**raɪt**]
Minju : Right. [**raɪt**]
T   : Great! Sometimes, Korean students pronounce the /r/ sound
        like the /l/ sound because the two sounds come from the same
        underlying consonant 'ㄹ' of the Korean language. So, you
        should be careful when pronouncing the 'r' sound.
Minju : I see. I will try my best. *(She looks nervous.)*
Juwan : Minju, were there many animals?
Minju : Yes, there were so many cute animals like pandas, monkeys,
        giraffes, zebras, and so on. Especially, I was so lucky ['rʌki] that
        I could feed a baby lion ['raɪən] by myself. *(After the teacher's
        correction, Minju starts to pronounce both 'r' and 'l' sounds into
        the 'r' sound.)*
Juwan : Feeding a baby lion ['laɪən]? Wow, that's amazing!

Based on the information in <A>, identify TWO types of errors the students show in <B>. Then, explain each type of the identified errors using concrete evidence from <B>.

Your Answer

_____

_____

_____

_____

02 Read the passages and follow the directions.

─┤ **A** ├─

Motivation in language learning has proved to have an important impact on learning success in both classroom and naturalistic learning environments. A specific approach that considers the importance of individual factors is Self-Determination Theory (SDT). SDT supports a dynamic view of motivation and is able to represent the different states of L2 learner motivation as a result of changes in a variety of internal and external factors. SDT framework classifies different types of motivation on a continuum (Figure 1) according to the extent to which the motivation is self-determined and internalized within the learner.

[Figure 1]

Motivation	Extrinsic motivation				Intrinsic motivation
Regulatory Styles	external regulation	introjected regulation	identified regulation	integrated regulation	intrinsic regulation
What regulates the motivation?	rewards, punishment, obedience, compliance	ego-involvement, competing, pride, guilt	high perceived value, personally important	integrated into self-concept	interest, enjoyment, satisfaction

Extrinsic motivation can be divided into four subtypes based on the extent to which their regulation is autonomous: external regulation, introjected regulation, identified regulation, and integrated regulation. Lastly on this continuum is intrinsic motivation which refers to motivation stemming from internal factors such as interest, enjoyment, and satisfaction. Learners here are the most self-determined.

---------------------------------| B |---------------------------------

Below is the survey questionnaire results conducted by 30 students who are taking Mr. Kim's lessons.

Item	Questionnaire	SA	A	D	SD
1	I study English because other people say that I should do so.	3	2	10	15
2	I study English because others will not be pleased with me if I don't.	1	4	11	14
3	I feel under pressure from friends/family to study English.	2	3	15	10
4	I feel guilty when I don't study English.	7	8	8	7
5	I feel ashamed when I don't study English.	8	8	6	8
6	I value the benefits of studying English.	18	9	2	1
7	It's important to me study English continuously.	15	12	2	1
8	I study English because it's fun.	9	8	7	6
9	I get pleasure and satisfaction from studying English.	8	9	6	7
10	I enjoy my English lessons.	12	10	6	2

SA=strongly agree, A=agree, D=disagree, SD=strongly disagree

Based on <A> and <B>, choose each regulatory style that Mr. Kim's students have answered as the most and the least appropriate for them, respectively. Then, support each of your choices by identifying all item numbers from <B> related to each chosen style.

Your Answer

_____

_____

_____

_____

03 Read <A> and <B> and follow the directions.

---| **A** |---

Two high school students are doing a speaking activity introducing their favorite beverages.

Suji　　：So, Minwoo. What's your favorite beverage?

Minwoo：Hmm, I like to drink Pocari Sweat. It supplies lost water and ions. So, it's good to drink after playing soccer.

Suji　　：Nice.

Minwoo：How about you, Suji?

Suji　　：Oh, I like coffee. Every morning, I drink a coffee with two shots of espresso.

Minwoo：Two shots? It must be a powerful coffee!

Suji　　：Powerful? You mean, a strong coffee?

Minwoo：Oops, I made a great mistake.

Suji　　：Haha, you mean, you made a big mistake.

Minwoo：Ah... it's so confusing because, in my first language, Korean, a powerful coffee and a great mistake totally make sense.

Suji　　：I know. It happens. It's alright, though. You can practice some word combinations, one by one. By the way, two shots are good for me, not too strong. It wakes me up really fast.

Minwoo：Yeah? Then, I should try coffee in the morning, too.

---| **B** |---

Below is a lesson procedure based on the _____ approach given its heavy emphasis on teaching words and word combinations.

Lesson Procedure

1. T introduces some examples of word combinations and explains them.

> • make the bed
> • do homework
> • take a risk

2. T shows a short text from a travel journal including various word combinations. T asks Ss in pairs to find the lexical chunks and fill in the table.

[Text] Thunder Bay Experience

We'll spark your imagination! Your days and nights will be filled with captivating entertainment - whether you're enjoying blockbuster movies, or the excitement of casino gaming. ... *(ellipsis)* ...

[Let's do it in pairs]
※ Can you find the word combinations?

1	spark your imagination
2	days and nights
3	captivating entertainment
4	blockbuster movie

...

3. T asks Ss to create an advertisement for the school using at least 3-word combinations from today's lesson.

※ Let's Create an Advertisement for School!
• Do in pairs.
• Use at least 3 collocations from today's lesson.
• After, we will share your advertisement.

(e.g.)

Welcome to Seoul High School!
Spark your imagination in Seoul High School!
We provide the first-rate education for ...
(ellipsis)

Fill in the blank in <B> with the ONE most appropriate word. Then, identify the major source of errors that Minwoo has made in <A> and write how the lesson procedure in <B> can help Minwoo avoid making the same type of errors.

Your Answer

_____

_____

_____

_____

_____

04 Read <A> and <B> and follow the directions.

A

The theory of multiple intelligences was developed in 1983 by Dr. Howard Gardner. It suggests that the traditional notion of intelligence, based on I.Q. testing, is far too limited. Instead, Dr. Gardner proposes eight different types of intelligence to account for a broader range of human potential in children and adults. These types of intelligence are:

- Linguistic intelligence ("word smart")
- Logical-mathematical intelligence ("number/reasoning smart")
- Spatial intelligence ("picture smart")
- Bodily-Kinesthetic intelligence ("body smart")
- Musical intelligence ("music smart")
- Interpersonal intelligence ("people smart")
- Intrapersonal intelligence ("self smart")
- Naturalist intelligence ("nature smart")

B

Jaesuk's Learning Log

I have learned English for approximately four years and have been writing a log to record my learning experiences. While reviewing the log, I figured out that there were certain learning situations that I especially enjoyed with high performance. First, I learned best in group works rather than individual works. It is because I enjoy sharing thoughts and giving and receiving feedback within a communicative context. Next, I prefer to help others who have trouble completing a task. That's why my partner or other group members frequently ask me for some help during pair works or group works. I, also, am willing to be a good leader and then try to carefully listen to group members' opinions and understand their feelings. By doing so, I can be more concentrated on my study.

Based on the categorization in <A> and the log in <B>, identify the type of remarkably high intelligence that Jaesuk seems to have and provide TWO reasons for your choice from <B>.

Your Answer

_____

_____

_____

_____

_____

05 Read the passages and follow the directions.

A

Negotiation of meaning refers to interactional work executed by interlocutors to achieve a mutual understanding when a communication problem occurs. This type of interaction has drawn considerable attention in Second Language Acquisition (SLA) research because it gives language learners opportunities to receive comprehensible input and produce comprehensible output. The strategies for negotiation of meaning that are most generally identified by researchers are confirmation checks, clarification requests, and comprehension checks.

B

Below is a conversation between Isaac, an American student, and Minju, a Korean student who is studying in America.

Isaac : Minju. You are from Seoul, right?

Minju : Yes!

Isaac : Then, is it true that Kimchi is the soul food for Koreans?

Minju : Hmm,,, many human?

Isaac : Many human?

Minju : Most Koreans. We eat Kimchi a lot. We use kimchi a lot. Like for soup, fried rice, or dumpling. Understand?

Isaac : Oh, okay. So, you mean, Koreans like Kimchi itself and also for cooking?

Minju : Right, right.

Based on <A>, write the role of meaning-negotiation occurred between interlocutors and identify all negotiation strategies that Issac and Minju employ, citing each utterance from <B>, respectively.

Your Answer

06 Review the two teachers' conversation below and follow the directions.

Two middle school English teachers, Ms. Park and Ms. Kim, are discussing the result of the writing test administered last week.

Ms. Kim : Ms. Park, did you check the writing test score?

Ms. Park : Yes, I did... The results were not so satisfactory. You did?

Ms. Kim : Yeah, and same here. I was disappointed with the results. For the last month, I fully focused on improving their writing ability but their writings in the test were just full of errors. Especially, the grammar part.

Ms. Park : Hmm, what did we miss?

Ms. Kim : I think the cause of grammatical errors is due to their native language. When I checked the errors, errors were frequently affected by their native language.

Ms. Park : Can you give me one example?

Ms. Kim : For instance, they kept dropping articles for nouns because Korean does not have articles. It's an entirely new item to them. So, I concluded that I should have compared all grammar rules of English and Korean in advance and taught the differences preemptively. If I had done so, they would not have made any errors.

Ms. Park : Well, it might. But, not all errors are caused by the grammatical differences between English and Korean. Besides, we cannot predict all types of difficulties before the actual errors happen. So, I think, it is better to focus on the point that students' confusion between English rules matters even further.

Ms. Kim : You mean, the errors like 'intelligentest'?

Ms. Park : Exactly! 'Intelligentest' does not relate to the grammar rules of Korean at all. Rather, it is because they misapply the target language rule to where it does not apply. I think this is the major cause of errors.

Ms. Kim : Hmm... Whatever the reason is, we need to find some other possible errors and help students not to make any errors.

Ms. Park : You don't need to be too negative about their errors. I believe making errors is just a part of a language learning process.

Identify the cause of the error that each teacher exemplifies in the conversation, respectively. Then, addressing the hypothesis of Second Language Acquisition that Ms. Kim refers to, write her idea on how to deal with students' errors.

Your Answer

_____

_____

_____

_____

_____

07 Read the passages and follow the directions.

A

Language learners try to counterbalance their restricted linguistic and non-linguistic knowledge in the target language by employing Compensatory Strategies (CSs) which might enhance their communicative competence. A concise definition has been suggested by Rababah (2004) indicating that "language learners attempt to solve their communication problems when they lack adequate resources in the target language by resorting to CSs. Most researchers agree that compensatory strategies are used to bridge the gap that exists between the non-native speakers' linguistic competence in the target language and their communicative needs". CSs pertain to output, how we productively express meaning, and how we deliver messages to others. The concept of CSs refers to the use of a couple of strategic options designed to overcome self-perceived weaknesses, such as using avoidance, circumlocution, approximation, word coinage, non-verbal signals, prefabricated patterns, code-switching, appeal to authority, and keeping the floor.

| **B** |

Below is part of a student-student interaction during a speaking activity where they are talking about their best memory of the vacation. Last class, the teacher asked students to bring some photos taken during the summer vacation if they have any.

(Student 1 starts to talk about his good memory using his photos.)

Student 1 : So, look at this photo. Do you recognize what these are?

Student 2 : They are...trees? I don't recall the exact name.

Student 1 : They are called maple trees!

Student 2 : Oh, yes, that's right! Maple trees. Where is this place?

Student 1 : It's Canada! I went to Canada last summer with my family.

Student 2 : It looks fantastic! What did you do there?

Student 1 : I visited many places like, something like, I mean, ah! it's on the tip of my tongue!

Student 2 : Haha, take your time. I will wait.

Student 1 : Rocky mountains! and Niagara falls! Yes! Here, let me show you more photos.

Student 2 : *(looking at some photos)* Wow, it's Ni-a-ga-ra falls!

Student 1 : That's right! Have you been there?

Referring to terms in <A>, explain each type of compensatory strategy that Student 1 and 2 use in <B>, adding some evidence from the data.

Your Answer

08 Read the passages and follow the directions.

| **A** |

Ms. Ahn's Teaching Note

I am teaching English to the 3rd graders of a middle school, who have different proficiency levels. As shown below, I prepared a reading text of about 500 words long, which talks about 'The future of urban living.' Before the lesson, I intentionally omitted the ending of the story and asked students to write the ending during the lesson. However, I thought that writing the end of the story individually should be all right for advanced students but would be definitely problematic for low-level ones. So, I decided to provide language support and apply an appropriate grouping strategy for low levels. That is, I wanted to _____, or support classroom learning for lower-level students. Thanks to such efforts, consequently, all students could successfully complete the writing task. In particular, the appropriate grouping strategy I chose enabled advanced level students to actively help the low levels. It worked out pretty well!

B

Lesson Procedure

1. As a pre-reading activity, T asks Ss to watch a 2-minute English video clip related to the reading passage and then predict the content of the text, 'The future of urban living.'
2. T asks Ss to skim the text and gives Ss half a minute to underline previously learned vocabulary related to 'future'.
3. T provides Ss with a set of comprehension questions. Ss read the questions first and then read the passage individually. (The final 3 sentences are omitted on purpose.)
4. T forms mixed-level groups of three and asks Ss in groups to discuss the ending of the text and collaboratively write down their ideas in about 100 words. T asks some advanced-level students in each group to help the other students.
5. While Ss write the ending in groups, T circulates the classroom and gives feedback, suggestions, or language help Ss may need to accomplish the writing task.
6. When Ss finish writing, T asks each group to present their versions of the ending.
7. While listening to each group presentation, the other groups vote for the most interesting ending.

Fill in the blank with the ONE most appropriate word. Then, considering information in <A> and <B>, identify TWO types of support Ms. Ahn gives students to help them complete the task successfully. Write some evidence from the passages.

Your Answer

09 Read the passages and follow the directions.

┤ **A** ├

For open, smooth, and productive conversation, speakers need to manage the conversation based on the sequence that seems to govern normal interactions. There is a common sequence of a conversation as seen below:

1. Attention getting: open with a greeting.
2. Topic nomination: initiate an exchange with some gambits about the day's topic.
3. Topic development and holding the floor: use strategies for continuing the conversation.
4. Turn-taking: yield the floor to another speaker.
5. Topic clarification: ask questions for clarification.
6. Topic shifting: change a topic.
7. Topic termination: close a conversation.

B

Eric	: Hey, dude. What's up?
Mark	: Yo, nothing much.
Eric	: What are you reading?
Mark	: Well, I found this book at Borders. It's all about salt. Did you know that there are more than 10,000 uses of salt?
Eric	: Really? How so?
Mark	: It's not just for cooking. We can use salt as a health or beauty product. In addition, salt has many uses in modern aquaculture.
Eric	: By the way, why are you so interested in salt usage?
Mark	: As a matter of fact, I always wanted to write this kind of book about sugar.
Eric	: Sugar? Are you positive? Sugar is bad for you.
Mark	: I'm not talking about eating sugar. Sugar makes cut flowers last longer and also kills cockroaches.
Eric	: Wow, that's cool. I've never heard about that. Oh no, it's 10:50. I've gotta go now. I'll see you later, dude.
Mark	: Yeah, bro. Bye.

Identify each utterance from <B> that indicates 'Topic clarification' or 'Topic shifting' mentioned in <A>. And then, explain how each identified utterance functions within the communicative flow, respectively.

Your Answer

_____

_____

_____

_____

_____

10 Read the passages and follow the directions.

─┤ **A** ├─

Below are some of teaching strategies that teachers can use to help students to solve some reading difficulties before, during, and after reading lessons.

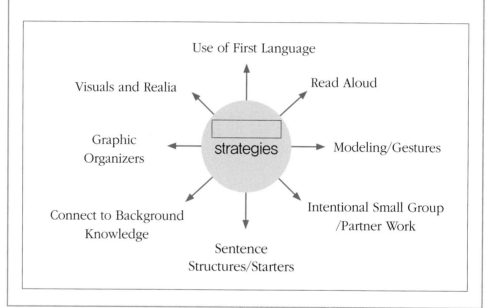

┤ B ├
Teacher's Note

I am teaching first-year middle school students whose proficiency levels are low intermediate or intermediate. Though some are at below intermediate level, I usually preferred using authentic materials. After conducting a needs analysis, however, I realized that my students feel them motivative but sometimes overwhelming. Thus, I decided to provide some activities to support new language features and contents from authentic materials. Today I, firstly, prepared a semantic map to visually display the connections between new words/phrases and new concepts. This map was made halfway, so students were asked to complete the map while reading the text. After that, I arranged group discussion where students worked together. While discussing in groups, they actively interacted and helped each other. So, they could clearly understand the difficult words and new concepts. Thanks to these two activities, students said, the reading lesson was not overwhelming them anymore.

Fill in the blank in <A> with the type of strategies in ONE word. Then, identify TWO examples of the identified strategies from <B> and explain how each of them functions to solve reading difficulties.

Your Answer

_____

_____

_____

_____

11 Read the passages and follow the directions.

 A

Methodologists and researchers of second language acquisition have identified a number of different ways in which students' errors can be corrected. More recently, researchers have developed hierarchical taxonomies of strategies based on a theoretical view of how corrective feedback (CF) works for acquisition. In the case of oral CF, two key distinctions figure: (1) explicit vs. implicit CF and (2) input-providing vs. output-prompting CF. These two distinctions can be combined into the taxonomy shown in Table 1.

[Table 1]

	Implicit	Explicit
Input -providing	• Recast	• Explicit correction
Output -prompting	• Repetition • Clarification request	• Metalinguistic feedback • Elicitation • Paralinguistic signal

---
B

Below is an excerpt from the conversation between a teacher and a student in a conversation class.

T : So, Jae-min. What did you do yesterday?

S : Yesterday, I go to the cinema.

T : *(using his right forefinger to indicate "past")*

S : Oh, I went to the cinema.

T : What movie did you see?

S : I see the Fast and the Furious.

T : You saw the Fast and the Furious?

S : Yes.

T : You must have lots of fun. Then, who did you watch the movie with?

S : I watch it with my sister.

T : I watch it with my sister?

S : Oh, I watched it with my sister.

T=teacher, S=student

Referring to Table 1 in <A>, identify the feedback utterance which is implicit and output-prompting in <B>. Also, explain how the identified utterance works for acquisition with evidence.

Your Answer

_____

_____

_____

_____

_____

12 Read the passages and follow the directions.

A

Lesson A

Step 1

- T shows a video clip related to 'Global Warming' and activates students' schematic knowledge.
- T pre-teaches new words before reading the text.
  (e.g. glacier, cloud forest, scramble)

Step 2

- Ss read the text individually and share ideas on what we can do to stop global warming in groups.
- T models how to make a poster promoting a global warming issue.
- Ss in groups make a poster using the ideas they have shared. While Ss carry out the task, T circulates and offers feedback, suggestions, or language help when Ss ask for.
- Ss in groups make a presentation for their posters.

Step 3

- T provides feedback with a clear explanation about the incorrect language usage Ss have in common.
- T provides quizzes dealing with the problematic language form.

[Text] What is global warming?

Glaciers are melting, sea levels are rising, cloud forests are dying, and wildlife is scrambling to keep pace. It's becoming clear that humans have caused most of the past century's warming . . . We call the result global warming, but it is causing a set of changes to the Earth's climate. Have we tried anything to save the Earth? What will we do to slow this warming?

. . .

[Sample Poster]

SLOGAN : Global Warming Does Not Hibernate!

What we can do to stop Global Warming :

1. Reduce water waste.
2. Pull the plugs.
3. Use public transportation.

─┤ **B** ├─

Lesson B

Step 1

• T begins the lesson by presenting a target language item through the text.

Flood Closes PMG Mall

Yesterday's thunderstorm and heavy rains caused a flood in the PMG Mall, 1.5 meter of water filled the lower level. The flood didn't hurt any shoppers, but the stores had to close early. Mr. Kim's store, Ice Cream Plant, was full of water. "I was talking on the phone when water started to pour in. It was so scary, so I ran," said Mr. Kim. "I haven't seen all the damage yet!" The most severe damage was in Jung's Meat shop. "I lost 300 kilograms of meat," said Ms. Jung. Luckily, shoppers haven't been discouraged by the flood. Repairs have already begun at PMG Mall. The mall will reopen next week.

• While reading the story, T explains the usage of the target form, 'have p.p.'

Step 2

T asks Ss to practice the target form in pairs.

1. I have already finished lunch.
   (He) has already finished lunch.

2. I haven't played with a dog.
(She) _____.
3. I have already eaten a candy bar.
(John) _____.

. . .

10. I have been to Japan.
(My mom) _____.

Step 3

Ss ask and answer the following questions in pairs.

Ask and answer the questions with your partner.

1. Have you traveled anywhere?

_____.

2. If yes, where and when have you been?

_____.

3. Have you experienced anything fun there?

_____.

T=teacher, Ss=students

Between the two lessons <A> and <B>, choose ONE lesson which helps students to pay attention to the gaps between their utterances and the correct forms. Then, provide the evidence from the data.

Your Answer

_____

_____

_____

_____

_____

13 Read the passages and follow the directions.

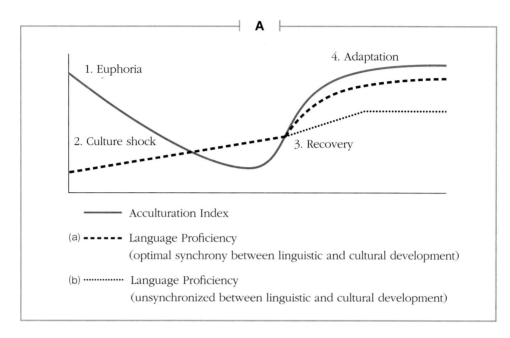

┤ A ├

- 1. Euphoria
- 2. Culture shock
- 3. Recovery
- 4. Adaptation

———— Acculturation Index

(a) ------ Language Proficiency
(optimal synchrony between linguistic and cultural development)

(b) ············ Language Proficiency
(unsynchronized between linguistic and cultural development)

┤ B ├

Soomin's Learning Log

After some modules about "American Culture," I got used to the Western culture different from Korean culture. Besides, the more I understood the culture, the more I put my efforts to improve my English ability. Before taking these lessons, I had not understood why the American people call their names regardless of the age difference. It was a culture shock, hindering me from studying English. However, I recovered from the culture shock thanks to the culture session. From my experiences, I got a lesson: the English language and English culture should be learned simultaneously, which helps me have a good command of English.

Jaewoo's Learning Log

I took the 'American culture' classes. Learning culture was fun and helpful. Before taking the class, giving a hug any time and anywhere looked so strange. However, as "American Culture" sessions went, I accepted it smoothly and even it looked great! What a change! The more I had cultural learning, the more I fell in love with the American lifestyle and their attitude. However, I did not study the English language as much as I was absorbed in learning American culture. That's my big problem. As a result, I got C– in English this semester even though I could understand American cultures well.

Considering two language proficiency graphs (a) and (b) from <A>, match each graph to the case of Soomin and Jaewoo, respectively. Then, explain the cause of language proficiency difference between the two students, starting from the Recovery stage.

Your Answer

_____

_____

_____

_____

_____

14   Read the passages and follow the directions.

┤ **A** ├

Activities

(a) **Summarizing**: Ss read a story called *The Ugly Duckling*. Ss first read the story as a whole group, then they read with partners. At the end of the lesson, Ss are asked to summarize the main idea and the sequence of events, not focusing on every detail.

(b) **Dialogue journals**: Ss can provide a personal and private connection to a trustworthy adult. Dialogue journals are an excellent way to keep up with their emotional changes and clarify information for them in a way that does not embarrass them in front of their peers. The dialogue journal provides a safe haven for building trust with an adult, naming and exploring feelings, and resolving issues.

(c) **Proofreading**: T explains to Ss that it is important to proofread their work and not rely solely on a spell check program. T passes out a sample page that T has created and gives Ss time to find as many of the incorrect words as they can. Review the page as a group and discuss any of the more difficult words.

T=teacher, Ss=students

┤ **A** ├

Soo-ah's Learning Log

Today, my teacher asked us to do a self-survey to find out my learning styles. It was a useful activity to know about myself. With the survey results, I had a consultation with my teacher. She said I have many good characteristics as a language learner. However, she pointed out that I have a 'tunnel vision.' Hence, she suggested me to practice finding the overall gist while reading or listening to a text. She said that I tend to focus on details too much. Thus, she prepared a compensatory activity for me to be a better learner with balanced learning styles.

Ji-eun's Learning Log

Through a self-survey, I found my learning styles. During a consultation about the survey results, my teacher told me that I am good at catching the overall meaning. For example, I can find the main idea and the implied meanings of a reading or listening text very well. For writing, I maintain the good flow of the whole contents. However, my weakness is incorrect expressions. To be specific, I make small errors a lot, which I do not notice. To solve this problem, my teacher gave me an activity to practice self-correction on small parts of a whole text. Through this practice, I hope I can get a balance in my learning styles.

Referring to <A> and <B>, identify the learning style of each student and choose a proper activity for each to be a better language learner. Then, provide the reason for your choice from the data.

Your Answer

15 Read Mr. Kim's teaching log and follow the directions.

Mr. Kim's Teaching Log

I am a teacher of students who are at the very beginning level of their English proficiency. A major part of my teaching philosophy is that language learners benefit from learning the target language in natural communication. So I try to maximize opportunities for my students to listen to and read the target language in meaningful contexts. Since my students are not able to talk or write in English, I do not force them to speak. However, after much exposure to English, I believe their speech will naturally emerge and then move toward full production where they can produce longer and more complex utterances. The following table shows the brief characteristics of language learners' development stages that I am assuming along with the kinds of activities that I will employ in those stages.

Stage 1	Stage 2	Stage 3
Meaning of words taught by: • Visual aids • Descriptions of pictures and people • Emphasize key words • Oral production not forced	Activities include: • Pictures • Charades • Role-playing • Open-dialogues • Charts, tables, graphs • Newspaper ads	Activities include: • Games and recreational activities • Content activities • Information/problem solving activities • Group discussions
Learners may respond by: • Physical contact with the pictures and objects being discussed • Pointing to an item or picture • Gesturing or nodding • Yes/no answers	Learners may respond by: • Sentence completion • Questions and answers • Two word strings and short phrases	Learners may respond by: • Complete sentences • Dialogue • Expended narrative

Identify the name of teaching approach (methodology) that Mr. Kim relies on. Then, write TWO of his teaching principles which aid students' comprehension of the target language.

Your Answer

_____

_____

_____

_____

_____

16 Read the passages and follow the directions.

─────────┤ **A** ├─────────

Types of Oral Corrective Feedback in Second Language Classrooms

Types Purpose	Implicit	Explicit
Reformu- lations	Conversational recast • a reformulation of a student utterance in an attempt to resolve a communication breakdown.	Didactic recast • a reformulation of a student utterance in the absence of a communication problem Explicit correction • a reformulation of a student utterance plus a clear indication of an error Explicit correction with metalinguistic explanation • In addition to signalling an error and providing the correct form, there is also a metalinguistic comment
Prompts	Repetition • a verbatim repetition of a student utterance, often with adjusted intonation to highlight the error Clarification request • a phrase such as 'Pardon?' and 'I don't understand' following a student utterance to indirectly signal an error.	Metalinguistic clue • a brief metalinguistic statement aimed at eliciting a self-correction from the student Elicitation • directly elicits a self-correction from the student, often in the form of a wh-question Paralinguistic signal • an attempt to non-verbally elicit the correct form from the learner

---
B

Below is an excerpt from a conversation between students and Ms. Kim during a speaking lesson.

T : Good morning, everyone!

Ss : Good morning, Ms. Kim!

T : How were your holidays? Did you have a nice time?

S1 : It was fantastic, Ms. Kim! I went to Jeju island with my family!

T : That's excellent! You can write about your vacation to Jeju today!

S1 : Sure.

T : How about you, Jin-ju? How were your holidays?

S2 : It was good. I was my grandma's house.

T : Excuse me?

S2 : Oh, I was at my grandma's house. I was there.

T : That's good. Where does she live?

S2 : She lives in Busan, so I leaves at 7 a.m.

T : You left home at 7 a.m!

S2 : Yes, so early.

T=teacher, Ss=students, S=student

Referring to <A>, identify TWO types of corrective feedback exemplified in <B>. Then, write the reason Ms. Kim uses each identified feedback, citing the line.

Your Answer

_____

_____

_____

_____

_____

17 **Read the passage in \<A\> and a teacher's note in \<B\> and follow the directions.**

┤ **A** ├

A researcher provides a brief sketch of the u-shaped curve, common in first language acquisition, and also found in second language learners. U-shaped learning denotes one frequent developmental path when new cognitive skills are developed. Imagine a curve shaped like a letter "U" in a graph with the x-axis depicting time, and the y-axis depicting the learner's level of skill. Learners often start out with seemingly high levels of skill, but then go through a certain phase in which students undergo a dip in performance. Then later, learners return to the high levels of performance once again. For example, a Korean student learned the expression 'Do you come to ~ ?'. But later, the student may use 'Do you go to ~?' instead of 'come to', and finally, she again uses 'Do you come to ~ ?'.

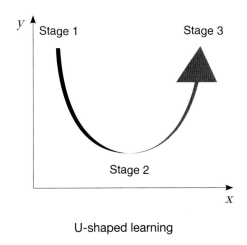

U-shaped learning

B

Teacher's Note

Whenever I teach a new target form to my students, interestingly, they show a three stage-based learning pattern. For example, when I taught the verb 'broke' in transitive and ergative contexts, in the beginning, they accepted both uses of the verb: they judged "He broke the vase" and "The vase broke" to be good English. However, at the next lesson, they rejected the _____ construction: they judged "The vase broke" to be incorrect English. Then, later they accepted both uses more correctly. While observing such a pattern of learning, I wondered why students go through regression. So I checked one research article. According to the article, this occurs when students' monitor is down due to either stress or relaxation. Besides, it usually lasts for very brief periods of time. Through this article, I clearly understand that this temporary regression is natural and inevitable for language learning.

Fill in the blank with the ONE word from <B>. Then, explain the "a certain phase" underlined in <A>, citing concrete examples from <B>.

Your Answer

MEMO

Build Up New
박현수 영어교육론 Ⅳ

Classroom Context (1)

기입형

서술형

Chapter

02 Classroom Context (1)

🔒 정답 및 모범 답안 p. 6

01 Review the lesson procedure and follow the directions.

Below is an overview of a new teaching model for the upcoming semester designed by a middle school English teacher, Ms. Song.

Day 1	T presents a whole group lesson to review foundational skills, introduce the overarching questions of the unit, and preview the unit's timeline and milestones.
Day 2-8	Students work independently in the online curriculum. Students who have questions put a red plastic cup on their desks to let the teacher know they need help.
	Based on students' questions and real-time data, the teacher works with students one-on-one, in a small group, or teaches a mini-lesson to the whole class.
	Once a week, the teacher dedicates a class period to a learning game, class discussion, project, or some activity related to the unit of study.
	Twice a week, students write their feeling and reflections about the class and send an email to the teacher. Then, the teacher responds to each student's email with her feedback and personal reactions.
Day 9	The teacher facilitates a study session to review for the unit test.
Day 10	Every student completes the unit test in their online curriculum during the class period.
...	...

Fill in the blanks with the most appropriate words.

The lesson presented above utilizes (1) _____ (ONE word) learning involving both online curriculums and in-person components such as one-on-one, or a small group lesson. The online learning goes with a written interaction between the teacher and an individual student. Also, twice a week, they regularly exchange e-mails about their ideas, feelings, or reflections about the class, which are called electronic (2) _____ (TWO words).

Your Answer (1) _____

(2) _____

02 Read the passages and follow the directions.

Below is an excerpt from a conversation between a teacher and students in a middle school English classroom.

T : Happy new year, everyone! It's great to see you again. Did you all set your New Year's resolution? How about Jimin? (1) <u>Do you have a New Year's resolution?</u>

S1 : Hmm, this year, I will do a diet.

T : Diet? You will start a diet?

S1 : Yes, I am have to.

T : (2) <u>AM HAVE? Should we need both verbs?</u>

S1 : Oops, I have to.

T : (3) <u>That's correct!</u> Then, how about Minsu? (4) <u>What's your goal for this year?</u>

S2 : I ... I play [fleɪ] ... game.

T : (5) <u>Huh?</u>

S2 : (6) <u>I will play [pleɪ] tennis game.</u>

T : (7) <u>Do you play tennis? How long have you been playing tennis?</u>

S2 : For 5 years.

T : (8) <u>Wow, you must be really good at tennis!</u>

T=teacher, S=student

As seen in the conversation above, a language teacher uses questioning usually to get students to actively engage in the classroom talk. Through effective questioning techniques, he or she can elicit responses from reluctant speakers or even prevent communication breakdowns. These questioning techniques consist of different teacher questions depending on the situation. In the classroom talk above, the teacher used three types of questions as the conversation went on. The one type in (1), (4) and (7) encourages students' higher-order thinking skills and authentic use during the conversation. Such type is called (1) _____ which require information unknown to the teacher. That's why the teacher shows a genuine reaction in (8) to the student's response following this question. On the other hand, another type in (2) leads the teacher to check and test students' ongoing learning as an important tool in the classroom. For the student's response to the second type, thereby, he or she provides evaluation as seen in (3). Finally, the other type in (5) is used for meaning negotiation because the teacher does not understand the student's previous utterance on account of wrong pronunciation. Thanks to this question in (5), he or she invites the student to reformulate their utterance as seen in (6), resulting in solving communication breakdown. The final question type is called a/an (2) _____.

Complete the comments on the conversation above by filling in each blank with TWO words.

Your Answer　　(1) _____

(2) _____

03   Read the passage and follow the directions.

Below are excerpts from a lesson plan for science, English, and art classes, respectively. After having a teacher's conference, teachers have decided to choose the same theme and prepare interrelated lessons where students can have a deeper understanding of the topic-related content.

Lesson 1. Science

- Ask students what they know about recycling.
- Talk about different ways people can recycle.
- Ask students what they recycle at home and school.
- Explain that objects can go into three categories when you need to get rid of them: trash, compost, objects that can be broken down and used in the soil, and recycling, which is generally glass, plastic, and paper that can be broken down and made into new items.
- Explain which items are recyclable and not recyclable using the table below.

What is recyclable?	What is not recyclable?
□ Aluminum and steel cans □ Plastic beverage containers (e.g. water and soda bottles) □ Clear glass bottles and jars □ Plastic six-pack rings □ Corrugated cardboard	□ Pizza boxes and wax-coated cardboard - The grease and/or wax on these boxes interferes with the recycling process □ Plastic bags - Recycle at your local grocery store.

- Ask students in groups to do research work about the relationship between global warming and recycling.

Lesson 2. English

- Have the students make a circle around the classroom. Tell the students that they will be tossing a globe/ball to brainstorm ways that people can help or hurt the environment.
- Begin with the topic of "helping the environment" and ask students to think of ways they can help the environment. Toss the ball to a student and allow that student to share.
- After a minute, transition to the topic of "hurting the environment." Use the same procedure as students brainstorm ways that individuals can hurt the environment.
- Tell the students they will be reading about the specific ways that an individual's actions can have an effect on the environment. Relate this to the reading skill of "cause and effect" and tell the students that they will be finding multiple effects in the text.

> [Text] Actions Around the House
>
> If you look very closely you will notice things that you can do around your house to make the Earth a better place to live. You might consider planting some extra bushes or flowers around your house. Plants can be a place where animals like birds and squirrels can live. Flowers can provide food for butterflies and bees. When butterflies and bees land on some flowers, they can transfer pollen and help pollinate other plants. (...)

Lesson 3. Art

- Introduce different digital posters on helping the environment.
- Have students partner up and make an awareness of how to create a poster using an ICT tool.
- In pairs, have students make their own poster.
- When students are done with their posters, ask them to release the posters on the school website.

[Example Poster]

Complete the comments by filling in the blank with the ONE most appropriate word.

> The above three lessons consist of different subjects, science, English, and art, but they are organized based on one united theme, how to help the environment. Such _____ lessons allow students not only to have a deeper understanding of the topic content based on each subject matter but to apply the learned information to a real-world situation.

Your Answer _____

04 **Review the dialogue below and follow the directions.**

Below is an excerpt of the conversation between Min-joon and his teacher.

T   : Min-joon, how was your weekend?
Min—joon : It was good!
T   : What did you do?
Min—joon : I go to Lotte world because it is my sister's birthday.
T   : When did you go?
Min—joon : I go to Lotte world yesterday.
T   : Oh, you went to Lotte world yesterday.
Min—joon : Yes. I went there yesterday.

T=Teacher

Fill in each blank with an appropriate term in ONE word.

The dialogue above shows the interaction modification between the teacher and the student. When Min-joon makes the tense error, the teacher asks for clarification by saying "When did you go?" leading him to make the utterance once again. However, Min-joon repeats the same error. Thus, the teacher uses a/an (1) _____ ("you went to Lotte world yesterday") as corrective feedback. Then, immediately following the teacher's feedback, Min-joon repaired his utterance, "I went there yesterday", which shows his successful (2) _____ of the past tense.

Your Answer   (1) _____

(2) _____

05 **Read the conversation and follow the directions.**

Below is a conversation between two English teachers talking about a new teaching method.

Ms. Kim : Hi, Mr. Park. What are you reading now?

Ms. Park : Hi, Ms. Kim. I am reading an article about a new teaching method.

Ms. Kim : Why? Are you thinking of changing your teaching method?

Ms. Park : Yes, well, for my 2nd-grade students. They used to enjoy my lessons very much but now they seem to have some problems in their learning process.

Ms. Kim : What kinds of problems?

Ms. Park : They said that they felt a high level of tension in the current classroom environment. So, I will try this new teaching method for them to feel more comfortable and have a successful learning experience.

Ms. Kim : That's nice! What should you do then?

Ms. Park : This article says that I should make the classroom atmosphere more comfortable, and help students to have good relationships with each other. More specifically, students can freely use their native language, Korean, during the lessons and I, the English teacher, need to translate what they have said into English.

Ms. Kim : Ah-hah! What an innovative method! Then, what should students do during the lessons?

Ms. Park : In such an environment, students can have a feeling of security and pay attention to what they are learning. The article introduces the detailed process of SARD.

Ms. Kim : SARD? What does it stand for?

Ms. Park : The SARD describes six factors that are essential for students to learn successfully. First, students need to feel Safe and Secure in the classroom. Then, they can pay Attention to what they are learning and, through Assertion (Aggression), become active in the learning process. Later, they work on Retention of the content and Reflection on the learning process. In the final stage, they Discriminate the difference between what they're learning and what they already know.

Ms. Kim : So, what is the title of this article?

Ms. Park : It's "an introduction of _____." It talks about non-defensive learning. In this learning method, the teacher is a counselor and tries to remove the fear and threatening factors in the class.

Ms. Kim : That sounds like true humanistic learning.

Ms. Park : You're right!

Based on the conversation between teachers, fill in the blank with the name of learning in THREE words.

Your Answer _____

06 **Read the passage and follow the directions.**

The three dialogues below show different types of responses from a student after the teacher's feedback.

1. Repetition
   S : She wear a dress.
   T : She wore a dress.
   S : She wore a dress.

2. Incorporation
   S : I love shopping, eye shopping.
   T : Window shopping?
   S : Yes. I go window shopping very often.

3. Acknowledgement
   S : I also like Gana art gallery. But my favorite one might be 'A-LA' gallery. It is....uh....I heard that the owner of the gallery is really really rich. They have Europe art.
   T : European art.
   S : Yes.

   T=teacher, S=student

Complete the comments by filling in blanks with ONE word in common.

The examples of interaction above show different cases of the _____. In the first interaction, the student simply repeats what the teacher reformulates based on his/her previous utterance. In the second one, the student incorporates the recast into his/her following utterance. Finally, the third case shows that the student responds to the recast by saying 'yes', suggesting simply an acknowledgement of the teacher's utterance. To sum up, the first and second cases can be defined as successful _____, whereas the third case as unsuccessful _____.

Your Answer _____

07 **Read the conversation and follow the directions.**

Below is an excerpt from a conversation between Ms. Kim and the students who are talking about plastic use in our daily lives.

(T shows photographs of various food items wrapped in plastic packaging.)

T : Do you know what they are?

S1 : They are bananas, kiwis, and bread.

T : Right! Look at the packaging. They are wrapped by ...?

S1 : Plastic vinyl.

T : Correct! These photographs were taken in a local supermarket. People from our neighborhood started a recent campaign that encouraged customers to stop buying anything in plastic packaging for one week! Plastic vinyl is a representative example we have to reduce in daily life. What are the other examples of plastic in our lives?

S2 : Plastic bottles!

S3 : Plastic straws!

T : Correct! Then, I will show you other photographs. *(T shows two photographs of eggs, one is wrapped in cardboard and the other is in plastic.)* One is the free-range eggs and the other is not. Yes, Young-ji?

S4 : Say that again, please? Free... what?

T : Free-ran-ge. Free-ran-ge which means the hens move around the field freely, not growing up in cages.

S4 : So the hens grow up in grass freely!

T : Exactly! The hens which grow up freely make healthier eggs than others! Do you get it?

S4 : Yes, thank you, Ms. Kim.

Complete the comments by filling in each blank with the TWO most appropriate words.

In the conversation above, when Young-ji does not understand the word 'free-range', Ms. Kim provides a brief explanation to help her understand the word considering her language proficiency. In the process of meaning negotiation, such language input that the student can understand is called (1) _____. Based on this, Young-ji can clearly understand the meaning of 'free-range'. Then, Ms. Kim adds one more fact that free-range hens are healthy and then uses a/an (2) _____ saying "Do you get it?" to make sure that the student understands the concept of 'free-range eggs'.

Your Answer   (1) _____

(2) _____

08 **Read the classroom technique in <A> and follow the directions.**

┤ **A** ├

Referring to a story she has just read aloud to students, Ms. Park has a conversation with her students in an English lesson.

Ms. Park : Did you enjoy it? Wow, you guys did it! All right! So, then, let's talk and write about the story altogether! Who goes first? Oh, yes, Jinhee?

Jinhee : I didn't like this story.

Ms. Park : You didn't? Why? Why didn't you like it?

Jinhee : I didn't like when Maria keep the ring. It didn't belong to her.

Ms. Park : Do the rest of you feel the same way? Did you not like it when Maria kept the ring? *(Five students raise their hands.)* How do some of the rest of you feel?

Jun-ho : It's okay.

Ms. Park : What's okay?

Jun-ho : To keep the ring. It was her mother's ring.

Jinhee : But her mother gave it to the neighbor.

Ms. Park : How many of you agree with Jun-ho that it was all right to keep the ring? *(Three students raise their hands.)* Okay, what should we write?

Jun-ho : Write "Some of us want Maria keep the ring. It belonged to her mother."

Ms. Park : Some of us wanted Maria to keep the ring? *(she looks at Jun-ho as she begins to write. Jun-ho nods. She writes "Some of us wanted Maria to keep the ring. It belonged to her mother.")*

Chapter

02

Complete the commentary in <B> about this classroom technique in <A> by filling in each blank with ONE word.

B

As shown in <A> the writing continues as Ms. Park guides the students, bringing out their ideas and helping them to express their own thoughts. She, in a sense, becomes a coauthor, as well as a/an (1) _____ who asks questions, clarifies meaning and makes a few contributions of his or her own. Moreover, she is providing language upon which the students can scaffold. Note also that indirect corrections are made through modeling. For example, she chooses a/an (2) _____ as a feedback type saying "Some of us wanted Maria to keep the ring?"

Your Answer   (1) _____

(2) _____

09 **Read the passage and fill in the blank with a suitable term.**

Below is an excerpt from the email sent by Mr. Kim, a new English teacher to Ms. Jung, a senior English teacher.

Dear Ms. Jung

I am writing this email to ask for your advice in my reading class. This week, I picked up a reading text about 'Deforestation' from the New York Times. During the lesson, my students were very interested in the reading topic. However, when they read the text, they looked so confused. I guess it was because I didn't give my students a general orientation to the reading topic. For the next lesson, I think I should recall what they know about the topic for smooth reading. Can you give me any advice to help my students?

Sincerely,
Jong-soo Kim

Dear Mr. Kim

Regarding the problem during your reading lesson, I recommend that you provide _____ (TWO words) before reading the text, pedagogical devices to activate relevant background knowledge relating to the topic. For example, you can show your students a short video or photos about the topic. Through these activities, you can help your students to fully comprehend the new information from the text based on what they already know. Try to take this action, and let me know if you still have an issue.

Best regards,
Sylvia Jung

Your Answer ⟩ _____

10 **Read the passage and follow the directions.**

> Below is an excerpt from a teacher's meeting where different subject teachers are talking about how to manage their lessons centering on one theme.
>
> **Academic Dean:** Last meeting, as you all are aware, we chose *Environmental Awareness and Action* as the topic to teach in our lessons. And, today we gather here to listen to your ideas on how to link different subject lessons closely. Then, Mr. Shin? Will you talk about your science lesson first?
>
> **Mr. Shin (Science teacher):** Well, in my science lesson, I can provide the environmental statistics to find out how severe the environmental pollution is. If they learn how scientists measure the Earth's temperature and check global temperature is actually rising year by year, it will be a great start to learn about environmental awareness and action. Then, if my lesson is followed by some practical action, students can easily make real-world connections based on a great synergy between subjects.
>
> **Ms. Park (English teacher):** That's a great idea! Then, after the students take the science lesson, they will participate in making group solutions on environmental pollution in my English lesson. After group works, they will make a slogan to protect environment. For example, there are 'Stop single-use plastic,' 'Save the Arctic,' 'Less boats more fish,' etc.
>
> **Ms. Jeong (Art teacher):** Making a slogan sounds perfect, Ms. Park. Then, after your lesson, I'll help the students to create their group poster about the slogan. This will be a great chance for them to raise awareness of environmental pollution.

Fill in the blank with a suitable term.

In the conversation above, teachers talk about how to manage an integrated curriculum, which connects different areas of study by cutting across subject-matter lines and emphasizing unifying concepts. They plan to teach a/an _____ (ONE word) unit that incorporates core content areas such as science, art, and English. Through this subject-integrated class of an environmental awareness and action unit, students can be engaged in far more than just a lesson on environmental pollution alone. Actually, they can attain actual information about environmental pollutions through oral language development and practice in English and have a chance to realize the concepts, which yields higher mastery of content standards.

Your Answer

11 Read the passages and follow the directions.

─┤ **A** ├─

Below is an excerpt from an Educational article provided for middle school English teachers participating in a teacher's conference.

Six ways to teach _____ in the classroom.

1. Emphasize the importance of critical thinking
2. Use social media for learning and collaborating
3. Provide guidance on how to avoid plagiarism
4. Teach students to manage their online identity
5. Help students manage digital distractions
6. Provide authentic contexts for practice

─┤ **B** ├─

Teacher's Note

Ms. Song and I read an article on teaching how to utilize, share, and create content using Information and Communication Technologies and the Internet in the classroom. According to the article, within the Internet-dominated world students should be equipped with computer literacy, information literacy, and knowledge literacy. With such skills, students can become digital citizens who are responsible for how they use technology to interact with the world around them. In the upcoming future, these skills will have become more and more important in some ways than reading and writing something. If so, how can we teach students these essential skills at school? This article suggests students can be equipped with _____ based on the following five transformative technology skills.

1. Social Media

   The power of social media cannot be denied. Most students are aware of the benefits of social media – now it's your job to harness it by equipping students with the right knowledge to use it properly.

2. Cloud Computing

Today's classwork means starting a report at school and finishing it at home. It means sharing a report with group members without worrying that they can't read the format you published in. Cloud computing makes all that happen. Students need to understand how cloud computing works and which "clouds" are used by their school.

3. Digital Databases

Digital databases are a new library. They're infinite, everywhere, and welcome visitors at all hours. Students should learn how to roam these virtual halls as soon as they're expected to research classwork.

4. Virtual Collaboration

Student study groups used to be hindered by finding a time that worked for all participants, agreeing on a meeting place, and then actually getting there (parents had to drive and pick up). Virtual collaboration has none of those problems. Many digital tools (like Google Apps) allow students to collaborate on a document from separate personal devices. Meetings can take place in the student's bedroom or their backyard, through virtual sites like Google, Hangouts, and Skype. Students should become comfortable using these.

5. Digital Citizenship

Because students spend so much time online, they need to learn how to act in that neighborhood. This includes topics detailing the rights and responsibilities of digital citizens, such as: cyberbullying, the legality of online material, buying stuff online, digital Footprint, privacy and safety while traveling the digital world.

Fill in the blanks in <A> and <B> using TWO words from the passages. Use the SAME words in both blanks.

Your Answer ⟩ _____

12 Read the passage in <A> and a teacher's note in <B>, and follow the directions.

───────┤ **A** ├───────

When students face a demanding reading, they want to do something which can help them comprehend the text better. Just then, teachers can ask them to check how to apply some reading strategies and to go beyond decoding the text. With any reading strategies-related problems, experienced teachers can present the following technique as a possible solution to teach reading strategies needed for effective reading comprehension.

_____ **Strategies**

Strategy	Sentence Stem
Predicting	I predict... In the next part, I think... I think this is...
Questioning	Why did?...When did...? What did?...How did...? Where was...? Should there...?
Visualizing	I see... I picture... I visualize...
Response	I feel... My favorite part... I like .../ I dislike ... I agree .../I disagree...
Clarifying	I got confused when I am not sure of ... I didn't expect...
Summarizing	This is mainly about... The summary of ...
Reflecting	I realized that... Next time I ... I wonder if...

| Connecting | This is like ...
This reminds me of ...
This is similar to ...
This connects .... |

B

Teacher's Note

As a middle school English teacher, I have three teaching principles to enhance students' reading comprehension: first, providing scaffolding, second, promoting higher-order thinking skills, and third, teaching learning strategies. Hence, in my reading lessons, students are asked to monitor their thinking and text comprehension as skilled readers usually do, whenever they have a problem in understanding a text. For example, with some opportunities and guidance, I lead students to verbalize why and when to use certain strategies and think and talk about whether these are appropriate or not. Then, with enough modeling and coached practice, they are on their way to becoming more independent and skilled readers. By doing so, they can recognize the difference between simply reading the words and comprehending the text.

Based on the information in <A> and <B>, fill in the blank in <A> with the ONE most appropriate content word.

Your Answer _____

13 Read the passages and follow the directions.

┤ **A** ├

Teacher's Note

For the last several years of teaching, I have been writing a journal about my lesson. It has been a great way not only to self-assess my own teaching, but strengthen the strategies, and identify areas for revision or improvement. Thanks to such _____ teaching, I am able to think more critically about my teaching and find solutions for recurring issues. As part of efforts to improve my lessons, I also have a one-on-one conference with my students or with my coworkers, regularly. Based on such diverse ways, I have looked back on my teaching, and it's been so worthy.

┤ **B** ├

Student's Log

Usually, I tend to decide on something without thinking about it deeply. Thus, I frequently make mistakes. Even in many learning situations, it is exactly the same. Thus, I really want to fix this problem. As I sought advice from the teacher, she gave some suggestions for me. Firstly, she told me to create my own learning goal this semester. If so, she said, I can recognize achievements and look back on the process at the end of the semester. Besides, she proposed me to make a scrapbook during the group project. For the scrapbook, I need to take pictures of the group work process, my group performance, and the final product. Through the scrapbook, thus, I will be able to reflect on my roles within the group, the process of collaboration, and the impact on the group's success/failure. These suggestions definitely will promote _____ learning where I can look back on what I have learned and achieved.

Fill in the blanks in <A> and <B> with the ONE most appropriate word. Use the SAME word in both blanks.

Your Answer _____

14   Read the passage and follow the directions.

Teacher's Log

My first-grade class has a wide range of ability levels; not all of my students need the same lesson delivered in the same way. So, instead of teaching a lesson to all students at the same time, I decided to give differentiated lessons for each group, customizing the delivery time, group needs and proficiency levels. The following is the sample lesson plan that I used to better engage the individual learners in my classroom. This lesson required students to use decision making skills in that they had to choose key words/phrases that would be best to search for their topic. Also, this lesson helped students equipped with ICT skills by leading them to utilize the search engine.

Lesson Overview

• Time: 135 minutes
• Grade Level: 1st grade of a middle school
• Goals: Decision making & technology skills
• Lesson Objectives:
  1) Students will be able to research and evaluate information through Google.
  2) Students will be able to write an informative text using the information they have selected.

Lesson Procedure

1. T introduces an informative writing and shows some samples written by senior students.
2. T asks Ss to choose the topic for the informative writing and plan their writing. Then, T puts Ss in groups of four.
3. T introduces four stations: teacher station, a tech station, an individual practice station and a group practice station. Each rotation generally lasts for 6-10 minutes. Ss in groups rotate each station and complete the given tasks across the station.

> **Teacher Station**: T re-teaches/extends how to write an informative text by groups. T can identify which groups may be struggling, and provide an additional guide.

> **Tech Station**: In this station, Ss watch a short video about how to use Google search engine for their topic. After watching the video, Ss choose keywords/phrases that would be best to search for their topic and then, gather, evaluate, and select information about the topic they have chosen.

> **Individual Practice Station**: Ss independently write an informative text using information they have gathered and selected in the tech station.

> **Group Practice Station**: Ss in groups share their first draft of the text with members and give and receive feedback on whether the information is well-located, organized, analyzed and synthesized. Based on feedback from each other, they revise the writing piece.

4. After rotating each station, Ss in groups meet T again with the final writing pieces.

T=teacher, Ss=students

Fill in the blank with the TWO most appropriate words.

The lesson plan above exemplifies the _____ Model. The class is specifically set up where students rotate to different stations, two of which are with technology tools and the others are face to face with the teacher or peers. Also, when the teacher takes care of one group, the other groups can engage in their own work at different stations.

Your Answer

15 Read the conversation between two teachers and follow the directions.

Two teachers are selecting a new reading material for the beginner and intermediate level students. The following is part of their conversation.

T1 : So, did you check the two texts? I went with Text A.

T2 : Text A? May I ask you why?

T1 : I think that the picture coming with Text A makes the text more attractive.

T2 : I agree! Text A contains a realistic photo to grab our students' attention and make them want to read it more.

T1 : That's it. So, you do pick Text A, don't you?

T2 : Well, actually no. I think Text B is better for my students than Text A.

T1 : Hmm... could you clarify your point a bit more?

T2 : Well, I mean, considering its vocabulary difficulty and sentence length, Text A is too demanding for my students.

T1 : That's true, but I think that Text A has more realistic language use.

T2 : You may be right. Authentic language can motivate students but not so effective for low-level students.

T1 : I see. Then, what should we choose? Text A or B?

T2 : Well, in my opinion, Text B is more appropriate and less difficult. Besides, with more elaborated expressions in Text B, students can comprehend the text more easily.

T1 : You're right! Then, let's choose Text B and add a more authentic visual.

T2 : That will be nice! Okay, what's next? Reading activities?

(ellipsis)

T=teacher

Identify the pedagogical criterion for selection of reading text that the two teachers focused on.

Your Answer

_____

01   Read the passages and follow the directions.

A

Below are excerpts from the comments about two English teacher's opinions on teaching pronunciation.

- Ms. Kim thinks that teachers should provide students with a model of native-like speech. By listening and then imitating the models, students improve their pronunciation. Thus, in her class, pronunciation is taught explicitly from the start. That is, she often uses a technique derived from the notion of contrast in structural linguistics. By using word with a single sound difference in the same position, she leads students to discriminate minimally distinctive sounds.

- Ms. Park thinks that students should work with language at the discourse or suprasegmental level if the ultimate goal is communication. Accordingly, she insists that some techniques and materials for teaching pronunciation at the segmental level be incompatible with teaching language as communication. Consequently, she directs most of her energy to teaching suprasegmental features of language (i.e., rhythm, stress, and intonation) in a discourse context.

Chapter

02

B

Teaching Materials

A	B
/iy/	/i/
sheep	ship
green	grin
least	list
meat	mitt
deed	did

Using _____, the teacher first has the students practice listening skills. The teacher says two words such as "sheep, sheep" or "sheep, ship" and asks the students to decide if they are the same or different.

1. **Listening**: Same or different?
   • Word Drills: "sheep, sheep", "ship, sheep"
   • Sentence Drills:　* Don't slip on the floor. / Don't sleep on the floor.
   　　　　　　　　　　* Is that a black sheep? / Is that a black ship?

Such listening discrimination practice is followed by guided oral production practice. Following the teacher's modeling, students read lists A and B first in isolation (i,e, reading list A and then list B), then in contrast (i.e., reading across columns A and B).

2. Guided Oral Production
  • Activity 1: Read down column A, then column B.
    (A)↓   (B)↓
    sheep   ship
    green   grin
    least   list

  • Activity 2: Read across the columns.
    (A)   →   (B)
    sheep   ship
    green   grin
    least   list

  Finally, the teacher asks individual students to read the lists without modeling.

Fill in the blank in <B> with TWO appropriate words. Then, identify the more appropriate opinion in <A> that the pronunciation technique and materials in <B> are based on. Also, support your choice with details from the passages above.

Your Answer

02   Read <A> and <B>, and follow the directions.

A

   Content-based Instruction (CBI) is designed to provide second-language learners instruction in content and language. More specifically, it refers to the concurrent study of language and subject matter, with the form and sequence of language presentation dictated by content material. Such instruction has a variety of models as presented below.

- Immersion model
- Sheltered-language instruction
- Adjunct model
- Theme-based instruction
- Competency-based instruction

B

Ms. Park's Teaching Note

   I am teaching English to 1st graders in a Korean high school. Ever since reading an article about the effectiveness of Content-based Instruction (CBI), I've been interested in teaching both language and content. The most impressive thing is, according to the article, students could be highly motivated when they learn language based on the content. So, students are willing to actively use various language skills as they do in the real world, which I, precisely, wished for. Meanwhile, through interviews with my students, I found that most students are interested in social media. Thus, I decided to organize all my English lessons based on a single topic, social media. First, I will prepare diverse activities and materials related to social media. This type of instruction, I believe, will boost my students' motivation and interest. Besides, it will encourage them to use all language skills (listening, reading, speaking, and writing) equally balanced while dealing with real-life issues. Below is an example of activities.

※ You are going to listen to a two-part recording. Discuss these questions with your partner. Then, listen to Part 1 of the recording and answer the questions.

- How many social media sites are there on the internet?
- Do all social media sites have the same status among internet users? Explain.
- What do statistics tell us about social media sites?

※ Listen to Part 2 of the recording. Then, complete the following sentences.

There were an estimated _____ users of social media in the world in 2015.

In 2018, the number of social media users is expected to reach _____ worldwide. Facebook has _____ active users. WhatsApp has _____ users, ahead of the Facebook messenger app, which has 700 million users. Twitter is _____ on the list and LinkedIn is last. In eighth place, we find Skype, Google+ and _____, with 300 million users each. In the second quarter of 2015, the number of mobile-only active users of Facebook reached _____, which is double of what it was the year before. This means that 62% of social networks users and _____ of Facebook users accessed the site on their mobiles.

※ Group Research

Choose one from the given questions and do group research. Use diverse sources such as books, videos, political campaigns, and online articles and websites.

1. How do schools benefit and lose when letting their schoolchildren use social media?
2. How do social networks make a person addicted to social media? How can a person treat that addiction?
3. Facebook and Twitter save lives: how social media helps when natural disasters occur?
4. Looking for a job on Facebook: is it safe or not?

(ellipsis)

Based on the information in <A> and <B>, identify the model of CBI that Ms. Park has chosen and write TWO reasons she takes the identified model.

Your Answer

_____

_____

_____

_____

_____

03 Read the passage in <A> and the activities in <B>, and follow the directions.

A

   Ms. Park found that most students who have studied a foreign language for years do not appropriately communicate with native speakers. Most of them, in short, say a perfectly grammatical utterance that the native listener can understand, but do not conform to the sociolinguistic norms of the target language. That's why they encounter communication breakdowns easily. So, she decided to teach appropriate speech acts to students to avoid such serious breaches in communication. In the first lesson, she chose the responses to the compliments which are essential to pragmatic functioning in social situations. So, she took special efforts to incorporate information on responding to compliments into my lesson plan. Firstly, she made a handout that outlined the responses to the compliment in American English and then explicitly taught these responding strategies to the class, using many examples of compliments and responses most native speakers have used. Proper responses to different situations were given during the class. After this, depending on the situation, students were asked to respond to the compliment by saying "thank you", returning a compliment, or downplaying some aspect of what is complimented called a self-praise avoidance strategy.

B

   The following conversation contains a way of responding to the compliments given by Ms. Park, which will help her students gain a high level of _____ competence.

A: Wow, you look so different today!
B: Do I?
A: Yeah! You have a new hat! That's why! Your hat is really nice!!
B: Oh! I got it on sale, you wouldn't believe how little it cost me.

Fill in the blank in <B> with the ONE word from <A>. Then, based on <A>, explain the way of responding to the compliment that is applied in <B>.

Your Answer

04   **Read the passages and follow the directions.**

────────────┤ **A** ├────────────

A new English teacher, Ms. Kim, is supposed to have her first class for the 2nd grade middle school students. Before preparing her lesson, she thinks about how to manage the classroom properly, and so, decides to ask her senior teacher, Mr. Song, for help.

The following are Mr. Song's classroom guidelines provided for Ms. Kim's first class.

Guidelines for Classroom Management
• Articulate unambiguous objectives and goals.
• Take a personal interest in students.
• Challenge students for both higher and lower levels of ability.
• Exhibit enthusiasm and a positive attitude yourself.
• Be fair to all students.

────────────┤ **B** ├────────────

Ms. Kim's Lesson Procedure

• **Unit**: 3. How do you stay healthy?
• **Periods**: 3/8
• **Skills**: listening, speaking, writing
• **Students**: 30 students, mixed levels, 2nd grade, middle school
• **Objectives**:
 1) Students will be able to express their healthy and unhealthy actions in pairs.
 2) Students will be able to use the 'Do/Don't' form.

<u>Step 1</u>

T introduces today's topic, 'Stay healthy' and asks Ss to guess what they will do today. Then, T shows the types of activities in a flow chart and clearly explains today's lesson objectives and their goals to achieve.

Step 2

T asks Ss to call out any ideas related to the topic. T writes down the ideas from Ss on the board.

(T: How do you stay healthy? Any volunteer? Yes, Minju? Oh, you go for a jog every morning? That's a good way to stay healthy! Any other good ideas? Yes, Sungjin!)

Step 3

T provides Ss with target words and expressions related to habits for good health and bad health. After talking about each of them with the whole class, T asks Ss in pairs to choose one habit for good and bad health, respectively, and talk about them.

Step 4

Ss listen to the story about five students talking about their habits and find the main idea. T checks the main idea with the whole class. T plays the story once again and asks Ss to listen to specific information and match the people to their ideas as seen in Activity 1.

Step 5

T plays the story for the third time and asks Ss to do Activity 2 from the worksheet. While Ss do the activity individually, T walks around the classroom and encourages Ss by showing positive body language. However, when advanced students finish the activity earlier than the others and feel bored, T asks them to wait for their friends, not giving any extra activities or exercises. When all Ss are done, T collects the worksheets.

Step 6

T gives corrections for incorrect answers and scores each student's performance. For advanced level students' incorrect answers, T observes them closely and sees if they come from a lack of knowledge or just minor slips. In the case of minor slips, T puts a check mark without taking off points.

Worksheet for Students

[Words and expressions]

Good Health	Bad Health
• do yoga • eat fruits and vegetables • lift weights • laugh • meditate • exercise • walk • relax	• get angry • smoke • eat fatty foods • drink soda • work too hard • mental stress

[Activity 1] Match the people to their ideas.

Students	Ideas
• Jade • Taweoo • Rosa • Anthony • Yuri	• don't get angry • exercise • laugh • don't eat fatty food • walk

[Activity 2] Listen again and complete the sentence.

1. Exercise at least _____ times a week.
2. Eat _____ fruits and vegetables. Eat _____ color.
3. Walk. Don't always _____ or a _____.
4. Learn to relax. Try _____ or _____.
5. Laugh. Babies laugh _____ times a day. Adults laugh only _____ times.

T=teacher, Ss=students

Based on the information in <A>, explain TWO classroom management principles that Ms. Kim does not implement with evidence from <B>.

Your Answer

_____

_____

_____

_____

_____

05   Read the passages, and follow the directions.

─┤ **A** ├─

Mr. Lee, an English teacher of 3rd graders in a middle school, evaluated Textbooks A and B using the evaluation criteria below.

Evaluation criteria	Textbook A	Textbook B
	Score	Score
1. The textbook provides speaking exercises for segmentals and suprasegmentals.	5	3
2. The textbook includes meaning-focused communicative activities.	2	5
3. The textbook contains lots of transactional and interpersonal dialogues.	3	3
4. Topics are up-to-date and relevant to students' interests.	4	3
5. The textbook introduces new vocabulary in reading texts and facilitates a guessing strategy.	3	5
6. The textbook provides many writing opportunities.	2	2

...

1=the lowest, 5=the highest

─┤ **B** ├─

Haesun's Log

Since last year, I have been taking Mr. Lee's English lessons and I am enjoying his lessons very much. However, the lessons have two things to be desired. First, he gives us too many words to memorize. Before starting each lesson, we need to memorize 20 new words within 15 minutes. Mechanically memorizing words, I thought, is meaningless because I easily forgot them. Another problem is the type of activities. What I need is speaking practices for actual communication with friends, but most of the activities during his lessons are about accuracy. For example, during group discussion sessions, he asked us to use target patterns of the day and he only observed if we used the form correctly or not. After all, I could not speak anything worrying that he pointed out my mistakes. Most of my friends also seemed to feel afraid of being pointed out and so, become quiet during speaking activities. Thus, I hope that, in the next speaking activities, he would let us share our ideas freely without concerning about using correct grammar forms.

Based on <A> and <B>, choose the textbook that can satisfy students' needs in Mr. Lee's next class and provide the reasons for your choice from the student's point of view. Do NOT copy more than FOUR consecutive words from the passages.

Your Answer

06 Read the passages and follow the directions.

---| **A** |---

Below are the evaluation results for a candidate textbook by a high school teacher.

Evaluation Criteria	1	2	3	4	5
1. Is language being used in a 'real-world' way?					✓
2. Are communication functions taught in previous units repeated in later units?				✓	
3. Do the materials provide opportunities for self-study?			✓		
4. Do the activities facilitate learning for students with different proficiency levels?	✓				
5. Is vocabulary chosen based on its frequency in daily English conversation?				✓	
6. Are grammar items presented based on their complexity?			✓		
7. Does the textbook provide opportunities for self-and peer evaluation?				✓	

1=Totally lacking, 2=Weak, 3=Adequate, 4=Good, 5=Excellent

B

Ms. Kim's Note

This semester, I chose one textbook among three candidates focusing on its language authenticity. After several years of teaching experience, I realized that authentic language use is the key element for teaching students English meaningfully. The textbook I selected reflects the real-world language the most among the three. However, in terms of level-differentiated learning, it does not provide diverse levels of activities. Since the textbook is aimed at intermediate-level students, the activities are also mainly designed for them. If so, the other students with higher or lower proficiency levels would not be motivated, which is a big problem. Hence, I will prepare extra learning materials for beginner and advanced level students. For beginner levels, I will provide a new vocabulary list and for advanced level students, extra writing exercises. Thus, I believe that all students can enjoy the lesson with high motivation.

Referring to <A>, identify the strongest and the weakest points of the textbook. Then, write ONE concrete solution that Ms. Kim thinks to compensate for the weakest point in <B>. Do NOT copy more than FOUR consecutive words from the passages.

Your Answer

07   Read the passages and follow the directions.

┤ **A** ├

Mr. Kim, an English teacher at a middle school, is teaching beginner-level students. According to his school curriculum, students should have an opportunity to build the comprehension ability. Accordingly, he wanted his students to listen to and read the target language in meaningful contexts as many as possible. Also, if his students are not ready to talk or write in English, he decided not to force them to speak. After enough exposure to English, he believed, his students would start speaking in English naturally. Also, they would move toward full production and then produce longer and more complex utterances. To help his students achieve sufficient comprehension ability, he makes efforts to ensure that they deal with large amounts of comprehensible language input within meaningful and communicative contexts.

┤ **B** ├

Activity 1

First, the teacher prepares a text that contains examples of the grammatical form to be studied. The teacher reads the text to the students at normal speed while they take notes. Students then work in small groups to prepare a summary of their work using the correct grammatical structures. Finally, each group presents their work to the rest of the class.

Activity 2

The teacher presents the statements to the class orally, accompanying them with a pantomime of the actions involved. Props are used for the activities. Then, students are asked to act out the statements the teacher produced.

[Topic] Making Fondue
I take the fondue pot. / I plug it in. / I pour the chocolate. / I put in some cream. / I stir it. / I smell it. / I taste it. / I say: "Yum, yum it's good!"

Activity 3

Give the class five minutes to brainstorm ideas relating to the topic of the reading. Then, give them five minutes more to organize their ideas and form sentences. Once they have completed this, encourage them to get up and move around the room and share their ideas with other learners.

Considering the information in <A>, choose the ONE activity from <B> you would recommend to Mr. Kim and write TWO reasons for your choice.

Your Answer

08 Read the passages and follow the directions.

---| **A** |---

Mr. Kim's Teaching Note

I am teaching 2nd graders in a high school. At the beginning of the semester, I conducted a diagnostic test to check my students' strengths and weaknesses in English proficiency. Based on the results, I found that most of the students have better listening and reading skills than speaking and writing. To figure out the reasons, I had a conversation with my students and checked previous lessons. It turned out that I had excessively focused on improving students' comprehension abilities last semester. This semester, thus, I decided to maximize Student Talking Time (STT). In other words, I will give them more group activities. Moreover, regarding language forms, not my choice but their task performance will decide what to learn before finishing the lesson. That is, instead of predetermined language items, students will focus on the language points they incorrectly used during the group activity.

---| **B** |---

Below are excerpts from different types of instruction.

[Type A]

Language and functions	Procedures	Time	Materials
Language: Keywords (a bargain, to bargain, cash, discount)	Warm up: T explains to Ss how they are going to work using posters of different colors and with different meanings. For example, T shows a red poster meaning "Silence please", a green poster meaning "Work in pairs", etc. First, T will show Ss all the posters in order to see if they understand how the class will be developed.	10'	Posters of different colors
Functions: Asking for and giving information about the right price of different things	Presentation: In order to understand the vocabulary that will be used in the lesson, Ss will work on a matching activity. *(T: Before you start matching the words with the definitions, use the Mini-dictionary if needed.)*	8'	Text-book

[Type B]

Steps	Stage 1	Stage 2	Stage 3
Details	Meaning of words taught by: • Visual aids • Emphasize keywords • Oral production not forced	Activities include: • Pictures • Charades • Role-playing • Open-dialogues • Charts, tables, graphs • Newspaper, ads	Activities include: • Games and recreational activities • Problem-solving activities • Group discussions
	Learners may respond by: • Pointing to an item or a picture • Gesturing or nodding • Yes/no answers	Learners may respond by: • Sentence completion • Two-word strings and short phrases	Learners may respond by: • Complete sentences • Dialogue • Extended narrative

[Type C]

Procedure		Details
Pre-task	Introduction to topic and tasks	T explores the topic with the class and highlights useful words and phrases. Ss are exposed to examples.
Task cycle	Task	Ss do the task in small groups. T monitors. Mistakes do not matter.
	Planning	Ss prepare to report. For accuracy, T can give advice.
	Report	Ss present report. T listens and takes notes for language errors.
Language focus	Analysis	Ss in groups examine and discuss the language mistakes observed during the presentation.
	Practice	T conducts practice for language errors.

Based on <A> and <B>, choose the ONE type of instruction that Mr. Kim wants to arrange for his students. Then, explain why the identified instruction satisfies Mr. Kim's needs. Do NOT copy more than FOUR consecutive words from the passages.

Your Answer

_____

_____

_____

_____

_____

09　Read the lesson plan and follow the directions.

Lesson Plan

- **Students**: 30 students, low-intermediate level, 2nd graders (middle school)
- **Unit**: Word parts
- **Key terms**: prefix, suffix, root
- **Lesson objectives**:

  1) _____ .

  2) _____ .

Lesson Procedure

1. Introduction
   - T writes the following word on the board:
     "ANTIDISESTABLISHMENTARIANISM."
   - T asks Ss if they recognize any word or word parts. Then, T makes them share the word parts they have found. As they share, T asks them to underline or circle those word parts. (e.g., Anti-dis-establish-ment-arian-ism)

2. Explicit Instruction
   T explains what each of the word parts (prefix, suffix, and root) means, and when people use those parts. T adds that word parts can be clues to figure out the meaning of the whole word.

3. Group Practice
   - T distributes worksheet #1 on roots and introduces the grid, pointing out the root word column, the meaning column, and the example column.

   [Worksheet #1]

ROOT (G=GREEK; L=Latin)	Meaning	Examples
−ast(er)−(G)	star	asteroid
−audi−(L)	hear	audible
−auto−(G)	self	automatic

- T makes Ss work in groups of three for 10 minutes to see how many additional examples they can generate using the roots provided.
- After 10 minutes, Ss share examples they have added.
- T distributes worksheet #2 on prefixes.

[Worksheet #2]

Prefix	Meaning	Examples
a–, an–	without	amoral
ante–	before	antecedent
anti–	against	anticlimax

- T makes Ss work in groups again for 10 minutes to see how many additional examples they can generate using the prefixes provided.
- After 10 minutes, Ss share examples.

4. Independent Practice
- T distribute worksheet #3 on suffixes and makes Ss work individually for 10 minutes to see how many additional examples they can generate using the suffixes provided.

[Worksheet #3]

Suffix	Meaning	Examples
–acy	state or quality	privacy
–al	act or process of	refusal
–ance, –ence	state or quality of	maintenance

- After 10 minutes, Ss individually present examples they have found.

5. Further Practice
- Using the backside of Worksheet #3, T asks Ss to draw lines splitting the page in half vertically and horizontally, creating four rectangular sections.
- T asks Ss to create four nonsense words (using word parts) and define them, putting one word in each box on their sheet. T gives Ss 10 minutes.

[Example] Nonsense words

reautographer (Definition) —————————	

- After 10 minutes, T points out Ss to present their nonsense words and asks the other students to guess the meaning of the words.
(e.g., reautographer = one who follows around a famous person who is giving autographs and signs their name again, more neatly).
- If anyone guesses its meaning correctly, he or she gets 1 point. Ss play the guessing game for 20 minutes, and the one who gets the most points is the winner.

T=Teacher, Ss= Students

Fill in the blanks of the lesson plan with TWO most appropriate lesson objectives.

Your Answer _____

_____

_____

_____

_____

10 Read the passages, and follow the directions.

A

Ms. Park's Teaching Log

To teach my 2nd-grade students who are at the low-intermediate level, I usually choose 20 new words and phrases for each lesson. I thought memorizing new expressions could help them improve their English proficiency and promote them to the intermediate level. After explaining the meaning of the target expressions, I give students 15-20 minutes to memorize them and then conduct a test before finishing the lesson. However, today, I received feedback from some of my students that memorizing new expressions did not help much in improving their proficiency. Then, they added that they want to learn how to speak and write their own ideas and opinions rather than memorizing words that I, as a teacher, already have chosen for them. I realized that I should have given them opportunities to learn something they actually need in their lives. Thus, I decided to change the whole syllabus. Instead of focusing on pre-selected target forms and words that they should learn as a result of lessons, I will let them experience language learning closely related to their real lives. In other words, I will give them chances to express their own ideas first and then choose target expressions for the day by themselves. For example, first, they will practice some meaningful activities related to their real lives. Then, based on their performance, they will learn specific expressions they need to know. I hope this new type of lessons can better motivate my students and help improve their proficiency levels.

B

Syllabus 1

Unit	Notions and Functions	Exponents
Unit 1	• Introducing your family • Expressing possession	• This is my... • What's your father's name? • My father's name is...
Unit 2	• Expressing existence • Counting	• What is there in your bag? • There's a ... • There are ... • Numbers: 1-20

Syllabus 2

Unit	Reading & Listening	Task	Grammar & Vocabulary
Unit 1	• Reading: Museum brochures • Listening: a discussion about major historical finds	Introducing three historical places to visit in Korea	• Grammar: TBD • Vocabulary: TBD
Unit 2	• Reading: SK ecoplant, the future of cities. • Listening: a radio programme about fear of flying	Describing the traffic problems in your city and suggesting solutions	• Grammar: TBD • Vocabulary: TBD • TBD: to be determined

Based on the information in <A>, choose ONE syllabus in <B> that you would recommend to Ms. Park and identify the name of the syllabus you have chosen. Then, write TWO reasons of your choice based on its characteristics.

Your Answer

_____

_____

_____

_____

11   Read the passages and follow the directions.

───────────────────┤ **A** ├───────────────────

　　Display and referential questions are opposing question types. A display question is asked when the teacher already knows the answer students will provide; commonly used to check their learning. It is typically associated with the retrieval of information, facts, and knowledge that the students already know. A referential question is asked when the teacher does not know the answer students will provide; commonly used to seek a greater understanding of a topic. It is typically associated with students providing a personal reflection on their own feelings, attitudes, and experiences that only they know.

───────────────────┤ **B** ├───────────────────

　　The classroom conversations between the teacher and students as shown below occurred in the middle of an ESL class.

Conversation 1

T　　　 : So, will you read question number two, Juna?
Juna　 : *(Reading from a book)* Where was Sabina when this happened?
T　　　 : Good. So, where was she?
Juna　 : Er, go out.
T　　　 : She went out, great job!

Conversation 2

T　　　　: Taewoo! What is your favorite type of social media?
Taewoo : Hmm. I like Instagram.
T　　　　: Do you have any particular reasons?
Taewoo : Well, I think it is easy to use and allows me to share many pictures.

T=teacher

Based on <A>, identify the type of question that the teacher asks in each conversation from <B>, citing ONE line, respectively. Also, write why he or she uses the identified type of question in each conversation.

Your Answer

12 Read <A> and <B>, and follow the directions.

---| **A** |---

Ms. Song's Note

For teaching English to students, I believe, the most important thing is motivating and exciting lessons. However, I often experience quite the opposite. Some of my students seemed to have no motivation and thus I had a one-on-one conference with them. They commented that they hope the lessons to be more student-centered. In other words, they want to learn and personalize the contents closely related to their real lives. Besides, they prefer to study new knowledge by themselves rather than being provided the knowledge by the teacher. Based on their comments, I will choose an appropriate textbook that can satisfy my students' wishes.

---| **B** |---

Below are the results of a high school textbook evaluation.

Prerequisites	Textbook A	Textbook B
Can the cover of the book and illustrations of the textbook be attractive to students?	2	4
Does the textbook offer chances for personal/real-world content creation or exploration?	4	1
Does the textbook introduce an appropriate difficulty level of grammar items?	5	3
Is the cognitive level of the contents challenging enough for learners?	2	5
Does the textbook provide various problem-solving activities?	5	2
Are new words used again in later sessions to help students understand their meaning and application?	2	5
Does every chapter include sufficient teacher guidelines?	4	3
Does the content provide a glimpse into the culture of the target language?	2	5

0=the lowest score, 5=the highest score

Based on <A>, choose ONE textbook that is more appropriate for Ms. Song's students from <B>. Then, write TWO reasons of your choice with evidence. Do NOT copy more than FOUR consecutive words from the passages.

Your Answer

_____

_____

_____

_____

_____

13 Read the passages and follow the directions.

───┤ **A** ├───

Below is the class observation checklist written by Ms. Kim, a middle school English teacher after observing a colleague's class.

Observation Checklist

- Level：Mixed proficiency level
- Grade：1st graders in a middle school
- Target skills：Reading, Writing
- Target language：(Grammar) interrogative sentence/Future tense
  (Vocabulary) dear/request/non-smoking room/
  check-in/check-out/confirm ...
- Period：4/6
- Date：Friday, 18 September 2022

Areas	Criteria	Scale*		
Teaching Procedures	Use an inductive approach.	A	B	Ⓒ
	Teach words and expressions necessary to understand reading texts.	A	Ⓑ	C
Teacher Talk	Give T's talk with proper speed and clear pronunciation.	Ⓐ	B	C
Teaching Methods/ Techniques	Use student-centered teaching technique or methods.	A	Ⓑ	C
	Provide real-life tasks.	Ⓐ	B	C
Teaching/ Learning Environment	Give equal opportunities for Ss' participation.	A	Ⓑ	C

A=good, B= okay, C= poor

B

Notes

- T gives a clear explanation for the target grammar rule with enough example sentences. However, some beginners seemed confused about the rule given in many metalanguages.
- T gives an activity where students can use the language form in a communicative context. For example, Ss are asked to write an email for the hotel reservation.

Based on both the observation checklist and the notes, write ONE strong and ONE weak point of the lesson.

Your Answer

_____

_____

_____

_____

_____

14 Read <A> and <B>, and follow the directions.

A

Ms. Nam's Teaching Note

I am teaching 3rd graders in a middle school who are intermediate level. During the lessons, I continuously try to have a conversation with my students by asking some questions to them. However, since most students mechanically give just a short answer to my questions, actually I have difficulty continuing a natural conversation. Thus, I discussed this problem with a senior English teacher, Mr. Kim. He advised me that I should change the classroom talk type. Usually, students respond to my questions and then I evaluate whether their responses are correct or not. However, he said that I should share my actual feeling and thoughts based on students' responses instead of giving a simple evaluation. For that purpose, he added, I need to provide open-ended questions that have no correct or wrong answers. In other words, if I ask a question requesting a broader answer different from closed questions, the conversation between my students and me will be more authentic and natural. Then, finally today, I was able to have a natural communication with my students following Mr. Kim's two suggestions.

B

Below are examples of classroom talks after listening to a story about a high school student who has difficulty making friends.

Example 1

T : Ji-won, what has the writer been feeling like?
S1: He has been feeling like... Hmm... A stranger.
T : Good job! Eunji, what is the most difficult thing about school for him?
S2: Making friends.
T : Excellent!

Example 2

T : Jaebum, have you ever had similar feelings as the writer? I mean... Feeling like a stranger?
S1: Yes, I have.
T : Really? When?
S1: When I went to one of my friend's birthday party, my other friends could not come because they were busy. So, there was nobody I know and I felt like I was the only stranger at that party.
T : You must've been so lonely.

Based on <A> and <B>, choose ONE example that satisfies Mr. Kim's two suggestions. Then, explain how the chosen example follows his two suggestions with evidence.

Your Answer

15 **Read the passages and follow the directions.**

┤ **A** ├

Ms. Kim, a middle school English teacher, has participated in Teacher's seminar to promote an English-speaking environment in school. The followings are some principles presented during the seminar.

- Speak only English in the classroom
- Use visual aids as many as possible
- Maximize interaction between students
- Use different types of questions based on students' proficiency levels
- Praise even the smallest efforts
- No interruption from a teacher during group works

┤ **B** ├

Ms. Kim's Teaching Log

After participating in a school seminar, I realized that I should make a learning environment where my students can be exposed to English as much as possible to facilitate their use of English. Thus, I decided to prepare an English-only classroom. I asked students to only use English in class. They are not allowed to use any Korean in class or a dictionary to find the meaning of unknown words. Besides, I designed the whole class as group activities to maximize their interaction with each other. I believe that the more English they use in class, the better the learning results would be. Lastly, during the activities, I decided not to interrupt the communication for correcting any errors from the students. According to the seminar, teachers' corrections during fluency-based activities can discourage them or make them lose their need to speak freely. However, after today's lesson, I got some negative feedback from my students. First, some lower-level students commented that the English- only classroom has raised the _____ which obstructs their language learning due to increased anxiety, stress, and cognitive load, resulting in declining their motivation. Moreover, they said they could not ask me for help because I already announced that I would only monitor their group performance without interrupting them. As opposed to my thoughts, they wanted to have some language help from me during group activities.

Fill in the blank in <B> with the TWO most appropriate words. Then, identify THREE teaching principles from <A> that Ms. Kim has applied to her English class in <B> and explain the actual problems that her students are experiencing in class.

Your Answer

_____

_____

_____

_____

_____

16   Read the passages and follow the directions.

┤ **A** ├

Ms. Song's Teaching Note

Before starting the new semester, I conducted a proficiency test to assess my students' current English abilities. The test results showed that they have a high-intermediate level in most skills except speaking skills. According to the test results, they have good knowledge of grammatical structures, but insufficient knowledge of lexical units which can help them have a natural conversation. I believe that lexical chunks are the key to learning a new language and having a fluent and natural conversation, not grammar rules. Thus, I decided to prepare speaking lessons where they can learn some conversational _____, common English expressions used to begin, continue, or end a conversation smoothly based on specific functions. Learning such words or phrases will help them effectively express what they are trying to say, and thus help them make more natural conversation.

B

Lesson Procedure

Level: High-intermediate

Step 1 Ask Ss in pairs to read the list below and put a tick next to the new words/phrases they have not heard before.

[Asking for information] I'd like to know....(   ) /
     I'm interested in...(   ) / Could you tell me...?(   )

[Asking for clarification] What do you mean by...? (   ) /
     what does...mean?(   ) / I'm not sure what you mean.(   )

[Interrupting] Excuse me (   ) / sorry to interrupt but...(   ) /
     Can I add something?(   )

[Actions in order] First of all (   ) / then (   ) / next (   ) /
     after that (   ) / finally (   )

[Telling a story] To begin with (   ) / so then (   ) / at the end (   )

Step 2 Put Ss in groups. Groups share the expressions they put a tick and discuss when to use the chosen expressions.

Step 3 Each group chooses at least two expressions from each function and has a group conversation using them as many as possible. Then, among the sentences actually used in their conversation, Ss choose one example for each function.

Step 4 Ask each group to present their example sentences.

Step 5 Talk about how useful the expressions are for having a conversation with the whole class.

Fill in the blank in <A> with the ONE most appropriate word. Then, briefly explain the teaching approach that Ms. Song applies to the lesson procedure in <B> and write the ONE major reason that she uses the identified teaching approach. Do NOT copy more than FOUR consecutive words from the passages.

Your Answer

_____

_____

_____

_____

_____

17 Read the conversation between two teachers and follow the directions.

> *Two English teachers in a middle school are having a conversation about an alternative type of learning.*
>
> Ms. Kim : *(sigh....)* Ms. Lee. Should I forbid students from using cell phones in class? I think many students cannot focus on lessons because they are busy checking their smartphones.
>
> Ms. Lee : It won't be easy. Smartphones already became a significant part of their lives.
>
> Ms. Kim : Then, what should I do?
>
> Ms. Lee : Hmm, how about teaching and communicating with them through smartphones during lessons?
>
> Ms. Kim : How? Do you have any ideas?
>
> Ms. Lee : Actually, I am using smartphones a lot for my lessons. There are many useful learning materials available for free.
>
> Ms. Kim : I know. I also use them to search for information in class. But I am not sure using smartphones for lessons is more effective than a traditional way of teaching.
>
> Ms. Lee : Hmm... To be honest, I think it is way better than a class using the blackboard. Using smartphones allows students to communicate more easily. So, I ask students to use smartphones during group projects which need a deep level of collaboration.
>
> Ms. Kim : For collaborative learning? Can you explain more about it?
>
> Ms. Lee : For example, they can share useful information such as articles, data, or videos related to the group project using smartphones. They also share their ideas more easily through smartphones.
>
> Ms. Kim : Hmm...That makes sense. But still not so persuasive to me. Can you give me one more good point?

Ms. Lee : Well, besides, I realized that using smartphones can give more choices for students, which enables students to self-learn. I don't have to prepare all options for students because they can search for them during the class and choose the best for them!

Ms. Kim : You mean, students can personalize their learning with greater options to choose from?

Ms. Lee : Correct!

Ms. Kim : But don't you think the screen of smartphones is too small for reading a text?

Ms. Lee : Right. That's the weak point of using smartphones during lessons. For reading or writing a long text, the screens are too small and uncomfortable to use a keyboard compared to computers. So, it is difficult to learn something at length.

Ms. Kim : However, as you said, there are reasons for utilizing smartphones for learning anyway. Thank you for your explanation!

Different from traditional classroom teaching, identify the alternative type of learning two teachers are talking about in THREE words. Then, write TWO benefits of the identified learning and ONE potential problem that the teachers are talking about.

Your Answer

_____

_____

_____

_____

_____

18 Read the passages and follow the directions.

┤ **A** ├

Below is part of the coursebook evaluation by two teachers. They decided to use the coursebook for the next semester. However, they will prepare extra teaching materials to compensate for the categories marked as 'Poor'.

Categories of Evaluation		Teacher A			Teacher B		
Components	Question	3	2	1	3	2	1
New vocabulary	Are the new vocabulary presented in an authentic context followed by the words that frequently occur next to each other?	✓				✓	
Grammar item	Are new grammar items presented within context?		✓				✓
Pronunciation	Is appropriate attention given to pronunciation?		✓		✓		
Discourse models	Are there enough authentic discourse models showing effective communication?	✓				✓	
Language styles	Does it introduce diverse language styles matching to social situations?		✓				✓
English language variety	Is more than one variety of English used to meet the demand for international English?		✓				✓

3=Excellent, 2=Good, 1=Poor.

---- **B** ----

Below is part of the conversation between Teacher A and Teacher B talking about extra materials after evaluating the coursebook.

Teacher A : Ms. Park. Do you have any ideas for the three categories marked 'poor'?

Teacher B : How about preparing extra activities to compensate for them?

Teacher A : That's a good idea. Shall we think about the first category then?

Teacher B : For grammatical items, I'd like to help students figure out how they are actually used within context.

Teacher A : That's good! So, what about looking for some authentic stories introducing target forms?

Teacher B : That's the point! Very good! Ok, then, what do you think about language styles?

Teacher A : I think we need to teach more diverse language styles than now. Most of the dialogues from the coursebook are about formal situations.

Teacher B : I agree. Let's prepare some informal dialogues, too. Then, our students can experience diverse language styles from formal one to informal one.

Teacher A : Oh, well, let's move on to the final category, international English. Our coursebook mostly deals with American English only despite the variety of English languages used across the world.

Teacher B : How about providing dialogues using British, Australian, or Indian English?

Teacher A : That sounds great. We can provide students with English language variety in class.

Based on the evaluation results in <A>, identify THREE components which both of teachers mark as "poor". Then, based on <B>, suggest extra teaching materials to compensate for the identified categories, respectively.

Your Answer

_____

_____

_____

_____

_____

19 **Read the passages and follow the directions.**

─┤ **A** ├─

Ms. Shin's Teaching Log

My low intermediate level students love to read short fairy tales for reading lessons. So, I choose one story for them but the level of language is a bit higher than their proficiency levels. Thus, I decided to modify the text to help them comprehend it better. Below is a list of methods for text modification that I refer to before modifying the text.

(a) Give Korean translation for new vocabulary to clarify key concepts.
(b) Elaborate the text to add information.
(c) Provide a summary of the text to focus on the key points of information.
(d) Rewrite the text with short/simpler/less complicated sentences.
(e) Reword the text with easier vocabulary.

─┤ **B** ├─

Below are excerpts from the original text of a fairy tale and Ms. Shin's modified version.

Original Text

The bird says "You cannot sell me. I won't be bought by anyone because I was in jail. I will lose my sweet voice" The bird's feathers slowly turned black. James' hopes of making money were shattered. Then, "I will kill you and I will eat your meat!" stated James.

Modified Version

The bird says "You cannot sell me. Nobody will buy me because I was in jail. I will lose my sweet voice." The bird's beautiful feathers slowly turned black. He looked like a crow. James' hopes of making money were broken. Then, "I will kill you and I will eat your meat!" said James.

Choose all methods of text modification from <A> that Ms. Shin applies to modify the text in <B>. Then, explain how the original text turns into a modified version, citing related sentences or words.

Your Answer

20 Read the passages and follow the directions.

┤ **A** ├

Ms. Kim's Teaching Log

Today's seminar was related to how the learning effect can be different depending on the type of syllabus. In the seminar, some panel of educators argued either for or against major types of syllabuses, *product-oriented syllabus*, and *process-oriented syllabus*. The former focuses on things learned at the end of the learning process whereas the latter aims at the skills and processes involved in language learning. From the seminar, I learned that I will not be able to gain the desired objectives without choosing the proper syllabus. Usually, I have taken the syllabus which focuses on outputs as a result of the instruction, which has not seemed to be enough for my intermediate-level students to gain communication skills. In fact, they just achieved some grammatical items or some isolated functions only. After attending the seminar, I decided to choose the new type of syllabus, which focuses on language skills in the process of language learning.

┤ **B** ├

Syllabus A

	Chapter	Functions	Example expressions
Week 1	1. Trip to America	Seeking information	I'm looking for~, I'd like to know.., Do you know...?, Do you have any idea...?
Week 2	2. Daily conversation	Changing a topic	So.., by the way.., speaking of.., That reminds me of...
Week 3	3. Do you agree or disagree?	interrupting	I'm sorry to interrupt but..., Do you mid if I jump in here?, Just a moment, I'd like to...

At the end of a learning section, the teacher tests Ss' knowledge on target expressions instructed by teacher.

Syllabus B

	Chapter	Skills	Lesson Objectives
Week 1	1. Shopping	(Reading) • how to skim • write down key words	Students will be able to find the main idea from a reading text about shopping habits.
Week 2	2. Relationship	(Speaking) • attention getting • topic nomination • topic developing • topic closing	Students will be able to speak their personal information to classmates.
Week 3	3. Environment	(Writing) • collecting information • drafting and revising	Students will be able to write a report on environment day.

In the process of each lesson, the teacher evaluates students' language skills they are using to complete the given task.

Referring to <A>, choose ONE Syllabus from <B> that Ms. Kim newly chooses and then write the reason for your choice with some evidence from <B>.

Your Answer

_____

_____

_____

_____

_____

21 Read the passages and follow the directions.

┤ **A** ├

Below are the evaluation results for candidate textbooks evaluated by a high school teacher.

Evaluation Criteria	Teacher A			Teacher B		
	1	2	3	1	2	3
1. Activities based on real-life situations		✓				✓
2. New vocabulary chosen by frequency of use			✓		✓	
3. Activities for diverse proficiency levels		✓			✓	
4. Opportunities to use integrated language skills			✓		✓	
5. Reading topics related to students' needs and interests			✓	✓		
6. Grammar items presented by grammatical complexity			✓		✓	
7. Opportunities for peer evaluation	✓					✓

1=poor, 2=average, 3=good

┤ **B** ├

Ms. Kim's Note

The goal of my class is to help students use authentic language. So I will spend most of my class time letting students authentic tasks they will perform outside the classroom. I also want to give my students sufficient opportunities to work together especially when they evaluate their own performance. While evaluating each other, I believe they can learn from each other and be more responsible for their own learning. Based on these two ideas, I will choose the best textbook for my students from the two candidates.

Considering the information in <A> and <B>, identify the textbook you would recommend for Ms. Kim and provide TWO reasons for recommending it based on its characteristics.

Your Answer

_____

_____

_____

_____

_____

22   Read the passages and follow the directions.

┤ **A** ├

Activity: Table Manners in Western Culture

Sit down at the table.
Pick up the napkin.
Unfold the napkin.
Put it on your lap.
Pick up your fork with your left hand.
Pick up the knife with your right hand.

. . .

┤ **B** ├

Mr. Lee's Teaching Log

For my beginner level students, I am preparing a command-based activity with short statements describing the actions. In this activity, I will present the statements to my students orally, showing the exact actions. Different from the other simple listening activities, it makes students demonstrate the corresponding actions while listening to the commands. Hence, it will accelerate students' listening comprehension. One more good point of this activity is that I can give commands to my students in a real cultural context. To be specific, the activity is useful to teach cultural knowledge and basic table manners in Western culture. While following the actions based on real context, they can increase their awareness of Western culture, immediately applicable in their daily lives. That's the reason why I prefer this activity to the typical Total Physical Response.

Identify the name of the activity in <A> which is different from the typical Total Physical Response (TPR) activity. Then, write Mr. Lee's teaching purpose that he chooses the identified activity from <B>.

Your Answer

23 Read Ms. Park's teaching reflection and students' reflection after a reading lesson. Then follow the directions.

─┤ **A** ├─

Ms. Park's Teaching Reflection

Today's English lesson aims for the intermediate levelled 2nd grader of a middle school. Although they have learned English for six years, they sometimes do not catch up the whole meaning of a five-paragraphed passage. Accordingly, I want to implement the following reading procedure because I need to model how good readers monitor their understanding while reading. Based on my demonstration, first, the students are asked to read five paragraphs about the festivals of the world and then, they are directed by a series of questions which they think about and answer aloud while reading as follows:

1. What do I know about this topic?
2. Do I understand what I just read?
3. What do I think will happen next?
4. What were the most important points in this reading?

Moreover, while reading, then, they are supposed to complete incomplete sentences at the end of each paragraph, such as "so far, I've learned . . ." "I think _____ will happen next," "I was confused by . . . " or "I think the most important part was . . . ."

Finally, after giving opportunities to practice the technique in small groups, I will offer structured feedback to students.

Through this teaching technique I want to demonstrate how good readers monitor their understanding by rereading a sentence, reading ahead to clarify, and looking for context clues.

B

Students' Reflection

Jinwha	During the lesson, I learned how to think and say about what I think and read from the teacher at the end of each paragraph. Then I engaged in the group discussion about how to complete the sentence. I thought I understood the flow of the passage pretty well but I realized that I frequently missed the key points through group discussion and teacher' feedback. Thanks to to-day's lesson I learned how to improve my reading comprehension while reading.
Hyunsik	Actually, I didn't know what to do when I faced confusing points in the text. However, from today's lesson I learned how to reread a sentence, read ahead to clarify and look for some clues. It was quite helpful to improve my reading comprehension skills.

Based on <A> and <B>, identify one teaching technique that Ms. Park implemented in her reading lesson and write its two benefits. Do NOT copy more than FOUR consecutive words from the passage.

Your Answer

24 **Read the passages and follow the directions.**

─┤ **A** ├─

Materials can be adapted for many reasons. Materials adaptation can be carried out by using a number of different techniques as follows.

Types of Material Adaptation

1. **Addition**: Where there seems to be inadequate coverage, teachers may decide to add to textbooks, either in the form of texts or exercise materials.
2. **Reduction**: Where the teacher shortens an activity to give is less weight or emphasis.
3. **Extension**: Where an activity is lengthened in order to give it an additional dimension. For example, a vocabulary activity is extended to draw attention some syntactic patterning.
4. **Replacement**: Text or exercise material which is considered inadequate, for whatever reason, may be replaced by more suitable material.
5. **Reordering**: Teachers may decide that the order in which the textbooks are presented is not suitable for their students. They can then decide to plot a different course through the textbooks from the one the writer has laid down.
6. **Simplifying**: Teachers could be rewording instructions or text to make them more accessible to learners.

B

Mr. Lee's Teaching Log

I am teaching first-year middle school students whose proficiency levels are very low. After conducting a needs analysis, I have learned that the students find the reading sections of the textbook too difficult and that they are interested in animals. While I plan a reading lesson for the next week, I want to control the number of new vocabulary items and rewrite some complex sentences. In addition, to maximize students interests I consider substituting the topic "the reasonable consumption" in Unit 1 for the text about "the animals". I believe that this change will help my students become better prepared for reading and more engaged in English language learning.

Referring to the information in <A>, and <B>, explain the reason why Mr. Lee wants to adapt the materials, and identify TWO techniques, the teacher is going to use for materials adaptation. Do NOT copy more than FOUR consecutive words from the passage.

Your Answer

_____

_____

_____

_____

_____

25 **Read the passages and follow the directions.**

---| **A** |---

Communication Strategies

(1) Avoidance strategies

    ⓐ syntactic

    ⓑ phonological

    ⓒ topical avoidance

(2) Compensatory strategies

    ⓐ prefabricated pattern

    ⓑ appeal for help

    ⓒ code-switching

    ⓓ word coinage

    ⓔ nonlinguistic signals

---| **B** |---

   A student and a teacher are talking about what the student did last week.

S : I visited my grandmother's house in Busan last week because of the Thanksgiving day. She seemed to be very pleased to see me.

T : What did you do while visiting her?

S : I went to a park nearby the grandmother's house with my two little cousins. The weather was so nice and I really liked the cool *bleese*.

T : *Breeze.*

S : *Bleese.*

T : No. *Breeze.*

S : Hmm . . . (1) <u>*Bl* . . . Anyway, I liked the *wind*</u> and the sky was blue.

T : That must have been really beautiful.

S : I also bought . . . Hmm . . . Y'know (2) <u>*airballs*</u>? For my cousins.

T : You mean, balloons?

S : Ah, yeah! balloons. Thank you.

S=student, T=teacher

According to the categorization in <A>, identify the communication strategies used in the underlined utterances in <B>. Then briefly explain why each strategy is used.

Your Answer

_____

_____

_____

_____

_____

26 Read the passages and follow the directions.

─────────────── A ───────────────

Textbooks are probably the teacher's and student's most valuable resource. They are normally quite well organized and help us to progress step by step through chapters. However, we need to remember that textbooks are produced to be used by teachers in very different schools and with students whose knowledge and ability can be greatly different. Hence, if you want to plan lessons that work for your own students and their particular learning needs, you need to be creative in how you use it. Then, how teachers can adapt a material? They can apply SARS: Select, Adapt, Reject, and Supplement. Below are definitions of each way of adaptation.

- S : select the activities, from the textbook, you want your students to do.
- A : adapt the texts or activities, by adding or reducing the number, or changing the type to be suitable for your students' needs and proficiencies.
- R : reject texts or activities as not being useful for the purpose of your lesson.
- S : supplement the textbook by finding some extra activities to add in.

─────────────── B ───────────────

Below are the lesson plans designed by Ms. Song.

The Original Textbook Activities

1. T introduces the reading topic and activates students' schematic knowledge.
2. T explains new vocabulary from the text, using example sentences.
3. T provides pre-set questions that Ss will find the answers while reading the text.
4. Ss read the reading text individually, thinking about the answers for the preset questions.
5. Ss in pairs discuss their answers, and then T checks the answers with the whole class.

6. T provides a model writing of an opinion essay and asks Ss in groups to write their opinions on what the text describes.

7. Each group gives and receives feedback to edit their group writing using a checklist. T asks Ss to post their final version to a class blog.

The Revised Textbook Activities

1. T introduces the reading topic and shows a short video related to the topic. Through such a viewing process, Ss can obtain specific information related to the topic, which activates their schematic knowledge.

2. T provides example sentences to teach new vocabulary from the text.

3. T gives pre-set questions before Ss reading the text.

4. Ss read the reading text individually, finding out the answers for the preset questions.

5. Ss in pairs discuss their answers and then, T checks the answers with the whole class.

6. T provides a model writing of an opinion essay and asks Ss in groups to write their opinions on what the text describes.

7. Each group gets and gives feedback to edit their group writing using a checklist. When they are done, each group presents their group essay to the whole class. T asks Ss to post their final version to a class blog.

T=teacher, Ss=students

Referring to <A>, identify the type of material adaptation that Ms. Song has applied to 'the revised textbook activities' in <B> and provide TWO concrete examples from <B>.

Your Answer

_____

_____

_____

_____

_____

27   Read the passages and follow the directions.

┤ **A** ├

In class, students want to know about the new context of new learning material, needed to understand what they are learning and why it is applicable to their lives. However, without proper support for that, they easily lose focus during lessons. For that matter, one possible solution is providing students with a/an _____. It helps students to stay focused and teachers to provide a framework in which the lesson can be well understood. Below are the three examples that teachers can easily utilize to make their lessons more effective.

1. Textbook Headings

   Teachers can ask the students to skim the textbook and to write the headings and subheadings on the board as a numbered list of agenda items to cover in class.

2. Questions

   Instead of writing a to-do list on the board, write questions that will be answered or discussed in a given lesson. Again, this will give a context to the new information that students learn in the course of a lesson.

3. Graphic Organizers

   For example, teachers can give a KWL Chart and have students recall their prior knowledge about a topic. Complete the prior knowledge portion of the chart and refer back to it throughout the lesson. Teachers might also give students an incomplete graphic organizer or mind map.

─┤ **B** ├─

Ms. Jung's Note

Last week, I participated in a teacher's conference and realized that rote learning where students repeat the learning material over and over until they memorize it, is not effective. In fact, the learning process should be meaningful by helping students to connect any new knowledge with their existing knowledge. So, today, I began my reading lesson by giving the students some questions and a mapping activity. With the questions I wrote on the board, they made a guess what the text would be about. Also, I provided an incomplete map that they need to fill up later. With the map, they recalled what they know about the reading topic. After the lesson, I asked my students how helpful the pre-reading activities were. They commented that the activities helped them predict what the text would be about by recollecting their previous knowledge. Also, they felt that they were able to get the new information faster and remember it longer by visualizing the relationship between what they previously know and what they newly learn.

Based on the information in <A> and <B>, fill in the blank in <A> with the name of the tool in TWO words. Then, referring to <B>, write TWO benefits of the identified tool.

Your Answer

_____

_____

_____

_____

Build Up New

박현수 영어교육론 Ⅳ

Classroom Context (2)

기입형

서술형

Chapter 03 Classroom Context (2)

🔒 정답 및 모범 답안 p. 12

🔒 정답 및 모범 답안 p. 12

☑ 기입형

01 Read the passage and follow the directions.

> Mr. Kim prepares a speaking activity to help students communicate only using their own knowledge and skills even when they don't know exact words.

Speed game: what I am

1. Students make a pair.
2. Student A checks the given word. (Student B cannot see the word.)
3. Student A explains the word using definitions, descriptions, or examples.
4. Student B guesses the word and says it out loud.
5. For 3 minutes, the pair with the most correct answers wins the game.

[Example] Word : bedside table

> Student A : Well it... uhm ... how would you say, it's a piece of furniture which is just near your bed, er... where ... a bedlamp is staying on it and where I can put my books, for example, my jewelry and all my things.
> Student B : Hmm... bedside table?
> Student A : Correct! The next word! You use this when...
> *(ellipsis)*

Complete the comments by filling in each blank with ONE word.

The activity demonstrated above aims to increase students' (1) _____ competence as a significant part of 'communicative competence' as defined by Canale and Swain (1980). Through it, students are expected to practice a/an (2) _____ strategy by describing, exemplifying, or defining the given word. Thus, with this strategy, they will not hesitate or get blocked anymore when they don't know exact words. In short, they can reduce the possibility of communication breakdown by making up for their insufficient language ability.

Your Answer   (1) _____

(2) _____

Chapter

03

02 Read <A> and <B> and follow the directions.

A

Lesson Procedure

Step 1

  T asks Ss to brainstorm diverse types of social media they have used. When Ss call out the types, T writes down the names on the board.

Step 2

  T introduces a reading text titled "Is social media good or bad?". T asks Ss to skim the reading text individually and find the main idea. T checks the answer with the whole class.

Step 3

  T chooses sentences including new words and shows them through the screen. Then, T explains how to guess their meanings based on the surrounding clues.

Step 4

  T asks Ss to read the text again. This time, T makes Ss underline any unknown words from the text and guess their meanings from the context.

Step 5

  T shows a list of new words and their meanings on the screen. While presenting contextual clues given from the text, T checks whether Ss guess the meaning of the new words correctly.

Step 6

  T provides Ss with a worksheet including comprehension questions. While scanning the reading text, Ss find the answers to the questions. T checks the answers with the whole class.

T=Teacher, Ss=Students

─┤ **B** ├─

Student's Note

Today, my teacher asked us to practice various reading strategies such as skimming, scanning, and vocabulary guessing. Learning reading strategies was generally enjoyable except for a guessing strategy. When there were new words from the text, I had to figure out their meanings using some contextual clues. However, it was not easy for me to practice it. Also, since I was practicing a guessing strategy, I was not allowed to use a dictionary, which was very frustrated. It was like torturing me. Without knowing the meaning of new words, I could not continue to read. After all, I just looked them up in a dictionary without the teacher's permission.

Complete the comments by filling in the blanks with TWO words in common.

The student cannot stand the vagueness while reading the text and relies on a dictionary due to low _____. However, from the aspect of foreign language learning, learners who have a moderate level of _____ tend to be more successful in mastering the foreign language. Thus, the teacher needs to help him develop the ability to tackle ambiguous new stimuli without annoyance and without requesting for help.

Your Answer ▶ _____

03   Read the lesson procedure and follow the directions.

Lesson procedure

1. T makes Ss brainstorm cities they want to travel to and discuss why they have chosen the places.

> T : Ok, let's brainstorm places you guys want to travel to! Any volunteers?
> S1 : Sydney!
> T : *(T writes down Sydney on the board.)* Great, Eunji. So, say why...?
> S1 : Sydney harbour looks peaceful and clean!

2. T shows short videos of some popular cities in the world to visit.

> • Bangkok   • Singapore   • London
> • New York   • Paris   • Kuala Lumpur
> • Dubai

3. After watching them, Ss in groups talk about the cities they want to visit and the reasons using the given expressions. Then, Ss choose the most popular city in each group.

> • My favorite city to visit is .... because ...
> • I prefer .... to ... because ...
> • I agree with you because ...
> • I disagree with you because ...

4. T asks each group to present their choice and valid reasons. During the presentation, T writes down some common grammatical mistakes of Ss.

5. Before finishing the lesson, T gives Ss some exercises focusing on the grammatical mistakes that T has noted down during the task. The exercises are presented in a communicative context in order to give more meaning to the language.

Complete the comments by filling in the blanks with ONE or THREE words.

The lesson exemplified above is Task-Based Instruction. During the task, students talk about the countries they would like to visit and the teacher utilizes (1) _____ techniques by asking students to talk about their own opinions using the given expressions. Then, the teacher notes down some language errors that students have made during communicative tasks and then, encourages students to pay attention to the target forms within the communicative context. In the last stage (the fifth stage) of the whole instruction, he or she prepares the grammar activities based on the (2) _____ approach which refer to activities capturing learners' attention to form while maintaining meaningful communication.

Chapter

03

Your Answer (1) _____

(2) _____

04   Review the lesson procedure below and follow the directions.

- Level: Intermediate
- Grade: 2nd grade in a middle school
- Time: 45 minutes
- Objectives:
  1) Students will be able to find the main idea and specific information from the text.
  2) Students will be able to present their own healthy eating tips.

Lesson Procedure

<u>Step 1</u> T provides a reading text and explains some new vocabulary from the text.

> ※ Adjectives to describe the healthfulness of food. Read and listen.
> - healthy/healthful: is good for you.
> - unhealthy/unhealthful: is bad for you.
> - fatty/high-fat: contains a lot of oil.
> - salty: contains a lot of salt.

[Reading text] Get Smart! Eating on the go

We know a daily diet of fast food can be bad for us. But fast food is quick and easy, and when we're on the go, it's sometimes a necessary choice. So here are some tips for fast-food fans:
- Choose the chicken. Have chicken rather than red meat. When in doubt, order the grilled chicken - not the fried.
- Go light on the sauce. Mayo, salad dressings, and other sauces are loaded with calories. Cut down on them, or cut them out altogether!
- Fill up on veggies. Ask for tomato, lettuce, onion, or other veggies on your sandwich. These low-calorie choices can help you avoid fried and other high-calorie options.
- Go for the regular size, not the extra-large. Super-size portions can super-size YOU.

(ellipsis)

Step 2 T asks Ss to look at the title of the text and predict what the text is about. Ss present their ideas voluntarily. T checks the main idea of the text with the whole class.

Step 3 Ss are asked to independently read the text and answer the following comprehension check-up questions.

(1) What is the first tip that the text suggests?

(2) To cut calories, you should cut this. What is this?

(3) To avoid fried and high-calorie options, what should you include on your sandwich?

Step 4 T puts Ss in groups of four and makes them share the answers. T nominates a few groups to present the answers and then checks the answers with the whole class.

Step 5 T provides students with a discussion question as seen below. Ss in groups discuss healthy eating tips using vocabulary from the list.

※ Share healthy eating tips with your group members. Use the vocabulary list.

Categories of foods	Adjectives	Verbs
• grains • meat • seafood • sweets • dairy • products • fruit • vegetables • oils	• healthy/unhealthy • good/bad for you • high-calorie/low-calorie • fatty • salty • sweet • spicy	• skip • avoid • cut out • cut down on • fill up on

Step 6 Each group presents their eating tips. Ss listen to the tips and vote for one best tip.

Fill in each blank with the ONE most appropriate word.

The reading lesson demonstrated above provides lots of vocabulary related to food and health based on the topic, "healthy eating tips". Also, this lesson takes the (1) _____ approach to language skills by requiring students to read, listen to, and speak about eating tips. That is, in Step 3, students read a text and find specific information using a/ an (2) _____ strategy. Then, in Steps 5 and 6, students in groups speak about and listen to their own healthy eating tips.

Your Answer   (1) _____

(2) _____

05 **Read the passage, and follow the directions.**

> *Min-ji and Eun-hye, two middle school students, are having a casual conversation sitting on a bench in Han river park.*
>
> Min-ji : Look! There is a little cute dog!
> Eun-hye : It's so lovely!
> Min-ji : I love dogs. I want to have one in my family! Do you have one?
> Eun-hye : Unfortunately, no. My sister has an allergy to cats and dogs.
> Min-ji : Hmm...I am not sure if I have an allergy or not. I want to find it out! Eun-hye, can you go to a pet cafe with me today?
> Eun-hye : Hmm...I have my swimming class at 8 o'clock but it's only 4 now.
> Min-ji : Yeah~! Let's go then!

Complete the comments by filling in the blanks with appropriate words.

> The conversation above has good cohesion in that there is continuity between one part of the conversation and another based on (1) _____ (TWO words). For example, 'a little cute dog' from the first utterance is replaced or substituted by the pronouns 'it' and 'one' in the conversation. Sometimes, a conversation can be united without any connectors if another important qualification of discourse is met. In the conversation, you can see that the overall meaning is united in terms of functions (i.e., suggestion → acceptance) and creates (2) _____ (ONE word) of the conversation.

Your Answer (1) _____

(2) _____

06 Read the lesson procedure and follow the directions.

- Students : 3rd year middle school students
- Approximate Time : 45 minutes
- Lesson Objectives : Students will be able to
  1) visit an online gallery and describe artwork.
  2) write a paragraph about the artwork and the artists based on a graphic organizer.

	Teacher	Students
Artwork appreciation through online gallery	• Provide diverse artworks using online art museum, 'Google Art Project' • Offer key expressions to describe the artworks	• Appreciate some artworks through 'Google Art Project' • Practice describing the artworks in pairs
Guessing artwork game	• Help practicing key expressions through presentation and writing activities	• Select an artwork and present the description of it in groups • Listen to the other groups' description and guess the artwork
Completing a graphic organizer with pictures	• Ask students to complete a graphic organizer	• Complete a graphic organizer about the artwork and the painter
Formative evaluation	• Make students to write one paragraph referring to the graphic organizer	• Write one paragraph referring to the graphic organizer

Online Gallery Tour

Let's go on a museum tour through Google Art Project!

Please describe the paintings we appreciated through the website with your partners.

Title	Content	Tone	Feeling	My rating
				☆ ☆ ☆ ☆ ☆
				☆ ☆ ☆ ☆ ☆
				☆ ☆ ☆ ☆ ☆

Fill in the blank with the ONE most appropriate word.

The lesson procedure above is technically known as _____ learning which is a mixture of online and face-to-face course delivery in educational settings.

Your Answer _____

07   Read the passage and follow the directions.

Ms. Jo's Teaching Log

Today, I prepared a writing activity whose topic was 'Do you agree or disagree with the death penalty.' In this activity, different levels of students were expected to collaboratively work together. For example, they exchanged their own opinion about the death penalty. Then, they chose a side between agreement or disagreement in groups and wrote a paragraph about their group decision on the death penalty. To be specific, during the group writing, high level students provided low level students with language supports if needed. So, all groups could complete the writing activity successfully without any group members left behind. Then, after listening to each group's presentation, students voted for the best paragraph, which they had known from the beginning of the activity. Consequently, these two points seemed to motivate them to achieve the desired outcome. The following is an excerpt from the conversation between students on the way to a group outcome.

S1 : Okay. Let's win the first prize!
S2 : Yeah! Let's do it. How can we start the paragraph then?
S3 : We completely disagrees with the death penalty.
S2 : disagrees?
S1 : I guess *We completely disagree* is right.
S3 : Good.
S1 : Okay, then 'We completely disagree with the death penalty. There is three reasons . . .'
S2 : Wait, it should be a plural form. There are.
S1 : Oh, yes. You're right.

S=student

Referring to the passage above, fill in each blank with an appropriate term.

According to Ms. Jo, the two keys to successful task completion is to have (1) _____ (TWO words) and (2) _____ (TWO words). As for the former, when working together students collaboratively complete the writing task by providing language supports each other. If working alone, they could not achieve such an outcome. Regarding the latter, by informing them of voting for the best writing in advance, she creates a competitive atmosphere between groups, which accelerates helpful anxiety and then motivates them to make an extra effort for better performance.

Your Answer   (1) _____

(2) _____

08 **Read the passage and identify the type of academic scheduling that the teachers are talking about.**

Head Teacher : Let's start the meeting now. Today's agenda is the new scheduling system. If anybody has any opinion about this, please speak up.

Teacher A : Well. I think that this new system is very effective. Since each class is scheduled for a longer period of time than normal, I can let my students practice enough of the new forms they learn on the day. For example, for the first 50 minutes, I lead the lesson based on necessary interaction with my students and for the second 50 minutes, my students do a group activity the entire time. I help them whenever they need me. My students seem to be satisfied with this new system.

Head Teacher : Thank you for your sharing, Mr. Moon. Any other opinions?

Teacher B : I agree with Mr. Moon's opinion. Because I have 100 minutes for one class, I can spend enough time offering background knowledge using a video clip or a short article related to the topic for the day. It enables my students to understand the lesson much easier with more fun.

Teacher C : Might I add, this new system allows us to place students into different classes based on their English level. So I can plan the lessons with the right level of content for my students. Furthermore, I have more time to communicate with my students. For instance, before applying this new scheduling system, I could not talk with them one by one due to the time constraint. But now I interact with each student very often. Also, feedback from my students shows that they are highly satisfied.

Head Teacher : What great opinions from all of you. Through this new system, I believe that all students can have more recess. Also this system offers more concentrated experiences of subjects. Even after this meeting, if you have any further opinion on this system, please feel free to come to my office and talk to me. Now I'd like to finish this meeting.

Your Answer

_____

09   Read the two students' conversation, and follow the directions.

Below is the conversation between first-year middle school students. They are talking about their recent experience in speaking and reading classes, respectively.

Hyo–min : Hey, Jin-su. How was your speaking lesson?

Jin–su   : It was okay except my speaking partner, Yoonha.

Hyo–min : Yoonha? Why? What was the problem?

Jin–su   : Well, she spent too much time thinking! To top it off, she talks slow!

Hyo–min : Oh . . . Did you ask her to speak a little faster?

Jin–su   : Of course, I did. However, she kept hesitating before speaking. She didn't try to guess anything. Totally different from me! I don't care about making mistakes! Also, I prefer to answer something immediately, but she needs much time to answer my questions.

Hyo–min : That's not good. That lessons sounds so tough!

Jin–su   : It was actually tough! What about you? How was your reading lesson?

Hyo–min : Today, we were asked to find the main idea of a text while reading it. It was okay because I am good at it.

Jin–su   : That's nice! I am not good at it, though. What's your secret?

Hyo–min : Well, I usually read a text as a whole. At the same time, I use my background knowledge to imagine the story as a big picture.

Jin–su   : Sounds cool. I should try. Then, was it all good?

Hyo–min : Actually, I had one problem. Remembering details from a text was so difficult. It's not really my style. For example, in a table completion activity, I got so many wrong answers. I just could not remember the exact words and expressions.

Jin–su   : Well, don't worry. Keep practice! You definitely can!

Hyo–min : You think so? Thank you. That encourages me a lot.

Complete the comments by filling in each blank with the appropriate term.

According to the conversation above, Jin-su is a/an (1) _____ (ONE word) learner given that he responds immediately without thinking enough and does not care much about making mistakes. As for Hyo-min, she is a field dependent learner who processes the text holistically. Also, she is good at grasping the overall message of a reading text using her prior knowledge. In other words, she prefers to use (2) _____ processing (ONE word) by activating her world knowledge to facilitate the comprehension of the text.

Chapter

03

Your Answer (1) _____

(2) _____

10 Read the passage in <A> and the conversation between two teachers in <B>, and follow the directions.

A

There are several reasons why students avoid actively participating in and practicing speaking activities. All students in the process of acquiring a second language have an invisible filter inside of them. This filter can either facilitate or hinder language production in a second language. When the filter is high, individuals may experience stress, anxiety, and lack of self-confidence. On the other hand, a low filter facilitates risk-taking behavior in regards to practicing and learning a second language. Therefore, one solution to a high filter is creating a safe, welcoming, and affective classroom atmosphere. Additionally, teachers should encourage their active participation by giving them more compliments. Moreover, teachers should be patient and wait until they start speaking. There is little use pushing or forcing them to say something when they are unwilling or not ready to say.

B

T1 : What's that? *(indicating the pile of coins on the table)*
T2 : Oh, that's the fine my students paid whenever they use Korean in class.
T1 : How much do they pay?
T2 : They pay 100 won. My students recently set the English-only rule at the class conference.
T1 : So, is it going well?
T2 : I guess so. But there are some side-effects. A few students keep silent in class. They don't want to participate in any speaking activities.
T1 : Well, it sounds that the new rule raises their _____. I mean, they might have low self-confidence and feel stressed while using English. Why don't you encourage them more often?
T2 : I am trying. But, still, they are reluctant to say something in class. I have no idea how to help them.

T1 : Oh, what about applying the rule in a more flexible way? For example, depending on students' proficiency, you can allow them to use a little bit of Korean when they don't know how to speak certain expressions in English.

T1 : Will it be okay to allow less competent students to use both English and Korean but to ask more competent students to use English only?

T1 : Sure! Then, you can see them enjoy your lesson and have more fun!

T2 : You're very right!

T=teacher

Fill in the blank in <B> with TWO words from <A>.

Your Answer _____

서술형

01 **Read the passages, and follow the directions.**

───┤ **A** ├───

Many studies show that declarative knowledge can become procedural knowledge in the sense that "learners can lose awareness of the structure over time, and learners can be aware of the structure of implicit knowledge when attempting to access it". However, it is manifest that the development of procedural knowledge takes longer time than the development of declarative knowledge. Thus, teachers often use different types of corrective feedback to assist the development of procedural knowledge. With the help of corrective feedback, L2 learners can achieve native-like proficiency after going through three stages: 1) declarative knowledge stage, 2) procedural knowledge stage, and 3) automatizing stage. In the first stage, learners develop declarative knowledge of the language. Declarative knowledge is the learners' knowledge of all the conscious facts about the language and the learners' ability to articulate those facts. However, they may not necessarily be able to apply the knowledge correctly. In the second stage, learners are developing procedural knowledge. Procedural knowledge is the learners' intuitive application of linguistic knowledge to produce responses in the target language. They subconsciously use the language correctly. In the third stage, they eventually develop automatizing stage which enables them to automatize their knowledge and fluently use the language.

B

Suji's Learning Log

In today's class, the teacher asked us about our favorite places to go. I gladly volunteered to speak and said, "I like to go to the beach because my sister also like to go there." The teacher pointed out my errors saying that "Put '-s' after the verb 'like'. Say 'my sister also likes'". Then, I continued speaking and the teacher kept jumping in with feedback on the same kind of errors. I already knew the third-person singular rule but I just could not use it properly while speaking. I think, it was only a minor mistake. After several times of direct corrections by my teacher, I felt nervous and didn't want to continue speaking. I was really so embarrassed that I wanted to ask her not to correct my errors too directly. Only with indirect correction, I would have noticed my mistakes.

Ms. Kim's Teaching Note

I am teaching 3rd graders in a middle school, who are intermediate level students. Today, I asked my students to talk about their favorite places. Some students who are very passionate about speaking English spontaneously started to share their favorite places with other classmates. Most of them used correct grammar but, only Suji didn't. Surprisingly, Suji is also a high intermediate level student, but she kept dropping the third person singular '-s'. For the first and the second time, I just let her continue speaking hoping that she fixes her errors by herself. However, the third time of making the same error, I could not help giving direct correction. Although she is a fluent speaker, she was making the same mistake again and again. I was worried that such an incorrect form becomes permanently internalized into her interlanguage system. That's why I directly corrected her utterances. After several times of corrections, she started to use the correct grammar.

Referring to the terms in <A>, identify the knowledge stage of Suji and write the reason of your choice based on <B>. Then, explain why Ms. Kim could not help giving direct correction to Suji's error. Do NOT copy more than FOUR consecutive words from the passages.

Your Answer

_____

_____

_____

_____

_____

02 Read the passages below, and follow the directions.

---| **A** |---

Ms. Song's Teaching Note

My students, 2nd graders in a middle school, are mostly low intermediate levels. That's why they frequently make errors in most speaking activities, and, also, easily encounter communication breakdowns. So, I decided to teach some compensatory strategies such as approximation, nonverbal signals, foreignizing, circumlocution, and word coinage. These compensatory strategies, I believe, can make up for their limited English proficiency. Today, I prepared a role-play activity to help them practice the strategy they learned last week. Below is part of the activity procedure.

---| **B** |---

Activity procedure

1. Ss in pairs (Student A, Student B) are given a deck of role cards on which roles of Ss in diverse communicative situations are described. Each situation contains at least one communication problem, and Ss have to use a proper compensatory strategy to cope with the situation and complete the activity successfully. Examples of role cards are shown below.

Role A	Role B
• You are an English learner. • This Sunday is your wedding anniversary. • You don't know the word, anniversary. • Invite your neighbor to your home party at 5 p.m, Sunday.	• You are a native English speaker. • You live next to an English learner. • Have a conversation with the English learner and figure out what he/she tries to say.

2. Ss choose one pair from the deck of cards and engage in a role-play while performing the roles designated by the cards. For example, when given the role cards above, Student A plays an English learner and Student B performs a role of a native English speaker.

[Example]

Student A : Hi, Mr. Green! How's it going?

Student B : Hi, Sungjin. Same old, same old. You?

Student A : I am good. Well, do you have any plans this Sunday?

Student B : This Sunday? Probably.... nothing. Anything fun?

Student A : Yeah. It's ... it's a special day. Janny and I got married on the same date last year. So, I want to invite neighbors and have a home party.

Student B : Oh, you mean the day both of you got married? We say it's the anniversary! Great! What time?

Student A : Around 5. Can you make it?

Student B : Five. Cool!

---

3. After completing the role-play, Ss choose another pair from the deck of cards to start the next role-play.

4. Role-plays continue until each pair of Ss completes 5 situations.

Among the types of compensatory strategies in <A>, choose the ONE that students can practice through the activity in <B>. Then, write how Student A prevents the communication breakdown to be expected, and cite the concrete utterances related to the identified strategy from [Example].

Your Answer

_____

_____

_____

_____

_____

03 **Read the passages, and follow the directions.**

┤ **A** ├

A Typology of Learning Strategies

Strategy	Types
Cognitive	• Classifying: putting things that are similar together in groups • Inducing: looking for patterns and regularities • Inferencing: using what you know to learn something new
Interpersonal	• Cooperating: sharing ideas and learning with other students • Role-playing: pretending to be somebody else and using the language from the reading to interview the writer
Linguistic	• Using context: using the surrounding context to guess the meaning of unknown words, phrases, and concepts • Summarizing: picking out and presenting the major points in a summary form of text • Skimming: reading quickly to get a general idea of a text
Affective	• Personalizing: learners share their own opinions, feelings, and ideas about a subject • Self-evaluating: thinking about how well you did on a learning task, and rating yourself on a scale • Reflecting: thinking about ways you learn best

Mi-jin's Learning Log

Since last year, I believe my English proficiency has improved quite a lot. Even in the last year, I was only at a beginner level. However, this year, I am taking an intermediate-level class. As an intermediate-level student, I want to improve not only my reading but speaking and writing skills. For example, after reading a text, instead of simply finding answers to given questions, I want to express my real ideas and opinions about the reading topic either orally or in writing. While reading the text, I, sometimes, strongly agree or, at other times, disagree with some parts of the writer's opinion because I had similar or different experiences. Thus, in future English lessons, I hope my teacher gives me more chances to express my own preferences and opinions and communicate with others based on real information about myself.

B
Activity 1

1. T provides two reviews of a product from Amazon.
2. Ss check the photo of the product.
3. T puts Ss in groups of four and asks them to determine if each review is a positive or a negative one, highlight clues in the review, and guess what the rating would be based on the review.

Jamie ☆☆☆☆☆(Rate here!)
Has to be one of the worst experiences ever.
Reviewed in the United States on July 20, 2022

It requires you to use your real name and photos via a Facebook account to use essentially a video game system. This is beyond ridiculous. I do not want to upload pictures of my face. I just want to play some games. Shame on Facebook.

William G. ☆☆☆☆☆(Rate here!)
Fantastic, and no fuss.
Reviewed in the United States on August 26, 2021

Honestly, the best thing about this sort of VR is that there's no wire to deal with. Turn on, sign in with Facebook, and done. Also, Beat Saber is pretty much the greatest game ever. I did pick up the Elite headband/ battery/case and that finishes off the package, but it's by no means necessary - just nice to have. Overall, loving this thing.

Activity 2

1. T provides a photo of the Parthenon and asks the following pre-reading questions to the whole class.

   [Pre-reading questions]
   (1) Have you ever been to Greece and seen the Parthenon?
   (2) Do you know why Parthenon was built?
   (3) What is the Acropolis?
   (4) Do you think that the remains of the Parthenon are in good condition today?

2. T asks Ss to read the text individually.

   [Reading Text]

    Have you ever been to Greece? If so, have you seen the Parthenon? It is one of the most visited places in Greece. The masterpiece of ancient Greek Architecture was built to honor the goddess Athena. It was part of Acropolis, a collection of ancient temples and monuments found on a hill in the center of Athens, Greece. *(ellipsis)*

3. T explains the structure 'Have you ever ~ ?'.

4. T puts Ss in pairs and makes them practice the form in pairs using the given words.

   Italy, France, China, U.S.A, Australia, Jeju island, Busan, Gyeongju, Leaning Tower of Pisa, Eiffel Tower, Statue of Liberty, Sydney Opera House

5. T puts Ss in groups of four and provides them with further questions to ask each other such as 'When did you go?', 'Who did you go with?', 'What did you see?' etc. After sharing their experiences about when and where they have traveled, they are asked to write their story into one paragraph.

Considering the information in <A> and <B>, choose the ONE activity that satisfies Mi-jin's needs and write why. Also, provide all learning strategies that the chosen activity focuses on.

Your Answer
_____

_____

_____

_____

_____

04 Read <A> and <B> and follow the directions.

─────┤ **A** ├─────

Ms. Song's Note

I am teaching low intermediate level students in a middle school. Recently, I have noticed that some of my students have excessively oriented certain learning styles, which could be detrimental to improving their reading skills. Such learning styles seem to be cultivated in past reading habits. Those students used to look up the English-Korean dictionary to find the meanings of new vocabulary while reading. That is, they did not seem to endure such ambiguities whenever facing unknown words from reading texts. Moreover, they show a learning style with which they strongly tend to distinguish parts from a whole. Sometimes, it can result in "tunnel vision" not being able to see the forest for the trees. In other words, students cannot understand the context or the flow of a reading text. To help my students reduce such an imbalance in learning styles, I need to choose one appropriate textbook for my students.

| B |

Below are the evaluation results of Textbook A and Textbook B.

Evaluation Criteria	Textbook A	Textbook B
The language in reading texts is realistic and authentic.	2	2
The textbook promotes self-learning.	1	3
The topics of reading texts match up to learners' needs and interests.	2	3
The textbook encourages students to use a guessing strategy for unfamiliar words in reading texts.	3	1
The reading texts are attractive enough in appearance with illustrations or photos.	2	3
The textbook provides communication activities where students can summarize and share their own ideas related to reading topics.	3	0
The textbook provides diverse types of evaluation for checking students' understanding of reading texts.	1	1

0=the lowest score, 3=the highest score

Referring to <A>, identify TWO types of learning styles that Ms. Song's students excessively show in reading. Also, choose ONE textbook from <B> which can help them have balanced learning styles in reading and then write TWO reasons of your choice based on the main features of the chosen textbook. Do NOT copy more than FOUR consecutive words from the passages.

Your Answer

_____

_____

_____

_____

05 Read the passages and follow the directions.

A

Below is the cycle of one new type of learning which is an engaged learning process whereby students "learn by doing" and by reflecting on the experience.

Stage 1 Concrete experience

Students engage directly in an authentic situation.

Stage 2 Reflective observation

Students notice what happened and relate it to their past experiences and conceptual understandings.

Stage 3 Abstract conceptualization

Students convert perceptions into abstract concepts.

Stage 4 Active experimentation

Students test new ideas, practicing skills in a new experience. If necessary, students can go back to Stage 1 to repeat the cycle.

B

Student's Log

This semester, I had special English lessons. After reading an article about the purpose and the benefits of volunteering services, Ms. Park asked us to try it for real. Thus, for one month, I participated in volunteering at an Elementary school, where I taught the English alphabet to 1st graders. Before starting this volunteer work, I asked her what the purpose of this is. So, she answered that we could learn better what volunteering means by actually doing it. (through concrete experience). She, also, emphasized that we could better understand what we have learned in class by connecting classroom learning with real-world situations. Indeed, by participating in volunteer service I could better understand what I have read from the articles. Anyway, based on my learning experience about the English alphabet, I tried to find an easy and fun way to remember it. I passionately prepared teaching materials and planned tutoring lessons. After this one month of experience, I sincerely learned what volunteering is. Overall, it was a very meaningful time for me.

Based on <A> and <B>, identify the type of learning that the passages deal with. Then, explain how the identified learning type can help students better understand what they have learned(read) in the classroom.

Your Answer

---

06   Read the passages and follow the directions.

┤ **A** ├

Motivation is the key to almost every successful learning program. Some educators view motivation as outside of their control—something their learners either have or don't have. But if you understand learner motivations, you can talk to learners in ways that trigger those motivations, inspiring them to keep going. There are two broad types of motivations: intrinsic and extrinsic. As we'll see, there are different kinds of intrinsic and extrinsic motivations, and their pull can wax and wane over time. Let's take a closer look.

1. Extrinsic: Incentive

   The most straightforward extrinsic motivation is through an incentive. If learners receive some kind of reward for taking your course—and for doing well—then they're more likely to stick with it.

2. Extrinsic: Fear

   Fear-based motivations sound very negative at first, but it isn't necessarily. While the motivation of the learner might be fear, the positive thing your course provides could be security and reassurance.

3. Extrinsic: Power

   Speaking of empowerment, many learners sign up for courses because they want the ability to change something about the world around them.

4. Extrinsic: Social

   How many of us have signed up for a course because we had to, but stayed because of the social connections we've made? I know I have. The social bonds formed by a community are some of the most powerful motivations.

5. Intrinsic: Competence

The first of our intrinsic motivations is competence—or, the sheer love of learning for its own sake. Many people are simply natural-born learners. They like acquiring new skills and knowledge, and they will continue to do so without much outside prodding.

6. Intrinsic: Achievement

Achievement-oriented learners are more task-driven than those who are in it purely for learning's sake. These learners want something very specific and are probably tracking goals and milestones toward achieving it.

7. Intrinsic: Creativity

Many of us have felt the need for a creative outlet at different points in our life. As a motivation, finding a new form of creative expression can be even more fulfilling than mere curiosity or the desire to cross an item off a list.

8. Intrinsic: Attitude

Finally, some people are motivated by their desire to change the way they perceive the world. They want to learn more about others, grow in self-understanding, or help others change their perspectives.

Chapter

03

B

The following students' logs describe what motivates them to choose the English coursework.

Jaemin's Log

When I read or talk about something in English, I am usually a slow reader and talker. So, if possible, I want to learn how to read fast and how to speak fluently. Fortunately, a free talking course is said to be started for the upcoming semester. Needless to say, I will sign up for the course because I want to be a fluent speaker. Anyway, just even finishing the free talking course itself, I will be able to get a great sense of accomplishment. I would be all right even though I cannot be a fluent speaker.

Suhye's Log

For English lessons, this semester, I took a novel reading and a discussion course. Both courses were very helpful to improve my English proficiency and I really enjoyed the lessons. Especially, I liked the novel reading course because I met many new good friends there. Actually, I had three close friends during the coursework. We all are big fans of science fiction so, talked about the science fiction we read on the day after every lesson. We enjoyed this coursework. Thus, for the next semester, the three of us all decided to take the novel reading course again. I already looked forward to meeting them again in that course.

Referring to <A>, identify the type and the goal of motivation (e.g. Extrinsic: Incentive motivation) that each student in <B> exemplifies. Then, provide the reason of your choice with evidence for each from <B>.

Your Answer

_____

_____

_____

_____

_____

07 Read the passages and follow the directions.

┤ **A** ├

Textbook Evaluation

Evaluation Criteria	Textbook A	Textbook B
1. Does it provide authentic input materials?	4	3
2. Does it contain some topics related to scientific and cultural issues which stimulate students' interests?	5	3
3. Does it provide diverse genres of model writing and corresponding writing activities?	2	5
4. Does it use an appropriate level of language for intermediate-level students?	5	3
5. Does it provide sufficient chances for real communication?	1	5
6. Does it encourage students to evaluate themselves?	3	2

0=the lowest score, 5=the highest score

Chapter

03

B

Below are the learning logs written by two intermediate levels of students, who talk about their individual needs for English lessons next semester.

Sally's Log

I want to communicate with foreigners freely in English, so that's why I study English very hard. As an intermediate-level student, I can understand English pretty well but need more practice to express my own ideas. In other words, my listening and reading skills are around the intermediate level, but my speaking and writing skills are not so good. So, I hope I can have more opportunities to share my own ideas and opinions in class. Besides, not only through speaking but writing, I want to learn diverse ways of expressing myself. Especially, I am interested in writing a poem and a novel. Thus, for the next semester, I hope my teacher will choose the best textbook to meet my needs.

David's Log

Last semester, I didn't like the textbook because the vocabulary and grammar were so difficult. I am only an intermediate level but the textbook was for advanced-level students. Thus, I had to rely on a dictionary whenever I read every unit, which was a big burden to me. Besides, the textbook introduced many issues related to society and history. However, since I am more interested in science and culture, I could not enjoy the lessons that much. If I had studied scientific and cultural topics, I would have participated in the lesson more actively. Hence, for the next semester, I hope my teacher will choose the very textbook suitable for me.

Based on <A> and <B>, identify ONE textbook that you would recommend for Sally and David, respectively. Then, write your reasons of recommendation. Do NOT copy more than FOUR consecutive words from the passages.

Your Answer

_____

_____

_____

_____

_____

08 Read the passage in <A> and a teacher's note in <B>, and follow the directions.

┤ **A** ├

6 Strategies for establishing _____

- Show interest in each student as a person.
- Give feedback on each person's progress.
- Openly solicit students' ideas and feelings.
- Value and respect what students think and say.
- Laugh with them and not at them.
- Work with them as a team, and not against them.

┤ **B** ├

Teacher's Note

As a new teacher, I joined an in-service teacher training, in which I realized how important the positive classroom climate is. As I learn, these days I am creating a positive, stimulating, and energizing classroom climate. Firstly, I am trying to have a good relationship with my students. Next, I am trying to make a good balance between praise and criticism. Actually, I believe students who have gotten genuine praise easily welcome criticism without aversion. In every lesson, anyway, I am trying to regard them with special attention, to honor them, to show consideration toward them, to admire their strengths, and to care for them. Overall, I think that building _____, a close and harmonious relationship with my students, is the key to create a positive classroom climate. In this classroom atmosphere, students seem to feel much more capable, competent, and creative.

Based on the information in <A> and <B>, fill in the blanks in <A> and <B> with the SAME word. Also, identify the ONE of six strategies from <A> that the teacher considers most important in <B>.

Your Answer

_____

_____

_____

_____

_____

09   Read the conversation and follow the directions.

| **A** |

Strategies and Techniques for Teaching Culture

- **Culture cluster** is simply a group of three or more illustrated culture capsules on related themes/topics (about the target life) + one 30 minute classroom simulation/skit that integrates the information contained in the capsules (the teacher acts as narrator to guide the student).

- **Culture assimilator** provides the students with 70 to 100 episodes of target cultural behavior. Culture assimilators consist of short description of a situation where interaction takes place between at least one person from the target culture and persons from other cultures. The description is followed by four possible choices about the meaning of the behavior, action, or words of the participants in the interaction. Students read the description in the assimilator and then choose which of the four options they feel is the correct interpretation of the interaction. Once all students have made their individual choices, the teacher leads a discussion about why particular options are correct or incorrect in interpretation.

- **Audio-motor units** consist of verbal instructions for any cultural routine which requires physical actions. With an audio-motor unit, the classroom is set up in appropriate setting with required props. Then, based on a teacher's orally given directions in sequence, students carry out a series of actions within cultural context.

- **Mini-dramas** consist of three to five brief episodes in which misunderstadings are portrayed, in which there are examples of miscommunication. Additional information is made available with each episode, but the precise cause of the misunderstanding does not become apparent until the last scene. Each episode is followed by an open-ended question discussion led by the teacher. At the end of mini-dramas, some "knowing" figure explains what is really happening and why the target culture member was really not doing wrong.

―― **B** ――

In the English lesson, the teacher teaches students how to eat properly at a table using realia such as a fork, spoon, knife, napkin, and plate.

T   : Now, we are going to do an activity called 'time to eat!'. First, I will play a tape and follow the commands from it. Suppose I am in a fine dining restaurant, and observe what I'm doing as a customer.
          (The teacher acts out commands according to a taped version of a script while the students observe.)

T   : You've observed what I was doing in the restaurant. Any volunteer, to be the next customer?
          (Hyemin raises his hand.)

T   : Thank you. Come to the front, Hyemin. From now on, I will give you commands and you have to follow the commands.

Hyemin : Okay.

T   : And everybody observes what he is doing in the restaurant. Let's start! Hyemin, sit down at the table!
          (Hyemin sits at the table.)

T   : Pick up the napkin.
          (Hyemin picks up the napkin.)

T   : Unfold the napkin and put it on your lap.
          (Hyemin unfolds the napkin and puts the napkin on his lap.)
                    (Ellipsis)

T   : Leave the restaurant.
          (Hyemin walks toward the front door of the classroom.)

T   : Good job, Hyemin! Have you guys observed his actions in the restaurant?

Ss   : Yes!

T   : What did Hyemin do before a meal?

                              T=teacher, Ss=students

Considering information in <A> and <B>, explain the instructional technique for teaching a target culture that the teacher implements in the lesson.

Your Answer

_____

_____

_____

_____

_____

10 Read the passages and follow the directions.

── **A** ──

Below are excerpts from two syllabuses designed for second-year middle school students.

[Syllabus A]

	Real-world tasks	Pedagogical tasks
1st lesson	Write letters	• Check sample letters and find useful expressions. • Decide the type of language for letters: formal, semi-formal, informal. • Write a letter to the city mayor, a teacher or a friend.
2nd lesson	Write reports	• Brainstorm types of reports. • Analyze situations to choose the correct types of reports. • Write a report.
3rd lesson	Write notes and memos	• Brainstorm types of notes and memos. • Write a note about restaurant service.

[Syllabus B]

	Functions	Language
1st lesson	Ask for help	• Could you give me a hand? • Would you mind helping me out? • I need some assistance, please.
2nd lesson	Make & accept apologies	• I'm terribly sorry • Excuse me for... • I do apologize for ... • That's all right. • It doesn't matter. • Forget about it.
3rd lesson	Request direction	• Could you tell me...? • How can I get to...? • How far is the ... from the...? • How do I find...?

Chapter 03

---| **B** |---

Mr. Choi's Teaching Log

This year, I am going to teach 2nd graders who are at the intermediate level. When I taught 1st grade beginners last year, I focused on certain expressions to teach in class. However, for the 2nd graders at the intermediate level, I want to manage process-oriented lessons where they can learn language forms and skills used in the given works. Instead of memorizing pre-planned forms, thus, they will focus on key expressions learnt in the process of completing given tasks. Also, they will be asked to use diverse skills as they do in the real world. To achieve these ultimate goals I cannot but choose a/an _____ syllabus. I believe, this type of syllabus can help my students well perform real-life tasks they will encounter outside the classroom. Through this syllabus, students can experience in class what they will do in their real lives.

Fill in the blank in <B> with the type of syllabus in ONE word. Then, identify the Syllabus Mr. Choi needs to choose in <A> and write TWO reasons of your choice from the passages. Do NOT copy more than FOUR consecutive words from the passages.

Your Answer

_____

_____

_____

_____

11 Read the dialogue and follow the directions.

T1: Hi, Mr. Park. What are you reading?

T2: Hello, Ms. Choi. I am reading an article about how to teach English using online resources.

T1: That's interesting. What is it talking about?

T2: It says classic teaching mode only with chalkboards, books, and homework is outdated.

T1: That's true. So, I think that we should use online resources as much as we can. You know, online reading texts, audio files and videos and things.

T2: Right. The article, also, suggests using those online resources, not for the classroom but at home.

T1: You mean, they are used as homework? Can you clarify that?

T2: Actually here the homework is not to do after the lesson but before the lesson. At home, students preview and study the day's topic using various online materials.

T1: Wow, if so, they can have enough time to fully study the topic on their own pace, can't they? That's nice! Then, what do they do in class?

T2: During the class, students do group activities such as discussion or project work. We arrange students to have more time for collaborative works with others.

T1: That's good for them, too. Hmm, so, what do we do during their activities?

T2: We monitor their performances and check if they have any difficulties they encounter.

T1: Is that all?

T2: Furthermore, we plan the next class to deal with students' difficulties based on what we observe.

T1: Wow, this teaching approach has many advantages!

T2: Really it does.

T=teacher

Chapter 03

Identify the teaching approach mentioned in the conversation in TWO words. Then, write THREE benefits of the identified approach based on the teachers' conversation.

Your Answer

_____

_____

_____

_____

12 Read the passages and follow the directions.

A

There are many taxonomies for classifying errors. Errors can be classified according to the four main processes: **omission, substitution, addition,** and **permutation or wrong ordering**. In addition to these four types of errors, errors can be viewed as either **global** or **local**. Global errors are more serious than local errors because global errors interfere with communication, disrupt meaning of utterances, and thereby should be immediately corrected. Local errors, on the other hand, do not hinder communication and understanding the meaning of an utterance. Some teachers say that every error should be corrected but others advise that what is more important is to maintain communicative flow and focus on meaning even though some errors occur. Definitely, classroom feedback on students' errors is very important because it gives students an opportunity to examine and modify some hypotheses about the target language. Such feedback types as recast, clarification request, repetition and elicitation are frequently used in a language classroom.

B

An English teacher and a beginner level of English learner are having a conversation in front of the classroom.

T : Happy Birthday! Jisuk!

S : Thank you, Ms. Park.

T : Did you get your birthday presents?

S : Yes, a lot. From my parents and some friends.

T : You must be so happy! What did you get?

S : Well . . . (a) my parents were gave me . . . bicycle, a new bicycle.

T : Wow, (b) your parents gave you a new bicycle! That's cool!

S : Yes! That's the new model I have waited so long! And my friends gave me a soccer ball, a mobile phone case, and a hoodie.

T : Wow, you got lots of presents! So what's your plan for today?

S : I guess . . . I will invite some friends to my house and have a birthday party!

T : Great! I hope you have the best birthday today.

S : Thank you, Ms. Park.

T=teacher, S=student

Based on the information from <A> and <B>, first, explain the error types that Jisuk makes in the underlined (a). Second, identify the type of corrective feedback that Ms. Park uses in the underlined (b) and write ONE reason why she chooses the identified feedback. All information should be derived from the given data.

Your Answer

13   Read the passages and follow the directions.

A

Ms. Song's Teaching Log

Since I am a new teacher, I try my best to prepare a student-centered lesson for my students. As part of my efforts, first, I survey my students' needs and interest every month. Based on the survey results, my students are very interested in environmental pollution. So, for the next lesson, I chose a reading text related to environmental pollution. Another way to find out what my students like is observation. According to my observation, my students enjoy the lesson where they use English in diverse ways. To figure out the reason, I asked one of my students and he answered, "Using different skills in one class makes me feel that I am doing a real communication as in my life." Hence, I planned a lesson that students need to use various skills at the same time, rather than focusing on either reading or speaking through the whole lesson. Based on these two factors, I designed a lesson procedure.

B

Lesson Plan

• Topic: Habitat Destruction
• Skills: Reading, Writing, Speaking

1. T activates Ss' schematic knowledge on wild animals and their habitats. Then, T pre-teaches new words on the reading text. (e.g., habitat, endanger, destroy)

> **Do You Know about Habitat Destruction?**
>
> A habitat is natural region where wildlife can live. For example, there are forest, pond, marsh or desert. Most animals and plants which are endangered have become so, not because they have been killed on purpose but because their habitats are being destroyed. Human activities have changed habitats for thousands of years. The natural habitats in almost every country in the world . . .

2. T asks Ss to read the text quickly and find out the main idea. Then, T provides a pre-set questions and while re-reading the text in pairs, Ss find the detailed information from the text. T checks Ss' answers.

3. T puts Ss into groups of four and asks each group to do a group discussion based on the template below.

Group Discussion

There are many things we can do to prevent unnecessary damage to habitats:
- Reduce pollution that can damage wildlife and habitat.
- Before developing the land, make a plan to protect ecosystems on the land.

What are the other things you can do? Let's talk about it with your group members.

---

4. T provides a writing worksheet to each group and demonstrates how to make a poster. Then, Ss in groups make a poster for 'Earth Hour'.

(. . .)

Referring to the information in <A>, write TWO factors that Ms. Song applies in the lesson plan <B> and provide the evidence for each factor.

Your Answer

_____

_____

_____

_____

_____

14 Read the evaluation table in <A> and the conversation in <B>. Then follow the directions.

| A |

Textbook Evaluation

The below table is a part of a coursebook evaluation by two teachers. They are supposed to use the same coursebook next semester. So, they want to prepare extra teaching materials after talking about those categories that they both marked as "Poor."

Categories of Evaluation (Subskills & Skills)	Teacher Ms. Park			Teacher Mr. Bae		
	3	2	1	3	2	1
1. Compared to texts for native speakers, does the content contain real-life issues that challenge the teenagers to think critically at the age?			✓			✓
2. Is the listening material accompanied by background information, questions and activities which help comprehension?		✓				✓
3. Are the activities developed to initiate meaningful communication?	✓			✓		
4. Are the new vocabulary words presented at an appropriate rate in terms of readability and also reviewed and encountered in the next units?		✓				✓
5. Are the grammar points presented with brief and easy examples and explanations?		✓			✓	
6. Is there enough for writing practice like controlled and guided compositions in the early stages?		✓			✓	
7. Is there sufficient work on recognition and production of stress patterns, intonation and individual sounds?		✓				✓

3=excellent, 2=good, 1=poor

| B |

Ms. Park and Mr. Bae, who are the English teachers of a high school, are talking about the result of textbook evaluation.

Ms. Park : Mr. Bae, what do you think about the current textbook? Was there anything (more) that we should have added? Personally I found that my students didn't like the contents of this textbook.

Mr. Bae : Neither did my students. Maybe the contents have too much information irrelevant to students' real lives. That's why most students are not deeply involved as well as demotivated in class.

Ms. Park : How about preparing the concerns and interests of teenagers in other countries? I think all the concerns and interests could be similar within the same age range.

Mr. Bae : Definitely true. That's a good idea!

Ms. Park : Ok, then what about writing section?

Mr. Bae : I think it will be all right. It could prevent students from focus on the writing process if there is too much writing practice at the beginning. I guess we do not have to add some more writing activities at the beginning of the lesson. That's enough for writing practice in the early stages.

Ms. Park : Is that so? I want to add some more writing activities. Without enough writing activities, writing compositions is too demanding for low-intermediate students. Anyway, let's think about it later.

Mr. Bae : OK. what's the next? Yes, it's the pronunciation section. What do you think about this? Don't you think it has to modify this section? Activities and exercises are enough with the confusing individual sounds. However, how about the stress, rhythm and intonation?

Ms. Park : Oh, you are right! I didn't notice it. That's definitely problematic. Our students need to practice these features more carefully because Korean is syllable-timed language. What do you think about vocabulary learning?

Mr. Bae : I think it's not based on spiral learning. Too many new words blocks up students' reading comprehension. Making it worse, they are not reviewed and recycled in the next chapter. So, the current textbook gives few chances to repeat the unknown words in new context.

Ms. Park : That's true! We need to consider the rate of new words in terms of readability and the possibility of the spiral learning on vocabulary.

Considering the information in <A> and <B>, suggest extra teaching materials/activities for Ms. Park and Mr. Bae based on their consultation.

Your Answer

15 Read the activity procedure in <A> and the conversation in <B>. Then follow the directions.

┤ **A** ├

Activity Procedure

1. Ask students to take a sheet of paper and divide it into two halves: same and different.
2. Tell the students that they are going to watch a video clip which contains information about the different cultures.
3. Ask students to find three similarities and three differences between the Korean culture and others.
4. After watching the video twice, ask students to make a group of four to discuss the similarities and differences they found.
5. Ask each group to share their own experience about _____ caused by one of the cultural differences observed.

┤ **B** ├

Below is the excerpt from the conversation of one group during the group discussion.

Min : I cannot believe that Indian people use their left hands instead of a toilet paper to wash themselves in toilet.

Chul : I was a bit shocked while watching the video. Fortunately, they use their right hands to eat food.

Min : Exactly! Their lifestyles and the city look very modern but the reality was way different with my expectation.

Chul : You're right! Another difference is that women in the video clip always put a kind of scarf on their heads.

Jee-eun : Yes, I saw it. Well, it looks very unique and convenient. You know, they might not need to take a time to do their hair every morning. Instead, they would just use the scarp thing.

Considering the information in <A> and <B>, fill in the blank with a term in TWO words which means the conflict or discomfort coming from the different cultures. Then suggest the appropriate cultural learning activity which helps students to overcome the conflicts stemming from the differences between Korean cultures and others.

Your Answer

Receptive Skills

Chapter 04 Receptive Skills

🔒 정답 및 모범 답안 p. 16

01 Read the passage and follow the directions.

Ms. Park's Teaching Log

While teaching 1st graders in a high school, I realized that reading texts are authentic but not sufficient to draw my students' interests and participation. Thus, I decided to find out one effective reading technique in which students make their own text based on their own school experience. Also, through this reading technique, they can have a chance to practice not only reading, but speaking, listening, and writing simultaneously. Below is the new lesson procedure I prepared for my students.

Lesson Procedure

1. T asks Ss to talk about Gym festival which was held last semester and then adds that they will create their own text related to this school event.
2. T first writes down the title students have agreed on and then dictates students' own feelings, opinions, and ideas about gym festival. On the board, T writes down the exact words as they have said, but corrects them if there are some errors in their saying.
3. After the text is created, T reads it to the class, being careful to point to each word as T reads it.
4. T has Ss read the story several times. Because the ideas and language are their own and the topic is familiar, Ss will be able to read the short selection smoothly and fluently.

5. As Ss grow in their ability to read, T lets them begin to make comprehension questions on their own.
6. T puts Ss in groups of four and Ss in groups switch their comprehension questions and find the answers.
7. T points out some groups to present their versions of questions and answers.

Complete the comments by filling in each blank with the most appropriate words.

Ms. Park's lesson procedure above exemplifies the (1) _____ (THREE words) in which students create their own reading text with a shared experience such as a classroom event, hands-on activity, or excursions. Within her chosen reading technique, also, (2) _____ (ONE word) occurs in that students use language to express their own ideas and opinions about it soon after Ms. Park asks students to say their favorite school event, Gym Festival. As seen in the lesson procedure, Ms. Park dictates students' opinions and ideas about the school event to create a reading text with her students. While dictating students' words, she changes the language only when there are some errors. After creating the reading text, she helps students read it smoothly and provides a chance to write their own comprehension questions. Like this, through this reading technique, students have chances to develop diverse language skills such as speaking, listening, reading, and writing at the same time. Thus, these benefits of this reading technique highly motivate students so that they can actively participate in Ms. Park's new reading lesson.

Your Answer (1) _____

(2) _____

02 Review the two students' learning logs below and follow the directions.

Ms. Song is managing an after-school reading club and Suji and Woobin, her students wrote logs after taking her reading club as below.

Suji's Log

It has been three months since I took Ms. Song's reading club. I can enjoy it because I can choose the texts that I want to read. Different from other classes, I don't have to care about any new words, expressions, or grammatical forms. Actually, many pre- and after-reading activities are helpful to analyze the text itself but they seem to be far from reading for pleasure. After taking the after-school reading club, also, only then did I realize that maintaining reading flow without stopping or being interrupted by any reading activities is to improve my reading fluency. Below is the list of texts or books that I have read so far.

1. Cambridge English Readers Level 2 The Big Picture
2. Penguin Readers Level 3 Michelle Obama
3. Macmillan Readers Elementary The Mark of Zorro
4. Penguin Readers Level 3 Mr. Bean in Town

Woobin's Log

In Ms. Song's reading club, I can choose reading texts for myself. Usually, I did not even think about reading real English books because my English proficiency is quite low. Actually, most authentic books that I want to read include too many unknown words and unfamiliar structures, which make me overwhelmed. Moreover, some sentences are too long and complex for me to understand. So, I hoped that Ms. Song helps me choose some authentic books even beginners like me can enjoy reading without feeling burdened. From the next reading club, I wish I could find some books suitable for my proficiency level. Below are examples of books I read in Ms. Song's reading club so far.

1. Anna Karenina (Novel by Leo Tolstoy)
2. The Power of Habit (Book by Charles Duhigg)
3. Harry Potter and the Philosopher's Stone (Novel by J. K. Rowling)
4. 10 Steps to Earning Awesome Grades (Book by Thomas Frank)

Fill in each blank with the ONE most appropriate word.

As seen in Ms. Song's reading lesson, a good way to improve the learner's knowledge of a foreign language is "free and voluntary reading". Such type of reading that two students have experienced in Ms. Song's after-school club is a/an (1) _____ reading where they choose their reading books for themselves and read longer texts for pleasure during the extended period of time. According to the list of books, Suji has read graded readers that are reading books of various genres, specially created for false beginners or intermediate-level learners of foreign languages. On the other hand, even in Ms. Song's reading club, Woobin only read books with too many unknown words and complex sentence structures. Consequently, he was a bit overwhelmed while reading the chosen authentic books. Therefore, from the next reading club, he hopes that he can choose authentic texts considering the (2) _____ of the books according to his reading proficiency.

Chapter

04

Your Answer   (1) _____

(2) _____

03   **Read the passage and follow the directions.**

> *Below is the conversation between two English teachers talking about after-school programs.*
>
> T1 : Hi, Mr. Kim. What are you up to?
>
> T2 : Ms. Choi. I am planning an after-school program for 2nd graders.
>
> T1 : Oh, did you take one, too? What's yours? I am preparing an English speech club.
>
> T2 : Mine is a reading club.
>
> T1 : Reading club sounds nice.
>
> T2 : But I have one problem. I just checked the proficiency levels of students who have signed up for the program and they are all different levels. Some of them are advanced but the others are only beginner levels. How can I choose the very book that can satisfy them?
>
> T1 : Actually you don't have to!
>
> T2 : What do you mean I don't have to? I was planning to make them discuss after reading the same book. But, if their proficiency levels are so much different...
>
> T1 : I mean, you can help them read the same book! In our school library, there are sections for a wide range of _____.
>
> T2 : Are there? That's good for my students.
>
> T1 : Yeah, there are books about the same story with different vocabulary and grammar levels. For example, suppose you ask your students to choose a certain book to read together and then they choose 'Mother Teresa'. If so, beginner-level students can read 'Mother Teresa' Level 1 and the advanced ones, 'Mother Teresa' Level 5.
>
> T2 : You say these sections have simplified versions of original stories?
>
> T1 : You're right!
>
> T2 : Ms. Choi, that's exactly what I am looking for! How come I'd never seen them in the library?
>
> T1 : Come with me. I'll show you the sections in the library.
>
> T2 : Thank you, Ms. Choi!
>
> T=teacher

Fill in the blank with the TWO most appropriate words.

Your Answer _____

04 **Read the passage and follow the directions.**

At a middle school English listening test, students were given the instruction in the box and conducted the test.

Now, listen to the information about Lucy's schedule. Remember, for the first listening, you will hear the sentences without any pausing. Then, for the second time, you will hear each sentence separately with time to fill in your chart. The first row has already been filled in as an example.

Listening Script

Lucy gets up at 8:00 every morning except on weekends. She has English class on Monday, Wednesday, and Friday at ten o'clock. She has History class on ... *(ellipsis)*...

	Mon	Tue	Wed	Thu	Fri	Week-ends
8:00	get up	get up	get up	get up	get up	
10:00						
12:00						
2:00						
4:00						
6:00						

Complete the comments on the test above by filling in each blank. Write your answers in the correct order.

> The chart-filling test above exemplifies a/an (1) _____ (TWO words) task which asks students to convert aurally processed information into a visual representation. Such chart-filling task is a good example of aural (2) _____ (ONE word) strategy in that test-takers must discern relevant information from a number of pieces of information.

Your Answer (1) _____

(2) _____

05 Read the conversation between a teacher and a student, and fill in each blank with the TWO most appropriate words.

Bomi, who has an intermediate level of English, visits the office of her English teacher, Ms. Choi, to talk about reading lessons.

Ms. Choi : So, Bomi, what's up?

Bomi : I have something to talk to you!

Ms. Choi : Yeah, what is it about?

Bomi : I really enjoy reading books, so I read many books in Korean.

Ms. Choi : That's a good thing!

Bomi : Yes, it helps me a lot. So, I want to read English books a lot. But I have only a few English books that I can read at home. Besides, the texts in the textbook are excerpts from whole stories, aren't they?

Ms. Choi : So, you mean, it's not enough?

Bomi : Yeah, that's just it! And I want to read the entire stories, which are more interesting.

Ms. Choi : Okay. Let me see.

Bomi : I want you to come up with a great idea.

Ms. Choi : Well, how about having the reading lesson in the school library tomorrow? Then, you guys can have more chances to read stories in English. There are many books you can choose for yourself.

Bomi : That sounds great! I like the idea!

Ms. Choi : Yes, that's called (1) _____, whose purpose is reading for pleasure. Usually, all of you participate in a/an (2) _____ class where you read for information and practice reading strategies with some exercises.

Bomi : I see. Then, what's the difference?

Ms. Choi : For the next lesson, usually, you are not asked to gain every detail from the text. There is no comprehension test after reading. But I can ask you to review the book very briefly. How does it sound to you?

Bomi : Cool! I am already looking forward to it.

Your Answer   (1) _____

(2) _____

06   Read the passages and follow the directions.

---| **A** |---

Mr. Yu's Note

Today, I attended to a teacher's conference about how to help struggling readers. According to an article from the conference, there are seven cognitive strategies which students can use, when they struggle with understanding key contents in a text. The seven cognitive strategies of effective readers are:

• activating	• predicting
• questioning	• monitoring-clarifying
• searching-selecting	• visualizing-organizing
• summarizing	

I believe that these cognitive strategies will change struggle readers into skilled one. By using these strategies students could extract, construct meaning from text and create knowledge structures in long-term memory. Thus, I decided to directly teach and model these strategies during the lesson. The following lesson represents one of these strategies, which can improve students comprehension and retention.

---| **B** |---

Below is a lesson template that Mr. Yu has prepared to teach one of cognitive strategies.

Lesson Template

Lesson Template for Teaching Cognitive Strategies		Lesson Plan for Teaching _____
1. Provide direct instruction regarding the cognitive strategy	a. Define and explain the strategy	This is restating in your own words the meaning of what you have read-using different words from those used in the original text-either in written form or a graphic representation.

	b. Explain the purpose of the strategy serves during reading	It enables a reader to determine what is most important to remember once the reading is completed. Many things we read have only one or two big ideas, and it is important to identify them and restate them for the purpose of retention.
	c. Describe the critical attributes of the strategy	• It is short. • It is to the point, containing the big idea of the text. • It omits trivial information and collapses lists into a word or phrase. • It is not a "photocopy" of the text.
	d. Provide concrete examples/ non-examples of the strategy	• **Good example**: report of a basketball or football game that captures the highlights. • **Non-example**: a paragraph that is too long, has far too many details, or is a complete retelling of the text rather than a statement of the main idea.
2. Model the strategy by thinking aloud		Choose a section of relatively easy text from your discipline and think aloud as you read it, and then also think aloud about how you would go.
3. Facilitate guided practice with students		Practice the strategy using easy-to-read content text: (1) with the whole class (2) with partners (3) independently

Chapter

04

Fill in the blank in \<B\> with the ONE most appropriate word from \<A\>.

Your Answer

07 **Read the passage and follow the directions.**

Lesson Procedure

Step 1 T shows a photo of people having a party and asks Ss to make a prediction on what they are celebrating.

Step 2 T plays a listening script in three segments.

Step 3 After listening to each segment, Ss guess the answer and write down the clues which lead them to think so.

(1) Where is the conversation taking place?
(2) What is the purpose of this conversation?
(3) What will happen at the end?

Step 4 Ss in pairs discuss their answers.

Step 5 While listening to the conversation one more time, Ss find the answer to the following questions.

(1) What is the address of the party venue?
(2) Which bus should they take to get to the party place?
(3) What is the dress code for men and women, respectively?

T=teacher, Ss=students

Referring to the lesson procedure above, fill in each blank with the ONE most appropriate term.

The lesson procedure focuses on two major listening strategies necessary to comprehend the whole text. In Step 1 and Step 3, students are asked to predict what occasion is in the listening script using the given photo and guess where and why the conversation takes place based on some clues. During the steps, in terms of comprehending process, students need to employ a/an (1) _____ listening strategy in that they are asked to use their background knowledge and life experience. On the other hand, in Step 5, they need to listen to specific details including the party venue, the bus number, and requested dress code. Through this step, students can practice a/an (2) _____ listening strategy that they divide and decode the listening text piece by piece using their knowledge on vocabulary, grammar, and sounds.

Chapter

04

Your Answer (1) _____

(2) _____

08 **Read the passage and follow the directions.**

A

Lesson Procedure

Teacher	Students
While-reading	
• T puts Ss in groups of four. • T gives directions for reading. [Directions] 1. Pick one part of the text per person. 2. You are the expert on each part. Each expert gathers together, reads the part together, and finds key information. 3. Experts get back to their original group and teach the group members about their own parts. 4. After collecting information on each part from each expert, Ss in groups answer in the worksheet.	• Ss seat in groups of four. • Ss listen to T's directions.
• T asks Ss to read the text and answer the questions in the worksheet.	• Ss follow the directions to read the text and answer the questions in the worksheet.

[Worksheet]

1. When does 'Earth Hour' take place?
2. What do people on 'Earth Hour'?
3. What does '60+' logo represent?

. . .

[Answers]

1. It will be on 30 March 2019
2. People turn off non-essential lights for one hour.
3. It represents a commitment to add to 'Earth Hour' a positive act for the planet that goes beyond the hour.

. . .

T=teacher, Ss=students

Based on the excerpt from the lesson procedure above, fill in the blank in \<B\> with the most suitable pedagogical term in ONE word.

─┤ **B** ├─

　　The lesson plan above shows _____ reading, where students collaboratively answer the questions on a worksheet after reading each part of a text. Through this reading activity, students in groups have an opportunity to teach each other what they have read and discussed the implications of the reading. By doing so, they actively participate in and contribute to their learning process. Accordingly, they can attain a higher level, not possible if the students were to try and read a text on their own.

Your Answer _____

09 Read the passage and identify the type of learning strategies Ms. Park intends to teach students in the strategies-based instruction below.

| A |

Lesson Procedure

- Topic: How To Be An Successful Language Learner
- Level: Intermediate or above
- Time: 30-35 minutes
- Aim: For students to have habits of good language users classroom
- Preparation: Make photocopies of the task sheet (each set of good and bad habits of language learning)

- Procedure:
  1. Engage students in self-survey about good language habits and poor language habits.
  2. Set up the initial pair work and give the students five to ten minutes to discuss the characteristics of good language users and poor language users.
  3. After the self-survey and initial discussion are over, students in groups conduct a survey for a maximum of twenty minutes.
  4. Chair the report-back session in which each group presents group suggestions or conclusions. Make OHPs or posters available to help the groups present their ideas.

B

Ms. Park's Teaching Log

Today my students talked about some habits of successful and unsuccessful language users. Based on the task sheet I prepared, they did a self-survey about their own learning habits as language users and then, had a discussion with their partner on how to be successful in language learning. Soon after the self-survey and initial discussion, they in groups conducted a survey, leading to make a plan for their learning for a month. After each presentation, I asked students to carry out their plan for a month and also write a reflective journal every day. It starts with some questions like "What was the most difficult habit to follow?" or "What can I do to solve the problem?" After one month I will arrange time they can evaluate if they comply with their plan successfully.

Your Answer

_____

10 Read the dialogue below and fill in the blanks with TWO words in common.

> *Ms. Park and Mr. Lee who are English teachers are having discussion about how to improve their reading classes.*
>
> Ms. Park : I've heard from some of my students that my reading class has been challenging and boring. So, instead of teaching reading intensively, I'm encouraging the students to read books of their interest from the classroom library.
> Mr. Lee : That's a good idea. So how's it going?
> Ms. Park : It's not working well because of their wide ability range. Some students said that books in the library were too easy. But for other students, reading a book in English itself was a daunting task. They found too many unknown words and were presented with language way beyond their level which made understanding the books very difficult.
> Mr. Lee : Why don't you use _____?
> Ms. Park : How do they work?
> Mr. Lee : Those can cater for all levels from beginners through advanced. If you use _____, students won't have to stop while reading and look up lots of unknown words in the dictionary.
> Ms. Park : That's nice. Should I buy them from somewhere else?
> Mr. Lee : Our school has them. I used them once and it had an impressively large selection of books. Students can choose their own books according to their personal preferences.
> Ms. Park : Awesome! I should check them out!

Your Answer _____

11 Read the passage in <A> and the teacher's journal in <B>, and follow the directions.

A

The teaching and learning of reading skill in high schools, just like the other three skills, contains a lot of problems that have been criticized for a long time. Despite the fact that it is the most taught skill of the four, reading has not become any easier for students. As part of efforts to teach students reading skills effectively, researchers have provided several reading models. The first model takes a bottom-up reading process where the reader decodes, letter-by-letter, word-by-word the written symbols in the text and then reassembles the pieces to form meaning. The second model with a top-down reading process, suggests that efficient readers do not need to use all of the textual cues. Instead, they consider reading process as a "psycholinguistic guessing game". Lastly, the third model represents the interactive processing. Interaction refers to the constant interaction between the two processing skills. This model proposes that developing readers must work at perfecting both their language recognition skills and their interpretation skills.

B

Teacher's Journal

Mr. Kim and I read an article on teaching reading and discussed how we can improve the way we teach reading. We realized that, in our reading lessons, the students were asked to focus on understanding separate pieces of information from the text without considering any higher-order relationship between them. As a result, the fragmented memory and heavy memory load disturbed their reading comprehension. So, we came up with the following activities to compensate the current reading process, leading to the _____ reading model.

Chapter

04

Reading activities to be implemented:

- Graphic organizers to relate students' own experiences to the reading topic
- Activating vocabulary knowledge
- Visualizing what they read
- Finding moods and emotions

Fill in the blank in <B> with the ONE word from the passage in <A>.

Your Answer _____

✏ 서술형

01 Read <A> and <B>, and follow the directions.

┤ **A** ├

Comprehension Level

1. Literal level: Answers are directly and explicitly expressed in the text. Students can answer the questions using the words of the text.
2. Reorganization level: Students obtain information from various parts of the text by putting them together in a new way.
3. Inferential level: Students consider what is implied but not explicitly stated. They make conclusions about the material presented in the text to come up with insights that are not explicitly stated in the text.
4. Evaluative level: Students formulate a response based on their previous reading experience, their life experience, and their opinions on the issues relevant to the text.
5. Creative level: At this advanced level of response to a text, students have to be emotionally and aesthetically sensitive to what he is reading. It also requires some appreciation of literary techniques.

┤ **B** ├

Reading Text

On September 8th, the Korean national soccer team beat Brazil 2-1 in the World Cup championship game held in Qatar. The victory was the greatest moment in Korean sports history. As a matter of fact, it was the first time an Asian country won the World Cup. It was anyone's game as the score was tied 1-1 deep into the second half of the game. But, with just 26 seconds left in the game, one of the youngest members of the Korean team, Jeong Wooyeong (23) scored an incredible goal. When the game ended, Korean fans stormed the streets all over Korea. Fireworks and car horns could be seen and heard everywhere. Crowds that gathered around City Hall celebrated for hours after the game. On the other side of the globe, fans wiped away their tears from their painted faces in Brazil. Thousands of fans walked around with expressions of disbelief and disappointment.

Below is parts of the conversation between two English teachers teaching 2nd graders in a middle school.

T1 : Hi, Mr. Kim. What are you doing?

T2 : Hi, Ms. Park. I am reviewing my next reading lesson plan. I want to modify it a little bit.

T1 : So, what do you want to fix?

T2 : A few comprehension questions need to be fixed. These questions are too complex and difficult compared to students' current level.

T1 : On what level are they?

T2 : Low intermediate level. Can you check up the text and the questions I prepared?

T1 : Sure! *(T1 reads the text and checks the question.)* Okay, let's see. 'What is the author's attitude or tone toward Korea's winning of the World Cup?' Hmm...the author's attitude is not mentioned in the text. Isn't it?

T2 : That's the point. That's why it is too demanding for my students who are not ready to figure out hidden meanings yet.

T1 : How about asking for the information easily found in the text? Like, 'When did the Korean team score the second goal?'. It's clearly mentioned in the seventh line of the text.

T2 : That's good!! Thank you, Ms. Park.

T=teacher

Based the categorization in <A>, explain the comprehension level of the question that T2 originally plans to give. Then, write the comprehension level that T1 suggests to T2 and explain why the new question is more suitable for T2's reading lesson. Do not copy more than FOUR consecutive words from the text.

Your Answer

_____

_____

_____

_____

_____

02 Read the passages below and follow the directions.

---| **A** |---

Types of Classroom Listening Performance

- **Reactive listening:** The listener has the role of a "tape recorder" and is not generating meaning. While this kind of listening performance requires little meaningful processing, it nevertheless may be a legitimate, even though minor, aspect of an interactive, in communicative classroom.

- **Intensive listening:** Students listen for cues in certain choral or individual drills. The teacher repeats a word or sentence several times to "imprint" it in the students' minds. While the teacher asks students in a sentence stretch of discourse, students notice specified elements such as intonation, stress, a contraction, grammatical structure, etc. It requires bottom-up skills that are important at all levels of proficiency.

- **Responsive listening:** Short stretches of teacher's language designed to elicit immediate responses. (Asking questions: "How are you today?", Giving commands: "Open the window!" Seeking clarification: "What was the word you said?") Students process the teacher's talk immediately and reply.

- **Selective listening:** In longer stretches of discourse such as monologues of a couple of minutes or considerably longer, the task of the student is not to process everything that is said, but rather to scan the material selectively for certain information.

- **Extensive listening:** This sort of performance aims to develop a top-down, global understanding of spoken language. Students may listen to lectures and other teacher monologues. It requires a global understanding of spoken language and may require students to invoke other interactive skills (e.g. note-taking, and/or discussion) or full comprehension.

- **Interactive listening:** Finally, this listening performance must be intricately integrated with speaking skills in the authentic give and take of communicative interchange. Students actively participate in discussions, debates, conversations, and role-plays.

B

Ms. Shin is teaching 2nd-grade middle school students who have intermediate proficiency. She prepares a listening lesson using a spoken text about types of accommodation in Seoul.

Ms. Shin's Preparation for his Class

1. T shows students a few accommodation online ads and activates schematic knowledge on accommodation.
2. T chooses one interview video (approx. 3-4 minutes) between two people discussing:
   • information from the various ads and personal preferences.
   • a ranking of the flats in terms of preference.
3. T prepares a table as shown below.

Location \ Information	Noryangjin area	Yeouido	Gangnam	Shin-chon	Samcheong-dong
Number of bedrooms					
Rent cost					
Date available					
Features					
Person A's rank					

...

In Class

1. Students listen to the interview.
2. After finishing the listening, students individually fill out the table in the worksheet.
3. The whole class checks the answers together.

Based on the information in <A> and <B>, choose the type of listening performance used in Ms. Shin's class. Then, explain how the identified listening performance corresponds to Ms. Shin's class with evidence.

Your Answer

_____

_____

_____

_____

03 Read <A> and <B> and follow the directions.

┤ **A** ├

Ms. Lee's Log

I'm teaching 2nd graders in a middle school. They had been very passionate about learning English but, these days, many of them looked uninterested, particularly, in the reading lessons. Accordingly, I had a one-on-one conversation with them and, then, found out the following two problems in my reading lessons. First, they complained that the reading topics have been unmotivating and unrelated to their lives. Because my school policy emphasizes scientific literatures, I had chosen many science-related texts. However, based on students' comments, I needed to find a different way. After careful consideration, I decided to apply one new reading technique that not only motivates students but also follows the school policy. Moreover, there was another complaint. They said that my reading classes excessively focus on reading itself. They, in short, wanted to practice various language skills during reading lessons. From the next reading lessons, thus, I will give them the chance to use speaking, writing as well as reading skills with the new reading technique. The following lesson procedure shows the new technique I will apply for the next reading class.

| B |

The following lesson procedure is based on _____ to maximize students' intrinsic motivation.

Step #1 A Shared Experience

The class begins with something the class does together, such as a field trip, a scientific experiment, or some other hands-on activities related to scientific issues.

Step #2 Creating the Text

Next, the teacher and students, as a group, verbally recall the shared experience. Students take turns describing situations, as in a large-group discussion. The teacher transcribes students' words on the board in an organized way to create the text.

Step #3 Read & Revise

The class reads the story aloud and discusses it. The teacher asks if the students want to make any corrections or additions to the story. Then, she marks the changes they suggest and makes further suggestions if needed.

Step #4 Read and Reread

The final story can be read in a choral or echo style, or both. Students can also read the story in small groups or pairs, and then individually.

Step #5 Extension

This text can be used for a variety of activities like illustrations or creating comprehension questions.

Fill in the blank in <B> with the name of the reading technique in THREE words. Then, explain how the identified reading technique is suitable for Ms. Lee's new class with some evidence from the passages.

Your Answer

04 Read the passages and follow the directions.

─────────────┤ **A** ├─────────────

When good readers involve themselves with any type of written discourse, they work on several processes simultaneously to produce understanding of the incoming text. The higher level of processing is driven by readers' expectations and understandings of the context, the topic, the nature of the text, and the nature of the world. The lower level of processing is triggered by the words, and phrases that the readers read as they attempt to decode a text and assign meaning. The text itself carries only some clues to the meanings that are encoded within it; readers must use their knowledge of the language to recognize keywords, phrases, and sentences.

─────────────┤ **B** ├─────────────

Below is part of the lesson plan that Ms. Choi prepared for her students.

Stage 1	• T shows a video clip of metaverse. • After watching the video clip, students in pairs share what they already knew about metaverse and what they newly learn from the video. • T previews some new words from the text.
Stage 2	• T asks Ss to skim the text about metaverse and think about the main idea. • T checks the main idea with the whole class.
Stage 3	• T provides Ss with comprehension questions on literal and inferential levels. • Ss read the text individually to find out the answers explicitly stated in the text and to infer the writer's intention beyond the text. • T asks Ss to present their answers and check them with the whole class.

Stage 4	• T provides a discussion question related to the metaverse and puts Ss in groups of four. (e.g. "Metaverse will have positive or negative effects on human evolution. What do you think?") • Ss in groups discuss the question while sharing their individual opinions. • Ss choose one group opinion.
Stage 5	• T asks each group to present their group opinion based on two supporting ideas. • Ss vote for one group that presents the most persuasive opinion.

Referring to <A>, identify TWO stages presented in <B> which require both levels of processing. Then, explain the reasons for your choice with some evidence. Do NOT copy more than FOUR consecutive words from the passages.

Chapter

04

Your Answer

05 Read the passages and follow the directions.

A

Mr. Kim's Teaching Note

While teaching 2nd graders in a middle school, I found that most of my students have lower reading proficiency compared to the other skills. During a one-on-one conferencing, I realized that they need to know how to monitor their own understanding while reading a text. Also, they need to learn some reading strategies for better reading comprehension such as predicting, visualizing, or guessing. Thus, I decided to prepare a reading lesson in which I can demonstrate how to monitor my comprehension and what strategies to use while reading the text myself.

B

Lesson procedure

Step 1 T states the purposes for reading and introduces the story.

Step 2 Ss predict what the story is about based on its title and cover illustration.

Step 3 T begins reading the story and says aloud how to build the text and what strategies to use as he reads every paragraph.

Step 4 T writes down some questions about his reading process on the board and talks about each of them with the whole class.
(*e.g.*) Do I understand what I just read?
Do I have a clear picture in my head about this information?
What more can I do to understand this?
What were the most important points in this reading?
Are there contextual clues to guess the meaning of new words?
What kinds of strategies are used?
How do I use the identified strategies to comprehend the text?

Step 5 Ss in pairs read a portion of a story and take turns vocalizing their thoughts while asking and answering the given questions.

T=Teacher, Ss=Students

Referring to <A> and <B>, identify the major teaching technique Mr. Kim chooses to teach how to build reading comprehension. Then, explain how the identified technique can help students build their comprehension with evidence from <B>.

Your Answer

_____

_____

_____

_____

_____

06 Read <A> and <B> and follow the directions.

┤ **A** ├

Mr. Choi's Teaching Log

To improve my students' reading competence, I want to help them practice and develop effective reading skills. As the first step for my reading lesson, I need to choose a reading text carefully. Thus, I prepared an evaluation sheet including important elements of a good reading text. Overall, I put emphasis on five main criteria: suitability of the content, exploitability, readability, authenticity, and presentation. I am thinking of using a reading text titled "What is Digital Security?" for tomorrow's lesson. Using the text, I am planning to teach inferencing and vocabulary guessing strategies.

┤ **B** ├

Below are the results of the evaluation of a text titled "What is Digital Security?"

	Questions	Yes/No
1	Does the text topic interest students?	Y
2	Can the text be used for teaching target reading strategies?	N
3	Does the text have a strong conclusion?	Y
4	Does the text include a wide vocabulary?	Y
5	Is the text level appropriate for the students?	Y
6	Does it represent the type of material that the students will encounter in the real life?	Y
7	Does it include illustrations to be attractive to students?	N

Y=Yes, N=No

Based on the evaluation results in <B>, identify TWO criteria mentioned in <A> that the chosen text 'What is Digital Security?' violates. Then, support your choice with evidence from the data. Do NOT copy more than FOUR consecutive words from the passages.

Your Answer

07 **Read the passages and follow the directions.**

┤ **A** ├

Authentic materials should be the kind of material that students will need and want to read when using the language outside the classroom such as traveling, studying abroad, etc. Authentic materials enable learners to interact with the real language and content rather than the form. Learners feel that they are learning a target language as it is used outside the classroom. When choosing materials from various sources, it is therefore worth taking into consideration that the aim should be to understand the meaning and not the form. Nuttall (1996) gives three main criteria when choosing texts to be used in the classroom suitability of content, exploitability, and readability.

┤ **B** ├

Ms. Park's Teaching Log

I am teaching English to 3rd-graders in a middle school. Last week, for my reading lesson, I chose a reading text titled 'How to write a poetry.' Since my students are at the low intermediate level, I chose the text including the appropriate level of vocabulary and grammar. However, during the reading lesson, many of them seemed to get bored. Later, I had a one-on-one conversation with some of my students and they commented that the topic was neither so useful nor related to their daily lives. Thus, to satisfy their needs, I decided to change the lesson. First, instead of the text about writing a poetry, I will use a new reading text titled 'How to write a text message'. Since my students use text messages every day, the new topic will be more appropriate to meet their needs. Moreover, after reading the text, I will give them a chance to personalize the text by asking them to actually send a text message to one friend considering the tips from the reading text. Writing a real text message of their own based on the text content will help them realize that they are learning the authentic language which they can actually use outside the classroom. Then, this would make them more engaged in the learning process. I believe these changes can provide my students with a successful and dynamic learning experience and thus produce excellent learning results.

Based on <A> and <B>, identify the criteria that Ms. Park originally has considered to choose the text and also the criteria that she newly takes into consideration after the conversation with her students, respectively. Then, write TWO changes of the newly designed lesson reflected in <B>.

Your Answer

08 **Read the passages below and follow the directions.**

┤ **A** ├

Ms. Choi, an English teacher in a middle school, uses a reading strategy in her class following the lesson procedure.

Step 1 As the first step, students look through a text and check the headings, pictures, summaries, etc. Students get an overall idea of what the text might be about.

Step 2 Students make questions using headings and subheadings about what they wish to get from the text.

Step 3 Students read the text to find answers to the questions and mark any sections which are unclear.

Step 4 After reading the text, students try to remember the main idea and key information. Then, they recite or rewrite them using both their own words and words from the text.

Step 5 Students review the text and look at the sections marked to see if they can now understand the sections.

B

Jaemin's Learning Log

Although I am an intermediate-level student, reading a text with an unfamiliar topic is still difficult for me. To level up my proficiency level, I want to overcome such a difficulty. Thus, I shared such concern with my English teacher and she prepared a new reading lesson today. She provided us with a reading text and a worksheet to help us understand the unfamiliar text better. There was one table including five steps. She asked us to follow the steps before, during, and after reading the text explaining that this would help us to be effective readers. Since it was my first time doing this, following the five steps, surveying, questioning, reading, reciting, and reviewing, took more time than my usual reading. However, after the reading lesson based on the five steps, I could better understand the text without being afraid of reading a new text anymore, resulting in being an effective reader. Moreover, different from the other reading lessons where I simply read the text, the reciting process helped me to memorize many new words. If I had no chance to recite or rewrite the contents of the text, I would not pay attention to the words and forgot them. After the reading lesson, I was able to have confidence that I can be an effective reader when I become familiar with the reading technique that my teacher taught me today.

Table in the worksheet

Scan the text and write down its title and subtitles	Make questions regarding what you wonder	Read the text and write answers to the questions	Recite and rewrite the text including key facts and phrases	Review answers and assess the importance of each piece of information
...	...	...	...	...
...	...	...	...	...

Identify the name of the reading technique that Ms. Choi uses in <A> and write TWO benefits of using the identified technique from the student's perspective based on <B>.

Your Answer

_____

_____

_____

_____

_____

09 Read the passages and follow the directions.

─┤ **A** ├─

Below is the list of lesson objectives for English lessons that are specified in the school curriculum.

Objective 1   Read from a variety of genres.
Objective 2   Build vocabulary by reading and use sentences to determine meaning.
Objective 3   Figure out the main idea of a story in groups.
Objective 4   Use technology to find information.
Objective 5   Gather information from graphs, charts, tables, and maps.
Objective 6   talk about how coherent texts are constructed.

─┤ **B** ├─

Lesson Procedure

1. T asks Ss to brainstorm any words, thinking about AI learning.
2. T asks questions and leads Ss to talk about what AI is and what they know about AI learning.
3. T provides Ss with a text about AI learning.
4. T puts Ss in groups of three and has them skim the text quickly, for about 30 seconds. Each group finds out its main idea without focusing on every word.
5. T checks the main idea with the whole class.
6. T asks Ss to read the text individually, but now more carefully.
7. T lets Ss know that the text is actually a combination of two shorter ones. T explains that she has chosen two different texts about AI learning from online news articles, scrambled the sentences randomly, and created the new text.
8. T puts Ss in groups of four and asks Ss to divide the text into two separate ones that make sense for 15 minutes.
9. When Ss are done, T asks Ss to discuss how and why they have divided the text the way they did. T asks each group to present what they have discussed.
10. T shows Ss the original versions of the two texts and has Ss compare them with their own.
11. T has Ss vote for the most accurately restored versions.

Identify TWO lesson objectives from <A> that the lesson procedure in <B> focuses on. Then, explain how each identified lesson objective is addressed with evidence from <B>.

Your Answer

10 Read the passages below and follow the directions.

┤ **A** ├

Ms. Lee prepares a reading lesson using the _____, the visual strategy for the extension of knowledge. Below is part of the lesson procedure of Ms. Lee's reading lesson.

Lesson Procedure

Step 1 T introduces today's topic, mental health. Then, T asks Ss in pairs to discuss how they can look after their mental health. Ss share ideas for two minutes.

Step 2 T asks Ss to present their ideas and fill in the map on the board with the ideas. Ss are asked to draw the same map on their notebooks, too.

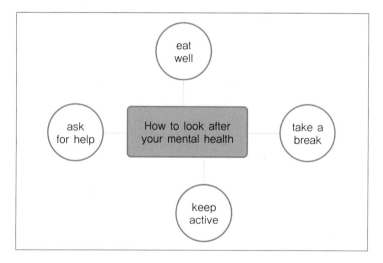

Step 3 T presents and teaches a few new words that will appear in the reading text.

Step 4 T provides a reading text about mental health and Ss read the text silently for five minutes.

Step 5 After Ss finish the reading, T reviews the ideas from the text about how to look after mental health.

Step 6 Based on the contents in the reading text, Ss individually expand the previously-drawn map as follows:

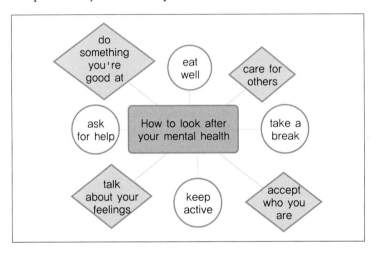

Step 7 T puts Ss in groups of four and asks them to discuss how the ideas would be helpful to care for their mental health and choose one best idea.

Step 8 Each group presents their map on the board and their group discussion results to the whole class.

T=Teacher, Ss=Students

B

Ms. Lee's Teaching log

I am teaching 2nd graders in a middle school. At the beginning of the semester, I conducted a proficiency test to check their current proficiency level. Most of them are low intermediate level and the test results showed that their reading ability is lower than the other skills. Thus, for this semester, I decided to focus on improving their reading skills. I thought that practicing diverse reading strategies can help them have a better understanding of a reading text. As the first lesson of this semester, today, I conducted a lesson using a visual strategy. I prepared two different visual aids for before and after reading, respectively. While filling up the first one, students were asked to guess what the story would be about before reading the text. While activating their prior knowledge about the topic, mental health, they shared their ideas in pairs and predicted what the text is about. Then, after reading the text, they used the visual map once again. This time, next to the ideas written in the earlier stage, students added some new ideas they received from the text. Through this activity, they were able to link the prior knowledge and the new ideas effectively, which helps them understand the text more deeply and better retain the contents of the text. After the reading lesson, I received positive feedback from my students that the visual aids were very useful to improve their reading abilities.

Chapter

04

Fill in the blank in <A> with TWO words. Then, based on the information from <B>, write how the mentioned visual strategy helps students understand the text through steps 2 and 6 in <A>, respectively.

Your Answer

_____

_____

_____

_____

_____

11   Read the passages and follow the directions.

A

Lesson Procedure

1. T distributes a worksheet to each student and introduces the activity 'Listen and choose'.
2. T asks Ss to listen to a monologue about Tom's day. The monologue only includes words that students already learned and the expressions of time such as yesterday, last week, this morning, tomorrow, etc.
3. While listening to the monologue, students write down the order of Tom's schedule. If needed, Ss can listen to the monologue again.

   ※ Listen and write the order of Tom's schedule.

4. T checks Ss' answers with the whole class.

B

Mr. Lee's Teaching Log

Since my students are beginner-level, I am very careful in designing activities not to overwhelm them. For example, when I prepare an activity, I choose one which does not require diverse skills at the same time. Today, I prepared a 'Listen and Choose' activity to check their vocabulary knowledge on expressions of time such as yesterday, last week, this morning, tomorrow, etc. During this activity, they don't need to use any language skills such as reading, speaking, or writing except for listening skills. Since they only focus on listening skills to review the vocabulary they have learned, they looked more comfortable in today's lesson without being overwhelmed cognitively.

Identify the name of the activity exemplified in <A>. Then, based on <B>, write ONE major benefit of the identified activity for beginner-level students.

Your Answer

_____

_____

_____

_____

12 Read the passages and follow the directions.

⊣ **A** ⊢

Five Types of Reading Comprehension

1. Lexical comprehension: understand key vocabulary in the text.
   - Preview vocabulary before reading the story or text.
   - Review new vocabulary during or after the text.

2. Literal comprehension: answer who, what, when, and where questions.
   - Look in the text to find the answers written in the story.
   - Ask questions from the beginning, middle, and end of the story.

3. Interpretive comprehension: answer what if, why, and how questions.
   - Understand 'facts' that are not explicitly stated in the story.
   - Illustrations may help to infer meaning.

4. Applied comprehension: relate the story to your opinion.
   - Not a simple question that can be marked right or wrong.
   - Challenge students to support their answers with logic or reason.

5. Affective comprehension: understand social and emotional aspects
   - Preview social scripts to ensure understanding of plot development.
   - Connect motive to plot and character development.

B

Below are two examples of reading activities.

Activity 1

※ If something is true, or it really happened, it is a fact. If something is what someone thinks or believes, it is an opinion. As you read Marco's letter from Uncle Ben, think about what parts are fact and what parts are opinion.

> [Text]
>
> *Marco got a letter from his Uncle Ben, the airplane pilot. Uncle Ben has traveled all over the world.*
>
> Dear Marco,
> This is my third time visiting Paris, and I think it is one of the most beautiful cities in the world. Paris, as I'm sure you know, is the capital of France. Today I walked along the Avenue des Champs-Elysees, which is the most famous street in Paris. I think it may be the most famous street in the world. It is lined with beautiful trees, fountains, and flowers. There are shops, theaters, restaurants, and many sidewalk cafes. *(ellipsis)*

※ Here are some things Uncle Ben said in his letter. Which ones are facts and which are Uncle Ben's opinions? Circle the word "fact" or the word "opinion."

1. This is Uncle Ben's third time visiting Paris.   (fact) (opinion)
2. Paris is one of the most beautiful cities in the world. (fact) (opinion)
3. Paris is the capital city of France.   (fact) (opinion)
4. The Avenue des Champs-Elysees may be the most famous street in the world.   (fact) (opinion)
5. On the Champs-Elysees, there are shops, theaters, and restaurants.
                                                            (fact) (opinion)

Activity 2

※ As you read the story, think about what you already know and what you newly know from the story. Try to figure out what the story means by thinking about what makes the most sense.

[Text] The Kingly Lion

The animals of the field and forest had a Lion as their King. When anyone had a problem, he took it to the Lion King, and the Lion King helped to solve it. When anyone had an argument, they took it to the Lion King, and he helped to settle it. The Lion King never made demands that were in his own interest. He wanted only what was best for each and every animal. Day after day, the Lion King thought about nothing but the animals who were his subjects. Then he sat down and wrote out a Royal Order. He called all the animals to come before him. He stood on a hilltop and watched the animals come together from far and near. He waited for them to settle.

"Hear ye, hear ye!" the Lion began, in his deep and rumbling voice. "I have written out my orders for a new way of doing things that will be better for all. From this day forward, the Wolf and the Lamb shall agree to live in peace. The Panther and the Goat shall live in peace. The Tiger and the Deer, and the Dog and the Rabbit—all shall live together in perfect peace and harmony.

※ Use what you already know and what the story says to make inferences:

1. Why did the animals bring their problems to the Lion?
   A. The animals knew the Lion was powerful.
   B. The animals knew the Lion was fair.
   C. The animals feared that the Lion would punish them.

2. Why did the Lion write a Royal Order?
   A. The Lion wanted the best for animals.
   B. The Lion was tired of the animals bringing their problems to him.
   C. The Lion wanted to be King of the field and forest.

Based on <A>, identify the level of reading comprehension that each Activity in <B> exemplifies and write the reason for each with evidence from <B>.

Your Answer

13 Read the passage and follow the directions.

---| **A** |---

In extensive reading, students read large quantities of texts, and they do so for pleasure. They are able to read quickly without relying on a dictionary. It means that they can read as easily and enjoyably as they can in their mother tongue. Extensive reading promotes fluency, reinforces vocabulary and teaches new words in context. As part of extensive reading, _____ are books written for foreign language learners. They encompass any genre and they are sometimes a simplified version of an existing book. They, also, are adapted to different levels: beginner, intermediate and advanced.

---| **B** |---

Minjin's Learning Log

Today, my English teacher took us to a school library and asked us to choose any English books as we want to. However, I doubted if I can ever read English books by myself, because I do not have enough a good command of English. At that moment, the teacher took me in the front of a certain library section whose books are divided into different levels from level 1 to level 5. Books in level 1 were for beginners and ones in level 5 were for advanced learners. Thus, I chose one book from level 3. It was about Chinese foods which are my favorite. As soon as I began to read the book, I was so concentrated that I read it to the end without stopping. Even I did not stop reading to look up to unknown words in the dictionary. On this experience, I could gain confidence that I can fluently read English books. If the chosen book had not been fit for my level, definitely, I could not have finished reading it. After reading, also, I realized that I easily picked up some new words from the book such as *cuisine, wok, pak choi, etc.* Different from vocabulary instructions given in class, the repeated exposure of new words within context seemed to naturally lead to vocabulary learning. Overall, today's reading lesson was very satisfying and enjoyable to me. I hope my teacher will give us this free reading time more often.

Fill in the blank in TWO words. Then, referring to <B>, explain TWO benefits of reading the identified books on the part of Minjin.

Your Answer

_____

_____

_____

_____

_____

14 Read the passage in <A> and the teacher's log in <B>, and follow the directions.

A

When we engage in listening, we are doing so for many different reasons depending upon the goals in which we are trying to achieve. There are five different strategies of listening that are essential to learning to reach your goal as a skilled listener: predicting, listening for gist, listening for specific information, listening for detail, and inferential listening.

• Predicting: this is for generating the learners' schemata. This strategy gets the learners to think about and talk about the content of what they are about to hear.

• Listening for gist: this refers to the general idea of what is being said, as well as who is speaking to whom and why, and how successful they are in communicating their point.

• Listening for specific information: this is when we don't need to understand everything, but only a very specific part. Specific information is often factual, for example, a name, a place, a profession, an object, a number or a quantity.

• Listening for detail: this refers to the type of listening we do in which we can't afford to ignore anything because we don't know exactly what information of the listening passage will be necessary to complete the task.

• Inferential listening: you need to listen for clues in the text or use general knowledge to guess the meaning of what the speakers are saying. We do this by working out the relationship between the speakers, the tone of voice and the words they use.

B

Teacher's Log

 To assess students' listening competency, I usually have my students listen to a story and then talk about what they have listened in their own words. However, it is not easy for students to listen to a new story and summarize it without using any strategies. Thus, I prepared listening tasks to teach specific listening strategies. Each listening task is designed to practice a single listening strategy so that they can pay attention to the target strategy. For the first task, before listening, students were asked to check the text title and given visuals. Then, they guessed what they were going to hear. After listening to the file several times, students in groups did the second task. They attempted to figure out the speaker's intention for speech based on some clues they have listened to from the text. Also, they identified the speaker's emotion which is not directly mentioned from the text, using their prior knowledge. After completing the strategies-based tasks, students commented that these tasks helped them improve their listening abilities very much. With their comments, I realized the effectiveness of these strategy training activities. Thus, I will provide them with more useful tasks focusing on specific listening strategies for the later lessons.

Based on <A>, identify the ONE listening strategy that the teacher focuses on in each listening task in <B>. Then, support your answer with evidence from <B>. Do NOT copy more than FOUR consecutive words from the passages.

Your Answer

_____

_____

_____

_____

_____

15 Read the passages and follow the directions.

┤ **A** ├

Below are the evaluation results of three different reading texts for intermediate level students based on five criteria.

Criteria	Text A	Text B	Text C
• Suitability of content: Is the text interesting enough for students and relevant to their needs?	2	2	3
• _____: Can be the text developed to achieve the purpose of the reading lesson?	2	3	1
• Readability: Does the text include the appropriate level of vocabulary and structure for students?	1	2	3
• Presentation: Does the text include interesting and appropriate images and illustrations?	3	1	2
• Authenticity: Is the language of the text authentic enough?	2	3	1

3=excellent, 2=good, 1=poor

B

Ms. Song's Note

The goal of my reading class is to help students improve their reading skills and learn the authentic language. So, I want to make them practice diverse reading strategies such as skimming, scanning, and inferencing. To compensate for their reading proficiency, I also consider teaching a guessing strategy for new vocabulary. Thus, the reading text should be appropriate to learn these reading strategies. Also, I want to help them learn the authentic language as much as possible. Although the language level is above their current proficiency, authentic reading texts introduce real-life language and interesting topics and thereby enhance students' motivation. Hence, I need to choose one reading text satisfying these two conditions.

Referring to <B>, fill in the blank in <A> with the ONE most appropriate word. Then, identify the Text you would recommend for Ms. Song and provide TWO reasons for recommending the identified text based on its characteristics.

Your Answer

_____

_____

_____

_____

_____

16 **Read the passages and follow the directions.**

┤ **A** ├

Worksheet A

Choose one sentence from ① to ⑤ irrelevant with the other sentences.

When photography came along in the nineteenth century, a painting was put in crisis. The photograph, it seemed, did the work of imitating nature better than the painter ever could. ① Some painters made practical use of the invention. ② There were Impressionist painters who used a photograph in place of the model or landscape they were painting. ③ But by and large, the photograph was a challenge to painting and was one cause of painting's moving away from direct representation and reproduction to the abstract painting of the twentieth century. ④ Therefore, the painters of that century put more focus on expressing nature, people, and cities as they were in reality. ⑤ Since photographs did such a good job of representing things as they existed in the world, painters were freed to look inward and represent things as they were in their imagination, rendering emotion in the color, volume, line, and spatial configurations native to the painter's art.

Worksheet B

Choose one word from ① to ⑤ different with the other underlined words.

Olivia and her sister Ellie were standing with Grandma in the middle of the cabbages. Suddenly, Grandma asked to Olivia, "Oh, you know what a Cabbage White is?" ① She answered, "Yes, I learned about it in biology class. It's a beautiful white butterfly,"

. . .

② She and Ellie started on the first cabbage. The caterpillars wriggled as they were picked up while Cabbage Whites filled the air around them. It was as if the butterflies were making fun of Olivia; they seemed to be laughing at ③ her, suggesting that they would lay millions of more eggs. The cabbage patch looked like a battlefield. Olivia felt like she was losing the battle, but she fought on. ④ She kept filling her bucket with the caterpillars until the bottom disappeared. Being exhausted and discouraged, she asked Grandma, "Why don't we just get rid of all the butterflies, so that there will be no more eggs or caterpillars?" Grandma smiled gently and said, "Why wrestle with Mother Nature? The butterflies help us grow some other plants because they carry pollen from flower to flower." Olivia realized ⑤ she was right.

B

Mr. Park and Jun-ho are talking about a mock test for the College Scholastic Ability Test conducted a few days ago.

Mr. Park : What was the most tricky question for you?

Jun-ho : Well . . . There was one question so difficult for me.

Mr. Park : What was it?

Jun-ho : It asked about whether the article is planned properly or not.

Mr. Park : You mean the question asking about the organization of the text?

Jun-ho : Yes! Right!

Mr. Park : Then, how about the question related to cohesive devices?

Jun-ho : Oh, I was okay with that.

Mr. Park : Great! Then, I can provide a worksheet for you.

Jun-ho : Thank you. By any chance, can you give me some advice about my difficulty?

Mr. Park : Well, think about whether ideas of the passage hang together or not. It will help you.

Jun-ho : Hmm . . . Okay, I will try. Thank you very much.

Mr. Park : Any time!

Referring to \<B\>, identify Jun-ho's difficulty in one sentence. Then, choose ONE worksheet appropriate for Jun-ho and write the reason based on \<A\>. Do NOT copy more than FOUR consecutive words from the passages.

Your Answer

_____

_____

_____

_____

_____

Plus ⁺

Coherence & Cohesion

Coherence means the connection of ideas at the idea level, and cohesion means the connection of ideas at the sentence level. Basically, coherence refers to the "rhetorical" aspects of your writing, which include developing and supporting your argument (e.g. thesis statement development), synthesizing and integrating readings, organizing and clarifying ideas. The cohesion of writing focuses on the "grammatical" aspects of writing.

One of the practical tools that can help improve the coherence of your writing is to use a concept map. The concept map is also known as "reverse outline" since you make an outline of your paper after you have finished the main ideas of your paper.

> ▶ Reverse outline
>
> Reverse outlining follows a two-step, repeatable process:
> In the left-hand margin, write down the topic of each paragraph. Try to use as few words as possible. These notes should tell you if each paragraph is focused and clear. In the right-hand margin, write down how the paragraph

topic advances the overall argument of the text. Again, be brief. These notes should tell you if each paragraph fits in the overall organization of your paper. You may also notice that paragraphs should be shifted after completing this step.

When rereading your own work, if you can't complete each step in 5-10 words, the paragraph may need to be altered. You should be able to summarize the topic and the manner of support quickly; if you can't, revise the paragraph until you can.

Cohesion is also a very important aspect of academic writing, because it immediately affects the tone of your writing. Although some instructors may say that you will not lose points because of grammatical errors in your paper, you may lose points if the tone of your writing is sloppy or too casual (a diary-type of writing or choppy sentences will make the tone of your writing too casual for academic writing). But cohesive writing does not mean just "grammatically correct" sentences; cohesive writing refers to the connection of your ideas both at the sentence level and at the paragraph level.

Here are some examples that illustrate the importance of connecting your ideas more effectively in writing.

Text A

The hotel is famous. It is one of the most well-known hotels in the country. The latest international dancing competition was held at the hotel. The hotel spent a lot of money to advertise the event. Because the hotel wanted to gain international reputation. But not many people attended the event.

⇒ The connection of ideas is not very good.

Text B

The hotel, which is one of the most well-known hotels in this region, wanted to promote its image around the world by hosting the latest international dancing competition. Although the event was widely advertised, not many people participated in the competition.

⇒ The connection of ideas is better than in the first example.

Text C

The latest international dancing competition was held at the hotel, which is one of the most well-known hotels in this region. The hotel spent a lot of money on advertising the event since it wanted to enhance its international reputation; however, it failed to attract many people.

⇒ The connection of ideas is better than in the first example.

Chapter

04

17   **Read the passage and follow the directions.**

> *Below is the conversation between two English teachers talking about a new type of listening.*
>
> Ms. Kim : These days, my students don't like listening lessons. They said the listening text from the textbook is so boring and unrelated to their interests. Also, the listening contents are out-of-date.
>
> Mr. Shin : Actually, I think the same. Also, I feel that using the listening materials of the textbook does not help my students improve their listening skills. Listening topics and sources from the textbook are so limited.
>
> Ms. Kim : Then, what is the alternative we can have? Hmm . . . How about encouraging students to listen more freely?
>
> Mr. Shin : Listen freely? You mean, they choose the topics they want to listen to?
>
> Ms. Kim : That's the point! For example, they do listening in a listening lab. Students can listen to what they want. How do you think?
>
> Mr. Shin : Good idea! They will love it!
>
> Ms. Kim : Then, what kind of listening sources they can have?
>
> Mr. Shin : I guess they can use up-to-date digital sources from YouTube, TED Talks, and other video clips. They will be able to access tons of authentic listening materials based on diverse topics and genres.
>
> Ms. Kim : Cool, then. Shall we start to plan?
>
> Mr. Shin : Yeah, why not!

Referring to the conversation, identify the type of listening that the two teachers talk about and provide TWO characteristics of the identified listening type compared to typical simplified classroom listening.

Your Answer

Productive Skills

기입형

서술형

Chapter
05 ▷▷ Productive Skills

🔒 정답 및 모범 답안 p. 20

 기입형

01 Read the passage, and follow the directions.

> *The activity below is a written conversation between Ms. Kim, an English teacher in a middle school, and her student, Sungjin.*
>
> **1st e-mail by Sungjin**
> July, 10
>
> Hello, mr. lee. Today, the class is very interesting. When you teach words, you show pictures, videos, and example sentences. *(ellipsis)* Thanks to these words, I can easily read the text, today. I love today's lesson!
>
> **Ms. Kim's Response**
> July, 15
>
> Hi, Sungjin. I also feel really glad that you could read the text in class. As you know, vocabulary knowledge is quite important in reading comprehension. Thus, in the next lesson, you will be taught some new words so that you can expand your vocabulary knowledge as well as review today's words. See you soon!
>
> **4th e-mail by Sungjin**
> September, 19
>
> Hello, Ms. Kim. Today's speaking class was very fun. I think Joon-ho did a very good job in making the presentation today. His PowerPoint slides and photos were very impressive. I want to learn how to use the program as well. Can you teach me how to use it? Or can you show us how to use it briefly? Thank you. :D

Ms. Kim's Response

September 25

Sungjin! Joon-ho did a good job but I think your presentation was amazing as well! I liked your story about the family trip to Japan. But, still, if you want to learn how to use visual aids for your presentation, I can help you! Of course, I can. Not only PowerPoint but there are also many useful tools for presentation! Next class, I will prepare a lesson introducing some of them. I hope you will enjoy the class!

Complete the teacher's note by filling in each blank with ONE word.

Ms. Kim's Teaching Note

This semester, I have been writing diaries with my students. It gives me more chances to communicate with them beyond the classroom. That's why I started this written conversation.

Actually, my class consists of 30 students, so it is difficult to have enough conversation with each of them during the class. While reading their diaries and then responding to them, I feel that I became much closer to my students than before. At first, they hesitated to write something and so did not enjoy writing dairies. Probably, they are bothered about making mistakes in writing. However, after several times of experiences, they realized that the content is more important than their grammatical mistakes. In their diaries, they usually like to talk about their daily lives to me. Sharing their daily routine with me, students and I are getting closer, which is the first purpose of this activity. I have thought establishing a good (1) _____ with my students like this is more important than anything in classroom teaching. Moreover, my second intention was to give them more chances to write and consequently improve their writing skills. During writing lessons, they usually feel a great deal of pressure for writing because they think their writing skills are not good enough. Hence, it is not easy to motivate them to write. However, as for this informal writing activity, students are willing to write something about themselves without being bothered about correct forms. Since they do writing regularly, their writing fluency as well as accuracy have improved a lot. Although their focal attention is placed on meaning, they pay peripheral attention to form. Such (2) _____ learning meaning unintentional or unplanned learning is the second aim of this writing activity. For example, Sungjin, at first, showed incorrect usage of the past tense and writing conventions like capitalization errors. However, he gradually acquired how to use them correctly while reading my written feedback with correct grammar and writing conventions.

Your Answer (1) _____

(2) _____

02 **Read the passages and follow the directions.**

---| **A** |---

 Dialogues involve two or more speakers and can be subdivided into those exchanges that promote social relationships, interpersonal, and those for which the purpose is to convey propositional or factual information, transactional. In each case, participants may have a good deal of shared knowledge (background information, schemata); therefore, the familiarity of the interlocutors will produce conversations with more assumptions, implications, and other meanings hidden between the lines. In conversations between or among participants who are unfamiliar with each other, references and meanings have to be made more explicit to assure effective comprehension. In this vein, interactional conversations can be trickier for students because they can involve some or all of the following features: a casual register, colloquial language, emotionally charged language, slang, ellipsis, sarcasm, and hidden meanings that require understanding "between the lines". Students would need to learn how such features are coded linguistically using authentic examples of interactional conversations.

Chapter

05

B

Activity

Choose the more appropriate version of expression and compare your answers with your partner's.

1. College Friends
   a. Fancy a beer afterward?
   b. I would like to invite you to come for a drink after work this evening.

2. Stockbroker to Client
   a. I'll tell you what to do - bung a couple of grand on HSBC. You can't go wrong. They're a dead cert investment, believe me.
   b. I would suggest you invest a couple of thousand dollars in HSBC. They're a very safe investment, I can assure you.

3. Family Members
   a. Ok, let's sort out the arrangements for the China trip.
   b. We are gathered here today to discuss the arrangements for the trip to China.

Based on <A>, write ONE feature that the lesson procedure in <B> focuses on. Use ONE word from <A>.

Your Answer _____

03 Read the students' learning logs and follow the directions.

A
Eunju's Learning Log

Today, my English teacher asked us to do a/an (1) _____, a kind of writing activity. First, my teacher read a short paragraph three times. After finishing the paragraph for the third time, she asked us to write the paragraph as we remembered it. To help us recollect what we heard, she put some keywords from the paragraph on the board. With keywords, then, we rewrote the paragraph as close as possible to the original sequence of events. After we completed our own paragraph, my teacher showed us the original text and asked us to compare our versions with the original text. Through this activity, I was able to use my listening and writing skills at the same time. Also, with some language support, it was a little bit demanding but enjoyable and exciting to me.

B
Minkyu's Learning Log

These days, I am writing a journal and getting the teacher's feedback on it every week. I enjoy it very much. There are several reasons that I like this writing activity. For this writing, I can choose the topics as I wish. Also, I can get my teacher's immediate feedback on what I write. Actually, this is a form of written communication but I feel as if it were a face to face conversation. Usually, my teacher does neither correct any errors from my writing, nor grade or evaluate the journal. Through the activity, I am having a good relation with my teacher and I can practice the mechanics of writing. With these various benefits, I like writing (2) _____ very much.

Identify the name of the writing activity that each student talks about in the learning log.

Your Answer   (1) _____

(2) _____

04 Read the passages and fill in the blank with the ONE most appropriate word.

> T : Okay, let's move on to a group activity. Guys, make a group of four!
>
> *(Ss sit in groups of four.)*
>
> T : This activity is called 'Let's go to Busan.' Have you been to Busan?
>
> Ss : Yes!
>
> T : How did you get there?
>
> S1 : I took a train.
>
> S2 : In my case, I took an airplane.
>
> T : Right, there are many different ways to get to Busan from Seoul. So, I will give you train, airplane, ship, and bus timetables. Based on the information from the timetables, find the best route to go to Busan.
>
> S3 : I have a question. The "best route" means the quickest way? Or the cheapest way?
>
> T : That's a good question! "Best route" means the cheapest way here. So, the budget to get to Busan is 200 thousand won for four people. Each transportation mode provides different discount types. For example, the train provides a 25 percent discount for four people travelling together. Also, the express bus provides a 20 percent discount for three people travelling together. Any questions? No? Okay, then I will give you 20 minutes. Let's start!
>
> *(T walks around the classroom to check the students' work and helps those who need help.)*

[Timetables]

Train	Departure	Arrival	Price per person
KTX 293	13:55	16:22	50,000
KTX 139	14:00	16:40	51,000
KTX 295	14:15	16:45	52,000

※ KTX provides a 25% discount for groups of four people.

Bus	Departure	Arrival	Price per person
Express Bus 407	13:00	17:00	50,000
Express Bus 364	14:05	17:55	49,000
Express Bus 486	14:15	16:45	51,000

※ Express Bus provides a 20% discount for groups of three people.

. . .

T=teacher, Ss=students, S=student

The activity above requires students to derive some new information by inferring it from the information they have been given. This type of activity is called a/an _____ activity. In this lesson, students are given timetables for train, airplane, ship, and bus routes. Then, the teacher asks them to work out the best route to get from Seoul to Busan.

Your Answer

05 Read the passages and follow the directions.

Lesson Procedure: Long Time No See!

Stage	Procedure
Listening	(. . .) • Ask Ss about two questions, 'what is the situation?' and 'what are they saying to each other?' for each scene. Then Ss play each conversation and contrast them to their predictions. • Give Ss Handout and draw attention to the gap-fill exercise. Ss complete together. **Handout** **Conversation 1** A: Good evening. B: Hi. A: Is anyone sitting here? B: No. A: Would you _____ if I joined you? B: Not _____. That would be lovely. A: Can I get you a drink? B: That's very _____. I'd love one. **Conversation 2** A: It was lovely to see you again, Sue. We really enjoyed ourselves. Thank you so _____ for having us to stay. B: Not at all. It's _____. A: But it was really kind of you to put up with all of us, and the animals. B: It's no problem at all. • Listen and pause after each conversation. Ss check. • Ask any questions about vocabulary.
Focus on pairs	• Lead Ss to focus on the functions of the pairs and show the function of each pair. • Ss match all the functions and check with their partner.
Speaking	• The whole class goes through each cue and then Ss practice the pairs individually. • Then Ss in pairs practice all the cues, paying attention to stress and intonation. • Ss switch the role and repeat the practice focusing on stress, rhythm, and intonation.

Ss=students

Scene 1.	A	B
	Would you mind if I joined you?	Not at all, that would be lovely.
Scene 2.	Thank you so much for having us to stay.	Not at all. It's my pleasure.
Scene 3.	Guess what? I passed the test!	What? Congratulations!
Scene 4.	Are you going to the theater tomorrow?	I'd love to, but I've already made plans.

Chapter

05

Considering the lesson procedure above, fill in each blank with a suitable term in ONE word.

The lesson procedure above is a speaking lesson teaching (1) _____ pairs for intermediate/upper-intermediate students aimed at helping them to respond more appropriately to each other's utterances. It highlights the importance of listening carefully and how to reply with focusing on (2) _____, not segmentals, for more natural stress, rhythm, and intonation.

Your Answer   (1) _____

(2) _____

06 Read the passage and follow the directions.

Lesson Procedure

1. T presents one of the paragraphs that students submitted last Friday and asks students to find two problems relating to text discourse.

   T: Hey, guys! Look at this! This is one of yours. So, I need your help to make this paragraph better. Read it first in groups and think hard on how to fix the paragraph in terms of text discourse. I will give you 5 minutes! Let's get started!

   > [Example]
   >
   > It was my birthday. I ask for a red bike. My parents bought me a red bike. I like the purple color too. It has white stripes on the fenders. I like to ride my bike everywhere. I like to ride on smooth pavement best. I am not allowed to ride on the sidewalk. People walk on the sidewalk. If I have time. I ride on the bike trail in the park. (*omitted*)

2. In groups, Ss discuss how to revise the paragraph and rewrite the paragraph.
3. After the group works, each group leader presents their findings.
4. T presents the best revision through an overhead projector to share with the whole class.

   > [Best revision text]
   >
   > It was my birthday, so I ask for a red bike. My parents bought me a red bike which has white stripes on the fenders. I like to ride my bike everywhere. Especially, I like to ride on smooth pavement best. However, I am not allowed to ride on the sidewalk where people walk on. Whenever I have time, I ride on the bike trail in the park. (*omitted*)

Chapter

05

T: Did you notice the changes in this revised paragraph? Right! There are two points! First, by deleting the sentence 'I like the purple color too,' all sentences are geared toward the one main point, his red bike. Also, there are some conjunctions, commas, and relative clauses to connect the sentences logically.

T=teacher, Ss=students

Referring to the lesson procedure above, fill in the blank with the ONE most appropriate term.

In the lesson procedure, the teacher helps students focus on text discourse to arrive at well-paragraphed writing. Firstly, after reading the given first draft in groups, students find out two problems to be improved. Based on the group discussion, then, they write their better versions. During the revision step, students discuss how each sentence is combined and how the given topic is logically developed. For example, they delete unrelated sentences to the topic and combine sentences with _____ (TWO words) such as *a red bike, so, however,* etc.

Your Answer _____

07 Read the conversation between the teacher and the students, and fill in the blank with ONE word.

T : Today we are going to do a writing activity. Are you ready? Okay, now, let's take out a piece of paper. I will read you a short story three times. How many times?

Ss : Three times.

T : Great! While you are listening to the story, try to remember what you hear. After three times of listening, write down what you remember individually. Then you will reproduce the story. Everyone, are you ready?

Ss : Yes, we are ready.

    (*Teacher reads the story three times.*)

T : (*Teacher writes some words on the board.*) Here are key words from the story. You can refer to them while reproducing the story. Now, it's time to write.

T : Okay, times up! Now, let's look at the screen. This is the story that I read you three times. Compare your versions with the original text and make a list of the differences.

    (*Ss compare their versions and the original story.*)

S1 : Mr. Moon. We have done this activity before, right?

T : You're right. It's our second time. Do you remember what this activity is called?

S1 : Hmm . . . Let me think. Yes! it's a/an _____.

T : Correct!

                                      T=teacher, S=student, Ss=students

---

Chapter

05

Your Answer _____

08 Examine the table and follow the directions.

Below is the correction symbols that Ms. Park, an English teacher of K-High school, will use to review her students' weekly journals.

Table of Correction Symbols

Symbol	Meaning	Incorrect	Correct
P	Punctuation	I live work, and go to school in Walnut.	I live, work, and go to school in Walnut.
=	Capitalization Needed	The dodgers play in los angeles.	The Dodgers play in Los Angeles.
VT	Verb Tense	I never work as a cashier until I got a job there.	I never worked as a cashier until I got a job there.
SV	Subject-verb Agreement	The manager work hard.	The manager works* hard.
TS	Tense Shift	After I went to the store, I eat the ice cream I bought.	After I went to the store, I ate the ice cream I bought.
⌒	Close Space	Every one works hard.	Everyone works hard.
#	Space Needed	Going to class is awesome.	Going to class is awesome.
SP	Spelling	The maneger is a woman.	The manager is a woman.

*This is just one correct tense that can be used.
Depending on the time of the action, conjugate accordingly.

Complete the comments by filling in each blank with suitable terms.

(1) _____ (THREE words) is a common tool to optimize students' learning opportunities from mistakes they make in writing homework and to encourage editing in the process of writing. Using symbols, the teacher indicates the types and the locations of the learners' mistakes. While looking at the symbols, the learners receive information on where they have gone wrong and try to detect the patterns of structures. Therefore, this way of marking allows students to use the (2) _____ (ONE word) approach in terms of teaching grammar.

Your Answer   (1) _____

(2) _____

09 Read the passage, and follow the directions.

Activity

Step 1

 On one side of the worksheet, there are several sentences of varying length. On the other side, the sentences are represented by a series of numbers; The teacher reads out the sentences, and students underline the number(s) for the word that is (are) stressed. For example：

 I bought my **sister** a **present**. ⇒ 1 – 2 – 3 – <u>4</u> – 5 – <u>6</u>
 Mike didn't break the window. ⇒ <u>1</u> – 2 – 3 – 4 – 5

Mix up the order in which the sentences appear on the left side. Say each sentence out loud, emphasizing the stressed word. Students must then match each sentence with its representation in numbers.

Step 2

 Students in pairs discuss where to put stress in sentences according to different situations. After the discussion, they practice reading the dialogues out loud with their partners.

e.g., 1. A：Did you lose your credit card?
   B：No, <u>Mike</u> lost his credit card.

  2. A：Did you lose your credit card?
   B：No, I lost my <u>wallet</u>.

  3. A：Did you lose your credit card?
   B：No, I <u>threw away</u> the credit card because it was expired.

Fill in the blanks with appropriate words.

The activity demonstrated above focuses on practicing the pronunciation of (1) _____ (ONE word) aspects. Since they can have an even greater impact on (2) _____ (ONE word) than the mispronunciation of individual sounds, the activity aims to raise students' awareness to the relations between stress patterns and the intended meaning for successful future communication.

Your Answer　(1) _____

(2) _____

Chapter

05

10 Read the passage in <A> and the teacher's journal in <B>, and follow the directions.

─┤ **A** ├─

Writing is sometimes used as a production mode for learning, reinforcing, or testing grammatical concepts. Such intensive writing typically appears in controlled, written grammar exercises. This type of writing does not allow much, if any, creativity on the part of the writer. A common form of controlled writing is to present a paragraph to students in which they have to alter a given structure throughout. So, for example, they may be asked to change all present tense verbs to past tense. Another form of controlled writing is a/an _____. Researchers suggest that teachers can expect some benefits by using this technique for their writing lessons as follows:

(1) It is challenging. Students listen to the passage twice/three times and have to use their own knowledge of language to rewrite it.

(2) Students focus on language accuracy as well as meaning.

(3) The technique not only requires students to write but demands careful listening and retention of the material.

─┤ **B** ├─

Teacher's Journal

To help a student become a good writer, teachers need to teach various genres of writing: descriptive writing, journals, narrative writing, persuasive writing and so on. Last semester, accordingly, I mainly focused on teaching narrative writings. This semester I am planning to teach descriptive writing so that they can express the accurate and vivid descriptions considering appropriate words and phrases. During the lesson, firstly, I will read a descriptive paragraph at a normal speed three times over. Then, I will ask students to rewrite it to the best of their recollection. Since my students are low intermediate level, I will put some keywords from the paragraph, in sequence, on the blackboard as cues that they can refer to. By practicing this _____ activity, I believe that they will be able to learn more about the characteristics of a descriptive paragraph such as generic structure, grammatical features, appropriate vocabulary, and expressions, leading to more dynamics during writing lessons.

Fill in the blanks in <A> and <B> with the ONE appropriate word. Write the same word in both blanks.

Your Answer _____

11 Read the passage in <A> and the teacher's journal in <B>, and follow the directions.

─────────────────┤ **A** ├─────────────────

   The process-oriented writing approach emphasizes the importance of developing students' ability to plan, identify issues and analyze, and implement possible solutions. In this approach, teachers train students to become self-aware and reflect on the activities and strategies they carry out while they write. In the classroom, teaching process writing means that students will engage in activities such as [figure 1] below. When students write, they do not follow a straight procedure. Instead, they can go back and forth in the stages allowing them to revise and edit even when the text has not been completed, engaging in a non-linear, exploratory, and generative process.

[Figure 1] A process model of writing instruction

       Selection of topic: by teacher and/or students
       Prewriting: brainstorming, collecting data, note-taking, outlining, etc.
       Composing: getting ideas down on paper.
       Response to draft: teacher/peers respond to ideas, organization and style.
       Revising: reorganizing, style, adjusting to readers, refining ideas.
       Response to revisions: teacher/peers respond to ideas, organization and style.
       Editing and _____: checking that the writing makes sense overall and then correcting spelling, grammar and syntax errors.
       Evaluation: teacher evaluates progress over the process.
       Publishing: by class circulation or presentation, websites, etc.
       Follow-up tasks: to address weaknesses

B

Teacher's Journal

   Normally, to make the written works, higher-quality writers should focus on revising and editing process as well as the drafting itself. Hence, during the writing lesson I have intentionally emphasized these processes. So my students always revise and edit their own writings before the submission. However, I found that some students' final papers still had many mistakes uncorrected even after revision and editing works. Through a one-on-one conference with students, I figured out that they do not check surface errors while editing their writings. Thus, I am preparing a lesson to teach students how to catch errors like misspellings and mistakes in grammar and punctuation. The following five strategies will be introduced to develop their _____ skills, which enable them to edit their writings as accurately as possible before finalizing their works.

Strategies to be taught for the students :
1. Work with a printout, not your computer screen.
2. Read slow, and read every word.
3. Circle every punctuation mark.
4. Check only one kind of error at a time.
5. Don't rely entirely on spelling and grammar checking programs.

Based on the information in <A> and <B>, fill in the blanks in <A> and <B> with the ONE most appropriate word. Use the SAME word in both blanks.

Your Answer _____

12 Read the passages and follow the directions.

The following is an excerpt from a lesson procedure of intermediate level writing course.

Lesson Procedure

Step A Modeling a text

1. T chooses a certain type of writing form to develop classroom activities. In this case, the type of text must match the students' needs and market needs where they will work later on.
2. T shows a model text and Ss discuss the text format by deconstructing, or manipulating the text.
3. Ss are directed to explicitly know and understand the function of the text (the communicative purpose of the text).
4. Ss, then, study the certain rhetorical structures, grammatical patterns, and vocabulary of the text, and then practice the procedure if necessary.

Step B Joint construction

1. Ss are guided and helped by the teacher before they become a real independent writer of a certain text format taught and learned through three practical steps:
   a) Ss reconstruct the certain type of text given. In this case, Ss may revise and paraphrase the vocabulary usage, the grammatical patterns, and textual devices, if necessary, by their own words.
   b) T continuously guides Ss to discuss so that they understand well the given text type.
   c) Ss review a modeling text and what they have practiced.

Step C Independent construction of a text

1. T makes sure that Ss fully understand the features of a certain text such as the communicative purpose, structure element of the text, grammatical patterns usage, relevant vocabulary usage, and textual devices as well.
2. Ss independently write the certain type of text as what they have learned before.

T=teacher, Ss=students

Fill in the blank with the ONE most appropriate word.

> The lesson procedure above consists of three steps which must be followed and implemented to teach and learn the target type of a text. According to the three steps, modeling a text, guided writing, and independent practice, the lesson procedure exemplifies cyclic teaching and learning writing focusing on _____ approach.

Your Answer _____

13 Read the passages and follow the directions.

---| **A** |---

What Makes Listening Difficult?

As teachers plan lessons and techniques for teaching listening skills, many characteristics of spoken language need to be taken into consideration. Second language learners need to pay special attention to such factors because they strongly influence the processing of speech, and can even block comprehension if they are not attended to. In other words, they can make the listening process difficult. They include some characteristics of spoken language such as clustering, redundancy, reduced forms, performance variables, colloquial language, rate of delivery, stress, rhythm, and intonation.

---| **B** |---

Listening Script

Simon : Hey, Janny. How's it going?

Janny : Pretty good, Simon. How was your weekend?

Simon : Aw, it was terrible. Really bad. I mean... the worst you could imagine. You know what I mean?

Janny : Yah, I've had those days. Well, like, what happened?

Simon : Well... you're not gonna believe this... my friend, you know Mike? — I think you met him at the party — anyway... he and I drove to Sydney Observatory, you know, the observatory in Millers Point? So, we were driving along when this dud in one SUV like a Hummer or something, comes up like three feet behind us and like tailgates us on these crazy roads up there, you know what they're like...

(...)

Below is an excerpt from the conversation between two English teachers talking about listening script above.

T1 : Hmm, Ms. Song. Is it too difficult for our students?

T2 : Difficult? Is it?

T1 : I mean, there are many reductions like gonna and I've.

T2 : I see. I agree that such reductions would not easy to hear for our students who are accustomed to only written English.

T1 : Also, the two speakers speak too fast. We need to slow down the speed when we play the listening file.

T2 : Do you really think so? Well, I understand what you mean but I think there are many pauses by the speakers. It would be okay for them to comprehend the conversation. Also, they can have more processing time and get more extra information with the little insertions like *I mean* and *you know* from the listening.

T1 : You mean, some _____ can help our students listening more easily, right?

T2 : That's right. For example, suppose the speaker repeats and elaborates his previous utterance, saying *"SUV, SUV like a Hummer or something."* Such spoken characteristic can give listeners one more chance to listen for it even though they miss and misunderstand the previous information.

T1 : Okay, then, let's remind our students of this spoken characteristic before listening and see how they perform. If they have a problem with this, then we can try another one.

T2 : That's exactly what I am saying.

T=teacher

Fill in the blank in <B> with the ONE most appropriate word from <A>.

Your Answer

✎ 서술형

01 Read the passages and follow the directions.

┤ A ├

Ms. Song's Note

I believe that the best lesson is a student-centered lesson. Thus, I try my best to make my English lessons as learner-centered as much I can. One of my efforts is having a conference with my students every month. Yesterday, I had a one-on-one conversation with my students again and found out their needs for activities. They commented that they want to do an activity using diverse skills simultaneously which will help them practice real-life communication. Besides, they added that they want to be more independent and responsible learners who make their own choices. Based on these two points, I prepared a lesson using one communication activity.

┤ B ├

Below is a/an _____ activity that Ms. Song prepares to facilitate diverse language skills in a student-centered learning environment. During the activity, students need to communicate to select one among five options to reach the best outcome.

※ For today's speaking activity, you will follow the given steps in groups.

(1) Identify the problem/conflict to be solved.
(2) Gather relevant information.
(3) Identify possible solutions.
(4) Identify potential consequences.
(5) Choose one best solution.

<u>Step 1</u> T provides guidelines for today's activity.

Step 2 T provides one situation as seen below and asks Ss to read the passage.

The digital footprint is a collection of data from a person's online activity that can be traced back to them. It's made up of data that can be found online. One day, you and your friend found out that the school website has a technical problem and allows you to access the digital footprints of some school teachers, which are classified. Then, your friend tempts you to see the classified information without telling the fact to your teachers. If you deny it, your friend says that you are no longer a friend of him/her. What would you do?

Step 3 T distributes a worksheet to Ss and asks them to choose one idea that they would do in the given situation, imagining its potential consequences. Additionally, T asks Ss to write the good and bad points of the idea they have chosen, individually.

※ Choose ONE option you would do if you are in the situation. Think about its potential consequence(s) and write down the information in one paragraph. Also, fill in the blanks with good and bad points of your choice.

① Tell the fact to your teacher immediately.
② Check the digital footprints of some teachers.
③ Blame your friend for the inappropriate behavior.
④ Pretend that you don't understand what your friend suggests.
⑤ Simply ignore your friend's suggestion.

I will choose to _____.
Then, _____ potential consequence(s)
_____.

Good points	Bad points
-	-
-	-

Step 4   T put Ss in groups of four. T makes Ss in groups share their ideas and good/bad points. Ss listen to their group members' opinions carefully and choose the best idea and relevant supporting ideas among good or bad points. Based on the group discussion, Ss complete the worksheet below.

> My group thinks the best idea for the situation is
> _____. Then, it will result in _____
> _____.
> There are three reasons we have chosen this idea. First,
> _____. Next, _____.
> Finally, _____.

Step 5   T asks each group to present their group decision and supporting ideas. After the presentation session, T asks the whole class to vote for the best answer. T finishes the lesson emphasizing the importance of making decisions on your own.

T=Teacher, Ss=Students

Fill in the blank in <B> with ONE word. Then, based on <A>, write TWO reasons that Ms. Song prepares the identified activity with evidence from <B>.

Your Answer

_____

_____

_____

_____

_____

02 Read the passages and follow the directions.

A

Pronunciation instruction was absent from the second/foreign language (L2) classroom for a long time due to the conventional beliefs that pronunciation is not important, cannot be taught, and can be "picked up" by learners. These beliefs have been questioned and pronunciation teaching has undergone a shift, so that, nowadays, many teachers put effort into developing pronunciation/speech activities, tasks, materials, methodologies, and techniques. At present, they recognize the importance of segmental phonemes and suprasegmentals in the teaching of intelligible pronunciation. Thus, their aim of teaching is to improve _____ by requiring students to work on segmental phonemes (i.e. vowels and consonants of a language), and suprasegmentals (i.e. such sound phenomena as accent and intonation) which may stretch over more than one segment.

B

Activity 1

Focusing on improving students' speaking skills, a high school English teacher prepares the following activity where students practice pronunciation using both their listening and speaking skills.

• Make Ss listen to a conversation. After listening, provide a list of sentences extracted from the conversation and make them check the intonation.

> 1. I'll be back in a minute.
> 2. Which of them do you prefer?
> 3. When does the meeting start?
> 4. Is John leaving on Thursday or Friday?
> 5. We've got a chairperson, speakers, a timer, and guests.
>
> ...

• Put Ss in groups of four and ask them to share their answers. Then, make Ss discuss when they use falling, rising, fall-rise, or rise-fall intonation.
• Make each group present their ideas and check the answers with the whole class.

Activity 2

After conducting a reading lesson, a middle school teacher prepares a game to practice oral intelligibility using words from the reading text.

List of words from a reading text
luck, look, lock, beat, bet, bad, bed, fur, far, for, fire, lug, leg, lake, lack, leak, hood, had, hoot, hit, hat, hot, pat, pete, pet, leap, lip, loop, line, loan, lane, lean, lamb, lime...

• Show the list of words and ask Ss to choose 20 words and fill in the blanks as they want.

Lug	pet		leg	
		hoot		lock
	lip		lean	
lime				
		...		

• While calling out minimal pairs, ask Ss to listen to, cross out the words called and make three horizontal, diagonal, or vertical lines.
• Have Ss raise their hands saying 'Bingo' when they make three lines.

Fill in the blank in <A> with the ONE most appropriate word from the passages in <B>. Then, based on the information in <A>, write the phonological feature that Activity 1 and 2 focus on, respectively, and provide evidence for each.

Your Answer

_____

_____

_____

_____

_____

03 Read the passage and follow the directions.

Below is the conversation between two English teachers in a middle school. Ms. Kim, a senior teacher, is listening to the problem of Mr. Lee's lessons and giving advice.

Ms. Kim : Good morning, Mr. Lee. What are you up to?

Mr. Lee : Hi, Ms. Kim. I am reviewing my English lesson yesterday because it was not satisfying that much.

Ms. Kim : Was it? What was the problem you thought?

Mr. Lee : Well, I've got most problems with group activities.

Ms. Kim : Can you clarify more about it?

Mr. Lee : After reading a text about the environment, I prepared a discussion session as a post-reading activity. So, in groups of five, students needed to share their ideas about the question, 'Can people save nature by using tech?'.

Ms. Kim : That's a good topic to discuss. Then, how did it go?

Mr. Lee : Turn-taking didn't go on exactly the way I expected. I mean, talkative students dominated turns to speak. So, reluctant speakers had fewer chances to talk.

Ms. Kim : Yeah, a discussion activity usually does not compel every student to participate. That's a typical problem in a discussion activity. How about preparing a group activity where students can have individual roles? What do you think?

Mr. Lee : Providing an individual role? That's a great idea! Can you give me an exemplary activity to do that?

Ms. Kim : Like a jigsaw activity. In this activity, every student receives one part of the text to read and fully understand the content. Then, they have to clearly explain it to the others. If even one student does not do their duty, the group cannot complete the task.

Mr. Lee : That's what I want! Well, I have another problem. Can you give me some advice on this, too?

Chapter

05

Ms. Kim : Of course! Go ahead.

Mr. Lee : While observing their discussion, I also found that some grammatical errors were repeated and reinforced. Especially, when advanced students made such errors, less proficient students could not notice the problems and just repeated the incorrect forms.

Ms. Kim : Hmm, that's a big problem. That often happens to my students. The errors from advanced students are just minor slips but lower-level students copy them without doubting. In that case, I conduct a grammar exercise as a treatment for the repeated errors. Through such a grammar-focused activity, students can clearly learn how to use the target forms correctly. You need to do what I do.

Mr. Lee : You mean that I should prepare a follow-up activity for my students?

Ms. Kim : Exactly!

Based on the conversation, write TWO problems of Mr. Lee's English lesson and the solution for each that Ms. Kim suggests with the concrete reason for the suggestion. Do NOT copy more than FOUR consecutive words from the passage.

Your Answer

_____

_____

_____

_____

_____

04 Read the passages and follow the directions.

─────── **A** ───────

Many approaches to teaching speaking have taken little account of the nature of spoken language but instead have tended to fall back on grammar which is essentially based on written text. Technological advances in recording speech and the establishment by linguists of corpora of speech utterances have led to much greater knowledge about the similarities and differences between the two modes of communication. It is very valuable for language teachers to be aware of the main differences and of the features that typically characterize speech, as this will allow them to make more informed decisions about what to teach. [Table 1] below summarises some of the key differences between the spoken and written language.

[Table 1] Spoken and written language: typical features

Features	Spoken language	Written language
Basic unit	clause	sentence
Formulaic chunks	Frequent use	Little use
Language formality	Informal language preferred	Formal language preferred
Performance effects (hesitation, pauses, repeats)	Range of noticeable performance effects	Few/no noticeable performance effects
Ellipsis (omission of grammatical elements)	Frequent use	Little use

---

B

Text 1

I was working in Turkey at the time um (3) I was lucky enough to have one of my colleagues doing the same program em (2) started at the same time as me so we used to get together regularly (3).

Text 2

I was working in Turkey. Fortunately, I was able to collaborate with a colleague who commenced the program simultaneously.

note=the number in brackets indicates the seconds of pause.

Based on the information in <A>, identify the type of language that each Text exemplifies. Then, explain TWO features that distinguish the identified languages with some concrete examples presented in each text from <B>.

Your Answer

_____

_____

_____

_____

_____

05 Read the passages and follow the directions.

---| **A** |---

One of the most significant contributions for the conversation skill development is the concept of the _____. They are composed of two turns produced by different speakers which are placed adjacently and where the second utterance is identified as related to the first. Once again, what is in the first part of the pair determines what needs to be in the second part. Thus, as a type of turn-taking, it is generally considered the smallest unit of conversational exchange because a single sentence usually cannot make for conversations. As shown in the following activity from <B>, the major aim of teaching this concept is to teach students how to respond more appropriately to each other's utterances.

---| **B** |---

Activity 1

※ Look at the 2 underlined pairs of phrases in the dialogue. What is their function?

A: I passed!
B: Oh, well done! Congratulations! We'll have to celebrate.
A: How about opening a party?
B: Brilliant idea!

Activity 2

※ Grade the expressions below based on the level of politeness.

☆ not very polite	☆☆ polite
☆☆☆ very polite	☆☆☆☆ extremely polite

How to ask for permission

- Could I use your phone?
- Might I possibly use your phone?
- Would you mind if I use your phone?
- May I use your phone?
- I'll use your phone, OK?
- Can I use your phone?
- I wonder if I could use your phone.

Fill in the blank with TWO appropriate words. Then, of two activities in <B>, choose the ONE that focuses on the concept mentioned in <A> and write how the identified activity can help students improve their conversation skills.

Your Answer

06 Read the passages and follow the directions.

───────────┤ **A** ├───────────

The word "text" refers to any instance of language, in any medium, that makes sense to someone who knows the language. We can produce text when we speak or write. A spoken language is in the forms of conversation, speech, and storytelling, while written language is reflected in the forms of newspapers, magazines, and books. Some researchers state that cohesion is the most important thing needed in the cohesiveness of a text or discourse, including in journalistic text. It shows that cohesion helps the process of understanding a text by using its connectives so that the information will be easy to understand. Within a text, if an item previously mentioned is referred to again and dependent on another element, it is considered a cohesive device. The cohesive devices are tools that when used appropriately enable the writer to hang sentences and text segments together. Cohesive devices consist of five elements such *as reference, conjunction, ellipsis, lexical cohesion, etc*. A cohesive device will help the readers in interpreting a text. Below is a brief explanation of each device.

- Reference is used to refer to things in your writing in order to create cohesion.
- Conjunctions operate within sentences and connectives relate to meaning between sentences.
- Ellipsis is simply characterized by "the omission of an item".
- Lexical cohesion can be subdivided into the categories, repetition of the same item, synonyms, superordinates, and general words.

───────────┤ **B** ├───────────

Below are example sentences extracted from a news article.

Did you know that soccer is the most popular sport in the world? The sport is the most popular in Europe and South America. It originated in China more than 2000 years ago. (...)

Chapter

05

Based on <A>, identify TWO types of cohesive devices exemplified in <B>. Then, explain the reason for your choice for each by providing the evidence.

Your Answer

_____

_____

_____

_____

_____

07   Read the passage and follow the directions.

A middle school teacher planned a lesson about informational essay writing. She designed the lesson plan as seen below.

Step 1 Introduction

T introduces an informational essay to the class, which consists of three parts, introduction, body, and conclusion. Then, T provides five topic questions for the informational essay and then asks Ss to choose one of them. T puts Ss in groups of four by the question they have chosen.

(*e.g.* Q1: Choose ONE influential person. What impact has he or she had on modern society?)

Step 2 Group Research & Outline

T gives Ss useful websites to search for information to be included in their essay and shows them how to use each website. Ss in groups research necessary information to answer the chosen question and make an outline for the essay by deciding where to put the information among the introduction, body, and conclusion.

Step 3 Writing the Essay

Based on the outline, Ss write a draft of the informational essay for 30 minutes focusing on giving topic-related information to readers. T walks around the classroom and observes their performance. T plays a role of a resource by giving the necessary information that students ask for. T tells Ss that today's writing lesson is based on product-oriented writing. T emphasizes they don't have to write their first draft perfectly because they have an opportunity to revise the writing.

Step 4 Peer feedback

Once each group completes their drafts, T asks students to switch theirs with others. T explains how to give feedback with a checklist and then has them do peer feedback with a checklist. Even more important is the fact that Ss provide comments about not the language but the contents.

Step 5 Revision

Based on the feedback from the other group, each group revises their essay in terms of contents. After revision, students proofread their own writing checking any spelling mistakes or grammatical errors, and finalize their essay based on the style of writer-based prose.

Step 6 Presentation & Evaluation

Each group presents the informational essay to the whole class and has a Q&A session. After listening to each group's presentation, Ss freely ask and answer questions about the information introduced. During the presentation sessions, T gives overall comments on each group's outcome. Before finishing the writing lesson, T asks Ss to post their group writing to the class blog. T gives students the final evaluation results of their writings.

Based on the passage above, identify TWO steps out of six that have a wrong description in the given lesson procedure. Then, support your answers with evidence from the passage. Do NOT copy more than FOUR consecutive words from the passage.

Your Answer

_____

_____

_____

_____

08 Read the passage in <A> and the conversation in <B>, and follow the directions.

A

What is that one needs to know and be able to do in order to speak another language? Of course, one needs to know how to articulate sounds in a comprehensible manner, one needs an adequate vocabulary, and one needs to have mastery of syntax. These various elements add up to (a) grammatical (linguistic) competence. Based on this, language users, also, need the ability to achieve communicative goals in a socially appropriate manner. Thus, the communicative competence one needs to speak in another language includes (a) *grammatical (linguistic) competence*, (b) *sociolinguistic competence*, (c) *discourse competence*, and (d) *strategic competence*.

B

NS : So what did you do last weekend?

NNS : I was busy. I go to a movie theater.

NS : Oh, did you? What did you see?

NNS : Batman. It is nice.

NS : It was good? You like watching movies?

NNS : Yes, very much. What about you? What did you do?

NS : Nothing much. I cooked meals, cleaned the house, and did the laundry. *(pointing out NNS's T-shirts.)* By the way, I like your T-shirts.

NNS : *(displaying modesty)* No, it's not good at all.

NS : *(looking embarrassed)* Well ... Okay.

NS=a native speaker, NNS=a non-native speaker

Referring to terms in <A>, identify TWO components of communicative competence that the non-native speaker in <B> lacks. Then, provide the reasons for your choice with evidence from <B>.

Your Answer

_____

_____

_____

_____

_____

09   Read <A> and <B> and follow the directions.

A

Jaeho's Learning Log

Based on the results of the proficiency test last week, my teacher told me that I belong to a low intermediate group. However, I think my English level is higher than the low intermediate one. If I had gotten a better score in the writing part, I would have been in a high intermediate group. Last semester, actually, I mechanically practiced sentence combining activities in decontextualized manner. That's why I didn't have enough opportunities to develop my writing skills, resulting in staying in a low intermediate group. For this semester, hence, I will apply myself to level up my writing skills somehow. For that purpose, I will give priority to paragraph writing instead of sentence combining. So, I want to practice lots of discourse-based compositions. However, since I cannot write a paragraph with perfect grammar yet, I prefer controlled or guided writing. In other words, I will be able to write a short composition only when language support is provided. For example, only after several times of listening, I can rewrite the text based on some keywords and my recollection.

Chapter

05

B

The following lesson procedure shows the _____ technique, a type of controlled writing. This activity is useful for low intermediate students who just learned writing at a paragraph level since it asks them to rewrite what they listen to based on some language support.

Step 1 T reads a short story to Ss.

Step 2 T reads the story two to three times and Ss listen carefully. (Note-taking is not required.)

Step 3 T puts keywords from a short story, in sequence, on the chalkboard as cues for the students.

Step 4 T asks Ss to rewrite the paragraph to the best of their recollection with some cues. Ss should write the story focusing on its meaning.

Step 5 T provides a script of the listening and Ss compare the reconstructed text with the original text.

Fill in the blank in <B> with ONE word. Then, explain how the writing activity can meet Jaeho's needs based on its TWO characteristics reflected in <B>.

Your Answer

_____

_____

_____

_____

_____

10 Read the passages and follow the directions.

---| **A** |---

Ms. Song's Teaching Note

The goal of my grammar class is to help students use the language to express their own ideas and opinions. I believe that using the language for real communication is more meaningful than mechanically memorizing patterns. So, I want to provide a grammar lesson where students can share their own ideas using the target form they just have learned. Also, I want my students to notice some examples of the target form within communicative context and then discover the rule by themselves so that they can actively internalize it. Based on these ideas, I am trying to plan a grammar lesson for my students.

---| **B** |---

Lesson A

T checks Ss' understanding of comparative forms.
T : When do you use the comparative? Yes, Minju?
S1 : When we compare two different things.
T : You're right! Then, do you know how to make comparatives? Any volunteer? (No responses)

T explains the rules of comparatives.
T : Don't worry! I will explain how to make it. As Minju said, comparatives are used to describe the differences between two people, things, or ideas. There are two ways you can describe the differences between two things.
T writes down the rules on the board.

[On the board]
(1) For one-syllable adjectives and two-syllable adjectives ending in –y: adjective + -er + than
(2) For adjectives that have two or more syllables: more + adjective + than

T checks Ss' understanding and gives some example sentences. Ss in pairs match the example and the rule.

T : Is it clear? Then, let's see some example sentences. Here, I will give you four sentences. With your partner, find out the corresponding rule relating to each example. I'll give you 10 minutes!

[On the board]

Ex 1. I think math is more difficult than history.

Ex 2. This recipe for banana bread is more complicated than my mother's.

Ex 3. Sending an email is easier than writing a letter.

Ex 4. Texting is faster than making a phone call.

Lesson B

1. T asks Ss to read the conversation.

A: Which do you prefer, London or Paris?

B: Well, I'm from Paris, so, of course, I love Paris.

A: London's a lot bigger than Paris.

B: It's true. Paris is much smaller, but it's more romantic! Parisians seem to live a happier life than Londoners.

A: Yes, this is what people say.

B: And the food is better.

A: Well, I'm not so sure about that...

(ellipsis)

---

2. T asks Ss to find the differences between London and Paris.
   (Possible answer: London's bigger than Paris.)

3. T puts Ss in groups of four and asks them to check the underlined forms from the dialogue. T asks Ss to answer the following questions after observing the underlined forms closely.

(1) When do we add '-er' to the adjective in making comparatives? (Possible answer: We add '-er' before adjectives that have one syllable. Also, for two-syllable adjectives ending in –y.)

(2) When do we add 'more' before the adjective in making comparatives? (Possible answer: We add 'more' before adjectives that have two or more syllables.)

4. T asks each group to present their answers.

5. T provides the following activity and asks students to complete the paragraph individually.

※ Which city do you like more between Seoul and Jeju (or Busan)? Write three reasons for your choice using comparative forms.

I like _____ more than _____. There are three reasons. First, _____ is _____ than _____ because _____ _____.
Besides, _____ is _____ than _____ in that _____. Finally, _____ is _____ than _____ so that _____.

Considering the information in <A> and <B>, choose the ONE lesson you would recommend for Ms. Song and provide TWO reasons for your choice based on its characteristics.

Your Answer

_____

_____

_____

_____

_____

11 Read the passages, and follow the directions.

A

Mr. Park is teaching English to 1st graders in a middle school. Last week, he taught 'articles and subject-verb agreement' and today, he asked his students to write about their best friend to practice what they had learned. The following is Saewha's writing and the teacher's feedback.

Saewha's writing

My best friend's name is Eunjung. Her favorite animal is <u>rabbit</u>.
ART

Her school isn't <u>Korean</u> school. She goes Lycée français de Séoul.
ART

It is <u>French</u> school. Her hobby is dancing. She <u>have</u> beautiful dark
ART   SV

eyes and hair and she's very tall. So, when she dances in a K-pop dance, she looks awesome. I really <u>likes</u> her... *(ellipsis)...*
SV

ART=article, SV=subject-verb agreement

B

Saewha's Learning Log

Last week, I learned two important grammar points, articles and subject-verb agreement. While explaining them, Mr. Park emphasized that it would take time for us to be familiar with those grammar rules because we don't have them in Korean. As the first practice, we wrote a short paragraph introducing our best friends. I wrote about my friend, Eunjung, and my teacher reviewed my writing. Usually, for reviewing students' writings, he directly corrects some grammatical errors and gives us a short comment on the content. However, this time, Mr. Park changed the way he corrects. Since this writing was to practice the two newly learned grammar forms, he used special symbols denoting errors for articles and subject-verb agreement. He added that he indicated errors only about articles and subject-verb agreement, even though there were other types of errors, so that we could focus on the target forms. Actually, I used to get overwhelmed with too many corrections without symbols. Cognitively, it was too much burden. However, this time it was totally different. One more good thing about this new feedback is that I can have a chance to correct the errors by myself. I could figure out where errors occur and self-correct them. Thanks to the new feedback type, I could internalize the target rules better and improve my grammatical proficiency.

Chapter

05

Identify the name of the feedback presented in <A>. Then, write Mr. Park's TWO correction principles mentioned in <B> which could make Saewha effectively internalize the target rules.

Your Answer

_____

_____

_____

_____

_____

12   Read the passages and follow the directions.

In a writing class, Eunji, an intermediate middle school student, wrote a persuasive essay about "online classes." After the class, Eunji and her teacher have a private conversation about her first draft. Below is part of the student-teacher writing _____.

T   : So, Eunji, what is your writing topic?

Eunji : Umm... it's about the online classes I am taking right now. I think online classes are more effective than offline classes.

T   : Good. When I read your essay, I could tell the main point clearly because of the good introduction and conclusion. That is, the thesis statement is obviously mentioned in the introduction. Also, the conclusion successfully recaps the key points. You did a very good job!

Eunji : Thank you, Mr. Kim. But there must be some points to be improved, right?

T   : Just one thing. While reading it, I found some sentences seem to have weak relation with the other sentences. But actually they should be closely related to each other to clearly convey what you want to say. Got it?

Eunji : So the sentences are not linked well to each other?

T   : That's the point! In terms of ideas, they are talking about the main idea. However, it's not easy to find the relationship between supporting details. Thus, for the second draft, I want you to use some linking words between sentences to show clear relationships such as comparing/contrasting, sequencing, or cause and effect.

Eunji : Ah-hah! You mean I need to make my essay have stronger cohesion?

T   : Exactly!

Eunji : Okay. Understood.

T   : Shall we revise some of it together? Here, I checked a red mark on some sentences that need to be revised.

Eunji : *(Skimming through the essay)* Hmm, how about the fifth and sixth sentences?

T : Cool! So, here are the sentences talking about the advantages of online classes. What is the relation between two sentences?

5th Sentence   Online classes give us great flexibility in that we can easily gain access to study material even at home.

6th Sentence   Online classes support us in setting our own pace for studying.

Eunji : Both are advantages of online classes. The first and the second advantages.

T : Yes! Then, what do you need between them?

Eunji : Moreover?

T : Excellent!

(Ellipsis)

T=teacher

Fill in the blank with the ONE most appropriate word and identify the strong and the weak points of Eunji's persuasive writing. Then, explain the solution that the teacher suggests Eunji to solve the weak point of her writing with evidence.

Your Answer

_____

_____

_____

_____

_____

13 Read the lesson procedure and a student's log and follow the directions.

⊣ A ⊢

- Students: 30 students, 2nd graders, middle school
- Level: Intermediate
- Speech act: Apologizing
- Lesson Objectives: Students will be able to express apologies based on the specific level of _____.

Lesson Procedure

Step 1

T: You need to be able to apologize appropriately if you hurt or offend someone. The social rules for when and how to apologize vary from one culture to another. Thus, simply translating expressions from Korean into English may not work well. How you apologize is significantly governed by the situation and your familiarity with the person you have hurt or offended.

Step 2

T: Look at the table below. The following expressions are often used after you make a mistake and feel bad about a situation. The mistake may be small (step on someone's foot) or serious (be a half hour late for a test).

	Apologizing	Responding
Informal	• Oops. Excuse me. • Sorry.	• That's okay. • That's all right.
↓	• I'm very sorry. • It was my fault. • I apologize.	• No problem. • Don't worry about it. • Forget about it.
Formal	• Please forgive me.	• I forgive you.

Step 3 T goes through the expressions and explains their degrees of politeness.

Step 4 T engages Ss in an activity for practicing English apologies.

T : Now, you and your partner sitting next to you will be given two packs of cards. One is for the person who apologizes and the other is for the person who responds. On each card, information about the context, age, and status of the participants is provided. For instance, you can apologize for bumping into an elderly lady, a five-year-old boy, a well-dressed business person, and so on.

T=Teacher, Ss=Students

B

Student's Log

Today, in my English class, I learned how to apologize. For apology, the only expression I know was "Sorry." However, my English teacher explained that saying "Sorry" for an apology can be inappropriate in some situations. At first, I didn't understand what she said. But, with her explanation, I was able to understand the diverse ways of expressing apologies. Especially, in today's lesson, I could practice how to apologize in different situations. I played the role of a person who makes a mistake, and my partner was a person who receives apologies from me. My partner pretended an elderly lady, a five-year-old boy, a well-dressed business person, and so on. Then, I apologized to him or her using the most proper expression in each situation. Through today's lesson, I learned how to smoothly and appropriately give an apology in real-life situations. That is, I could naturally internalize diverse expressions for an apology rather than repeatedly speaking the expressions to memorize them.

Fill in the blank in <A> with the ONE appropriate word. Then, identify the type of activity that the lesson procedure in <B> exemplifies and write its TWO advantages from the student's perspective.

Your Answer

14   Read the passages and follow the directions.

A

The communicative competence model we know and use today represents the ability to use language correctly to communicate appropriately and effectively in a variety of social situations. Currently, the communicative competence model is constructed of four competence areas: grammatical, sociolinguistic, discourse, and strategic. Two of them focus on the functional aspect of communication, and the other two reflect the use of the linguistic system.

B

Teacher's Note

After joining a teacher's conference about communicative competence, I realized that I had been heavily focusing on teaching the grammatical aspect. To improve students' actual communicative competence, however, I should have taught communicative functions considering the social context that the language is used. Thus, I prepared a new activity where my students can appropriately respond to one another when it comes to their turn to talk in a natural conversation. Additionally, through this activity, I believe, my students can enhance their _____ competence.

Activity

Here are parts of the conversation. Fill in the blanks with one of the given words/phrases.

1. A : Hey, James. Can you come to the party next Friday?
   B : _____.

2. A : Hey, Sara. How are you?
   B : Going well. _____.
   A : I'm good. By the way, I will open a party next Friday. Can you come?
   B : Well, _____.

3. A : Hi, Stella! Welcome to my house.
  B : _____.
  A : Take a seat. Coffee?
  B : _____.

> • How's it going?
> • Probably.
> • Thank you for inviting me.
> • I am sorry. I can't.
> • Yes, please.

Fill in the blank in <B> with ONE word from <A>. Then, define the example of conversational turn-taking that the activity in <B> focuses on. Also, based on the information in <B>, write the major reason that the teacher prepares the activity in terms of natural conversation.

Your Answer

_____
_____
_____
_____

15 Read the passage in <A> and the interaction in <B>, and follow the directions.

A

Texts provided to L2 readers are not just a sequential display of isolated words and sentences but are connected syntactically, lexically, and semantically. Therefore, L2 readers need the ability to understand relationships among text elements, which are signaled both explicitly and implicitly through two discourse features—coherence and cohesion. Coherence is challenging to study as it is greatly affected by learners interpretation, which cannot be captured by only studying the text. In contrast, cohesion is found in the use of devices in the text. Cohesive devices influence better comprehension because they explicitly integrate information between sentences in a text. Different types of cohesion are set out in the following figure.

Categories		Examples
Reference	Personal reference	I just met your brother. He's a nice guy.
	Demonstrative reference	You failed the test. This is bad news.
	Comparative reference	I asked for this bag, but I got the other bag.
Substitution	Nominal substitution	A: Can I have another drink? B: This one is finished.
	Verbal substitution	A: You look great. B: So do you.
	Clausal substitution	A: Is she happy? B: I think so.

Conjunction	Adversative conjunction	I didn't study. However, I still passed.
	Additive conjunction	He didn't study. And he failed.
	Temporal conjunction	She studied hard. Then she sat the test.
	Casual conjunction	They studied hard. Therefore they deserve to pass.
Lexical cohesion	Reiteration	Hand me the book. That book on the table.
	Collocation	The book arrived in the mail. The cover was ripped off and the pages were torn.

B

T : Sun-joo, you are so good at speaking English!

S : Thank you, Ms. Choi.

T : Can you tell me how you are so fluent?

S : Well, I practice speaking a lot with my friends. I think that's the only reason I can think of.

T : Cool. You use English in daily life occasionally.

S : I guess so.

T : Very nice. I think many students are curious about how to improve fluency. Can you share your experience a little bit?

S : Sure, I will.

T=teacher, S=student

Based on <A>, identify TWO types of cohesion exemplified in <B> and write what each cohesive device refers to. Then, explain how the cohesive devices function in the given dialogue.

Your Answer

_____

_____

_____

_____

_____

16   Read the passages and follow the directions.

┤ A ├

Do-Joon's Writing

My hobby is playing soccer. I love soccer. I think I can play soccer for 24 hours. Playing a video game is not interesting. Reading a book is boring. But I like reading comic books. So during weekends, I play soccer or read my favorite comic books. Sometimes, it is hard to choose what to do between two things. I want to play soccer and read comic books at the same time. I know it is impossible but I love soccer and comic books that much.

Dear Do-Joon,

I didn't know that you like playing soccer a lot. Your idea of playing soccer and reading comic books at the same time, actually sounds good. I don't think it is impossible. Did you ever consider writing a comic strip or a graphic novel about soccer? I really love your soccer ball picture. I think you have a great talent for drawing. If you make a comic strip about soccer players, you will feel like you are playing soccer and reading comic books at a time.

Ms. Song

- -

Dear Ms. Song,

That's such a great idea! I'd never thought about make a comic strip. That sounds so fun! Thank you, Ms. Song. I will try to make my own comic strips about soccer soon.

B

Do-Joon's Thoughts

I really enjoy having a written conversation with my teacher because of two reasons. First, different from the general lessons, I can feel closer to my teacher. She encourages me saying that 'Do-Joon, you can do it! and you are doing well!' I can feel how much she cares about me. Next, through this conversation, I can practice basic writing skills without pressure. I usually get pressured a lot during writing classes. At the beginning, it was really hard to write anything in English for me. So my writing had a lot of misspelling and incorrect grammars. However, with this regular writing, I became confident of applying the basic rules for spelling, punctuation, and capitalization correctly.

Identify the type of written interaction between Ms. Song and Do-Joon in <A> and write its TWO main advantages Do-Joon has reflected in <B>. Do NOT copy more than FOUR consecutive words.

Chapter

05

Your Answer

17   Read the passage and follow the directions.

A

Lesson Procedure

- **Aim**: Practicing sounds for words and stress in sentences
- **Materials**: Minimal pairs and a map
- **Level**: Beginner and above
- **Time**: 100 minutes

Step 1

To begin the lesson, T describes the differences between the production of /r/ and /l/. T pronounces them exaggerating the articulation to show the differences clearly. T provides Ss with the following table with minimal pairs for /r/ and /l/.

1. Right	Light	5. Rock	Lock
2. Fright	Flight	6. Ramp	Lamp
3. Fry	Fly	7. Wrap	Lap
4. Race	Lace	8. Rain	Lane

Step 2

T calls out a word from each pair. Then Ss listen to the word, and cross it out. T checks the answers with Ss.

Step 3

Then, T explains about content and function words. T makes Ss practice the following sentences with stressing the words in bold. T asks Ss to make groups of four and provides a map to each group.

How can I go to the **HOSPITAL**?
Please turn **RIGHT** on the corner.
Where is the **ICE RINK**?
It's the **RIGHT** side of the **SPORTS CENTRE**.

Step 4

Ss in groups color the content words in the following sentences and practice stressing the colored words. After the group practice, Ss do a role-play using the map and the sentences they practiced.

> Where is the stadium?
> Go straight. Then, it is on your right side.
> Then, is a hospital near there?
> Yes, it's right across the stadium.

T=teacher, Ss=students

┤ B ├

Mr. Song's Teaching Log

During the last semester, I focused on clear articulation of individual sounds. For this semester, however, I want to deal with the importance of intonation, stress, and rhythm along with segmentals. Thus, I planned to the lesson procedure in <A> whose purpose is to improve students' degree of _____, by raising the phonological awareness and thus enhancing students' understanding of what they listen to. Usually, I said to my students that if they can understand others and others can understand them, then their pronunciation is good enough. Besides, I added that they necessarily do not need to imitate Native Speakers' pronunciation.

Fill in the blank in <B> with the ONE most appropriate word. Then, explain TWO phonological factors and each type of activity chosen for the identified factors presented in <A>.

Your Answer ⟩ _____

_____

_____

_____

_____

18 Read passages <A> and <B>, follow the directions.

A

Mr. Park's Teaching Log

Usually my speaking lessons are based on pair work or group work. But for tomorrow, I will provide my students with opportunities to communicate not only within their groups but also with the other groups for expanded communication. While performing this activity, my students will be directly engaged with the material through peer-teaching which fosters depth of understanding. Also, each student can have an opportunity to develop an expertise which contributes to the group. Consequently, it will encourage their self-efficacy along with social skills.

B

Types of Activity

1. An information gap task is a technique in language teaching where students find missing information necessary to complete a task or solve a problem, and must communicate with their classmates to fill in the gaps. They must use the target language to share that information. For instance, one student has the key information and must give it to a classmate.

2. An opinion gap task is an activity that asks students to convey their own personal preferences, feelings or ideas about a particular situation. On a higher level, they can take part in a discussion about a political or social issue. On a lower level, they can complete a story. In these types of activities, there is no right or wrong answer.

3. Role-play is an excellent activity for speaking in the relatively safe environment of the classroom. In a role-play, students are given particular roles in the target language. Role-plays give learners a chance to practice speaking the target language before they must do so in a real environment.

4. The jigsaw technique is a method of organizing classroom activity that makes students dependent on each other to succeed. It breaks classes into groups and information into different pieces that the group assembles to complete the given task. During this activity, students interact with other students to attain necessary information and develop social skills within a classroom environment.

Referring to passage <A>, identify the type of classroom activity in <B> that reflects Mr. Park's intention. Then explain it with TWO reasons from <A>. Do NOT copy more than FOUR consecutive words from the passages.

Your Answer

_____

_____

_____

_____

19   **Read the passages and follow the directions.**

- Topic : Writing Character Descriptions
- Skills : Writing
- Time : 90 mins.
- Proficiency Level : intermediate
- Lesson Objectives :
  1) Students will identify the information needed to create a good character description.
  2) Students will write a character description.

1st period

Instruction : Explain to students that a good character description means painting a picture with words.

Step 1   T shows a short video of Iron Man and asks them to call out some words related to Iron Man and adds some new words under the three categories as follows :

Appearance	Personality	Weapon
sharp, handsome, tall, short, fat, thin, skeletal, giant, underweight	adventurous, helpful, affable, humble, imaginative	Stormbreaker, Infinity Gauntlet, shield, Thunderstrike, axe, Star-blazer

Step 2   T shows the questions below on OHP and students answer the questions related to Iron Man.

1. How tall would the character be?
2. What does he look like?
3. What do you think about his personality?
4. What type of weapon does he use?

Step 3   T, then, combines the answers of the questions into a phrase or a sentence.

Step 4   T shows students how to create a/an _____ text by connecting sentences with transitional words from the box.

Transitional words

Next, Moreover, However, Also, In addition, Besides, On the other hand

---

Step 5   T models how to write a description as a whole paragraph.

2nd Period

Instruction: Ask students to write a description about one of Marvel characters and post their 1st drafts on class blog for peer feedback.

T=teacher

Fill in the blank with ONE suitable word, and identify the way that the teacher uses to show students how to write a character description with some evidence.

Your Answer _____

_____

_____

_____

_____

20 Read the passage in <A> and part of a lesson procedure in <B>, and follow the directions.

A

Below are suggestions from a conference for teaching L2 speaking.

> ### To help students improve their speaking skills
>
> (a) Incorporate a "question of the day".
> (b) Attend to listening skills.
> (c) Model syntactic structure.
> (d) Explain the subtleties of tone which includes pitch, speed, and rhythm.
> (e) Check if students speak loudly and articulate clearly.

B

The following is part of Ms. Lee's lesson procedure for teaching how to do an interview effectively.

Steps

1. As an opening activity, T introduces students a question for the day to encourage a talk. T starts with a simple one-part question like "What is your favorite animal?". Once students successfully answer the simple question in a complete sentence, T gives a question that requires a more complex answer: "What is your favorite animal? Why?"
2. T provides a short interview video between a reporter (an interviewer) and an entertainer (an interviewee). Ss watch the video and jot down useful expressions used by the interviewer and the interviewee.
3. T encourages Ss to use complete oral language and models a short script with complete language.
4. Ss in pairs brainstorm and sketch their ideas and write the first drafts of an interview script.

5. T reviews Ss' drafts and provides feedback. T emphasizes that they need to revise their drafts carefully because the key in this activity is not how they say, but what they say. Ss revise their drafts and have rehearsal time.

6. T reminds Ss that she will not consider their voice volume and pronunciation for evaluation but check how much effort they put into preparing this interview.

7. Ss present their interview performance in pairs.

T=teacher, Ss=students

Identify TWO suggestions from <A> that Ms. Lee does not implement in <B>. Then, support your answers with evidence for each ignored suggestion from <B>.

Your Answer

_____

_____

_____

_____

_____

Build Up New

박현수 영어교육론 Ⅳ

Vocabulary & Grammar

기입형

서술형

Chapter

06 Vocabulary & Grammar

🔒 정답 및 모범 답안 p. 25

📝 **기입형**

---

01 Read the passage and follow the directions.

Ms. Song's Teaching Log

For teaching vocabulary explicitly, I often use a concordance program during lessons. Compared to incidental vocabulary learning, using a concordance program seems to be more effective to learn new words for my students in that it provides evidence of how the words are used in real situations based on millions of examples of the words. Besides, by analyzing the corpus data, I can teach students not only the meaning of new words, but also their collocations, frequency, and particular contexts they are used. Below is part of the lesson procedure for intentionally teaching vocabulary using a concordance program.

Lesson procedure

1. T tells Ss that they will learn some keywords related to Covid-19 and explains that the importance of words will be decided based on how often they are used in real life.

2. T introduces a concordance program and models how to use it. T searches for the words, *lockdown* and *pandemic* on the program and shows their example sentences. Additionally, she shows them that the program can find how often the word is used in real life. *(e.g., pandemic: 8493 times, lockdown: 6053 times (at CNN news from 2019~))*

---

3. T puts Ss in groups of four and shows some words related to Covid 19 (e.g. *Coronavirus*, Vaccine, Quarantine, etc.). Then, T asks each group to search for the example sentences using the program and guess the meaning of words.

4. T checks Ss' answers on word meaning.

5. T tells Ss that, this time, they will rank the words based on how often they are used in real life. T asks Ss to guess the rank of the words.

[Ss' guessing]

Your keywords ranking	Actual keywords ranking
1. Coronavirus	1.
2. Vaccine	2.
3. Social distancing	3.
4. Quarantine	4.
...	...

6. T asks Ss to search for how often each word is actually used in real life (at CNN news from 2019~) using the concordance program and compare their own rank and the actual rank.

[Actual keywords ranking]

Your keywords ranking	Actual keywords ranking
1. Coronavirus	1. Coronavirus
2. Vaccine	2. Quarantine
3. Social distancing	3. Social distancing
4. Quarantine	4. Vaccine
...	...

Chapter

06

7. T asks Ss to write down one example sentence of each word in order.

Actual keywords ranking	Example sentence
1. Coronavirus	In humans, coronaviruses can cause mild diseases like the common cold as well as more severe diseases.
2. Quarantine	
3. Social distancing	
4. Vaccine	
...	

8. T checks the target words once again by asking the higher-ranking words in order.

> T: What is the second important keyword?
> Ss: Quarantine!
> T: Good. What is the third important keyword?
> Ss: Social distancing!

9. T wraps up the lesson emphasizing the usefulness of a concordancer.

Complete the comments about the lesson procedure above by filling in the blank with the ONE most appropriate word from the passage.

The lesson above shows how to teach keywords related to Covid 19 effectively using a concordance program. Ms. Song first asks students to find authentic example sentences of keywords using the program. Based on the sentences, she makes them guess the meaning of each keyword. Then, she asks students to search for the degree of importance of keywords based on the word _____. As seen in the lesson procedure, a concordance program can provide much more useful information on vocabulary than a paper dictionary does and thus help students effectively broaden their vocabulary knowledge.

Your Answer

02   Read the passage and follow the directions.

Ms. Jung's Teaching Log

I participated in a teacher's seminar talking about how to teach grammar rules more effectively. In the seminar, the subject speaker explains three steps of how students learn the rules through the input, intake, and output stages. Before taking this seminar, I usually asked my students to practice grammar rules explicitly. Until I gave a sufficient explanation about the forms or the rules, I did not provide them with chances to practice the forms. So far, in short, I have focused on the output stage, in which they can practice the target form intensively, rather than the input and intake stages where they can internalize it. However, after the seminar, I decided to find out the activity which enables students to internalize the target form more effectively in the input and intake stages. Fortunately, Ms. Park, the senior English teacher at our school, recommended one activity, which leads students to focus on the meaning first and form second, resulting in facilitating the form and meaning relationship. Consequently, the activity forces students to concentrate on the input and intake stages rather than the output stage. Below is the part of the materials from the seminar and the new activity procedure I prepared.

Guidelines

• Keep meaning in focus.
• Use both oral and written input.
• Have the learners do something with the input.

Activity Procedure

• Watch the video about the story of Audrey and Camille.
• Based on the story from the video, check T/F below.

1. Audrey and Camille dance. (T/F)
2. Audrey and Camille watch television. (T/F)
3. Audrey listens to classical music. (T/F)
4. Camille talks on the phone. (T/F)
5. Audrey and Camille swim. (T/F)
6. Audrey introduces her cat, Arthur. (T/F)
7. Audrey and Camille play in the park. (T/F)
8. Audrey kisses her aunts. (T/F)

Complete the comments by filling in the blank with the TWO most appropriate words.

In Ms. Jung's Teaching log, she provides the guidelines and the procedure of a/an _____ activity usually used in Input Processing. To help students connect meaning and form in the lesson, she prepares *Binary options* activity where students can access the target form (the third person singular '-s') manipulated in particular ways. This activity can help students become dependent on form/structure to get meaning and derive richer intake from the input.

Your Answer _____

03   Read the passages and follow the directions.

| **A** |

Mr. Shin has prepared corpus data on Worksheet 1 to give an instruction about 'I mean.' He has found them through a special program.

Worksheet 1

Read the conversation and talk about the meaning of 'I MEAN' with your partner.

A: Where do you go? I mean, do you go somewhere nice?
B: Do you know Fabio's? It's ok. I mean, the food's good . . .

Referring to the collected data through online, complete the sentence below.

1) A: Do you even go out after class?
   B: Well, not very often. **I mean**, I usually go straight home.
2) A: How do you like the restaurants in your neighborhood?
   B: They're not bad. **I mean**, they're cheap.
3) A: Are you busy in the evening? **I mean**, do you have time to play basketball?
   B: Well, I take a lot of classes.
4) A: What do you do in your free time?
   B: Well, I don't have a lot of free time. **I mean**, I have 3 part-time jobs.

Conclusion:
You can use I MEAN to _____.

| B |

Mr. Shin tries to make the students infer the meaning of 'I mean' using Worksheet 1. The purpose of this activity is to study when the phrase, 'I mean' is used in daily conversation. To look up the authentic examples of 'I mean,' Mr. Shin has used a special program called a/an _____ which enables learners to see this phrase within context. This activity is an inductive approach to learning in which learners naturally internalize patterns and rules instead of studying them.

Based on the information in <A> and <B>, fill in the blank in <B> with the ONE most appropriate word.

Your Answer _____

04 Read the passage and follow the directions.

Lesson Procedure

T : Okay, guys. Today we are going to play one game. Let's make a group of five.
 (*Ss sit in groups.*)
T : Everyone is in your group?
Ss : Yes!
T : Great! Let me give you directions for the game first. Here we go. First of all, I will read out some words which have something in common. Then, you guys listen to the words and work out the missing suffix. Does everyone know what suffix means?
S1 : It is something we can add to the end of a word such as '-ly' and 'er'.
T : You're right! By adding suffix, you can form a different word with a different meaning. All right, then let's listen to the words and find out the missing suffix. If you guess correctly, it is five points. It will be minus one point for any incorrect guessing. And no points for a guess which is also true but isn't the answer that I am thinking of. I will give you this small whiteboard for each group. Write the answer and show me when I ask for. Is it clear? Yes? Okay, then, let's start!

[On the Board]

• broad + (   )
• wide + (   )
• length + (   )

(*Ss in groups figure out the suffix in common for the given words.*)
T : Did you find it? Let's check your answer! Show me the answer!
 (*Ss in group raise the whiteboard with their own answers.*)

T : Group 1, '-er'. Group 2, '-er'. Group 3, '-en'. Group 4, '-ness'. Group 5, 'en'. Okay, the correct answer is '-en'! Congratulations, Group 3 and 5! The others also made a nice try but the answer was '-en'. Those words take '–en' to make verb forms. Great job!

T=teacher, Ss=students

Referring to the passage above, fill in each blank with the ONE or TWO most appropriate words.

The lesson above deals with word-learning strategies, which is a form of a/an (1) _____ vocabulary learning contrasting with implicit vocabulary learning. In this learning process, students are involved in activities where they learn directly vocabulary words. For example, the teacher directs students' attention to three words (i.e. broad, wide, and length) and the suffix '-en' that he/she chooses beforehand. By figuring out the suffix in common for the given words, students learn the word-learning strategy which is (2) _____ by guessing the common suffix to change the given adjective words into the verb forms. Learning such a strategy can help students free from excessive dependence on the dictionary and develop confidence in reading.

Your Answer   (1) _____

(2) _____

05 Read the passage and fill in the blank with a pedagogical term.

Ms. Ra's Teaching Log

Teaching grammar rules is not easy work. However, I have secrets of making fun and meaningful grammar lessons. Here are some secrets. First, I teach only one thing at a time. I don't want to overburden my students until I am sure that they have worked out form-meaning relationships. Second, I keep meaning in focus. My students are asked to understand the meaning first to perform an activity. Last but not least, I make my students do something with the input. It is essential to give students a chance to use the grammar rule rather than simply repeating it. Based on my three secrets, I designed the _____ (TWO words) instruction, where students derive intake from the input.

Activity Procedure

1. Ss watch a short video clip titled "10 Steps from Seed to Cup."
2. Ss listen to the teacher's instruction about the activity.
3. Ss write the numbers for the following sentences in order in which they appear in the video clip.

※ Write the numbers in order.

_____	Coffee is ground by a grinder.
_____	The coffee cherry is harvested when it is ripe.
_____	The picked coffee cherry is processed.
_____	Green coffee is loaded onto ships.
_____	Defective beans are removed either by hand or by machinery.
_____	They are raked and turned throughout the day, then dried in the sun.
_____	Coffee is brewed.
_____	Green coffee is roasted by a roasting machine.
_____	Coffee is repeatedly tested for quality and taste.
1	Coffee seeds are planted.

4. Ss check the answers in pairs and talk about what they have watched. Then, T gives the answer to the whole class.

5. Ss match the picture and the correct sentence in the activity below.

The soils is
prepared.
(O)

The soil prepares.
(X)

The seeds are
planted.
(O)

The seeds plants.
(X)

The berries are
picked by hand.
( )

The berries picks
by hand.
( )

They take to a
factory.
( )

They are taken to
a factory.
( )

They are dried in
the sun.
( )

They dry in the
sun.
( )

They ship all over
the world.
( )

They area shipped
all over the world.
( )

T=teacher, Ss=students

Your Answer _____

Chapter

06

06 Read the passage and follow the directions.

> (*After reading one paragraph*)
>
> S1 : Mr. Oh. What's the meaning of "clumsy"?
>
> T : Okay, "clumsy". Does anyone know what the word means?
> (*T writes the word on the board.*)
>
> Ss : (*Silence*)
>
> T : Anyone? Okay, well, take a look at this sentence.
> "His clumsy efforts to imitate a dancer were almost amusing."
> Through the text we read so far, is Bernard a good dancer?
> (*S1 raises her hand.*) Okay, Sumi?
>
> S1 : Well, no. He is not a good dancer yet. We can see this in the earlier sentences.
>
> T : Excellent! So, what do you think "clumsy" might mean?
>
> S2 : Mmm . . . not cool?
>
> T : Good, what else?
>
> S3 : Not smooth? Not skillful?
>
> T : Great! Okay, so "clumsy" means careless and awkward.
> (*T writes synonyms on the board.*) Is that clear now?
>
> Ss : Yes! (*Ss nod in agreement.*)
>
> T=teacher, S=student, Ss=students

Considering the lesson above, fill in each blank with the ONE most appropriate word.

> In this lesson, students engage in (1) _____ vocabulary teaching in that it starts with the word appeared in a paragraph they are reading, not with a long word list to memorize in advance. When students request meanings of vocabulary during class or when the teacher realizes that a word needs to be clarified, such vocabulary teaching happens. However, this vocabulary teaching needs to be separated from incidental vocabulary learning that students read the text and pick up some words unconsciously. Further, when students face with the unknown word "clumsy" and ask about its meaning, the teacher encouraged students to use the strategy of (2) _____ to figure out the meanings of the unknown word through contextual clues not directly giving the meaning of the word, "clumsy."

Your Answer (1) _____

(2) _____

07 Read the passage and follow the directions.

───────┤ **A** ├───────

Computer Lab Worksheet
English Composition

Name : _____

1. Write down the problems noted in your paper.

> [Student's answer]
>
> a. Crazy mobs who contributed to ostracize her.
> b. bored and boring
> c. interested and interesting

2. Find a sentence from a corpus using a program on your computer, which uses the word/phrase (for each of the sentences you wrote above) in the desired way. Write the sentence below.

> [Student's answer]
>
> a. Levin makes a special case for Debord as a film-maker whose aim was to contribute to the ultimate destruction of cinema as a spectacular medium.
> b. I'm bored . . . wasn't that a damn boring game!
> c. Helen is not interested in making lists about her life.

3. Describe how this word/phrase is used lexicogrammatically.

> [Student's answer]
>
> a. After the phrase "contribute to" : most of the sentences have a noun, not a verb.
> b. If something needs to be bored, it should be a passive position. However 'being' accompanies something active.
> c. "interested" for a passive thing and "interesting" for an active thing.

4. Rewrite your sentences using the information that you learned.

> [Student's answer]
>
> a. Crazy mobs who contributed to ostracizing her.
> b. The students are bored because of the boring class.
> c. The audiences were interested after the singer made the show interesting.

Fill in each blank in <B> with a suitable term from the worksheet in <A>. You can change the form of the word if necessary.

 B

This sample activity was used in a composition class to help students recognize (1) _____ errors in their writing. A worksheet was provided for students to complete as shown in the sample. Students then followed the procedures below.

- List the (1) _____ problems that his/her instructor has marked.
- Find examples from an electronic (2) _____ that uses each item in the desired way and write one example down on the worksheet.
- Rewrite his/her original sentences using the information learned from the (2) _____.

Your Answer (1) _____

(2) _____

08   **Read the passages and follow the directions.**

┤ **A** ├

Teacher A : Mr. Kim. Did you check the notice from the English Department?

Teacher B : Yes, I did. We need to select 500 key words for our students.

Teacher A : Right, There are around 3000 key words already selected by the Ministry of Education. So we would be able to add 500 more considering our students' English proficiency.

Teacher B : Did you think about criteria to select the words?

Teacher A : Well, I think that our students need to learn vocabulary that they can listen, speak, read, and write more often in their real lives.

Teacher B : I agree. I have seen that some of my students are struggling to memorize vocabulary which is rarely used. Instead of an advanced level of vocabulary, my students need to learn words that they can use more in actual conversation.

Teacher A : That's true. Some vocabulary can be used in various contexts. But I will consider how often the words appear in daily life. Also, I am planning to offer the text in order to teach them inductively. The more authentic the text is, the more useful words are repeated.

Teacher B : That's a good idea. Since learning 3500 words is not an easy task for our students, we need to provide some support to help them enjoy learning new vocabularies.

Teacher A : I agree. I think we need to talk about this with Mr. Choi as well. I will ask him when he is available.

Teacher B : Of course. Let me know when the meeting time is.

Teacher A : Okay, I will send you a message.

B

Some Criteria for Selecting Vocabulary

Criteria	Definition
Range	the extent to which a word occurs in the different types of texts
Coverage	the capacity of a word to replace other words
Frequency	the number of occurrences of a word in the target language
Learnability	the extent to which a word can be learned without difficulty
Language need	the extent to which a word is regarded as "required" by the learner in order to communicate

---

Considering the information in <A> and <B>, identify the criterion of the most useful vocabulary that two teachers are talking about.

Your Answer

_____

Chapter

06

09   Read the dialogue and follow the directions.

The following is an excerpt from a teacher-student conversation talking about a grammar activity.

T : Take a seat, Jihye. How may I help you?

S : Well, Mr. Kim. I don't know grammar well, and grammar... is boring. I don't think we have to learn grammar.

T : Really? Why do you think so?

S : Because... I can learn grammar naturally when we listen and read texts a lot. So, I don't think learning grammar rules are necessary, which is so boring.

T : Well, Jihye. I understand what you mean. But actually, learning grammar can be fun!

S : Like how?

T : I guess, you feel that the grammar lesson was boring because you tried to memorize the rules. Am I right?

S : Exactly. I am tired of memorizing rules.

T : Well, then, how about taking the next grammar lesson and talking with me again?

S : Next grammar lesson? What will we do?

T : Rather than simply providing grammar rules, I am preparing a fun activity that you guys figure out the rules. Do you want to check it really quick?

S : Sure! I'd like to.

T : Okay. There is a brief plan for the next lesson. First, I will give you a text which is a sheet of a tour leaflet of the city of London.
(T shows S the following activity plan.)

Activity Procedure

1. Presenting a leaflet with the following words:

William spent his summer vacations in London for the first time in 2012. When he arrived at Clink Hostel, the receptionist gave him the leaflet below. Take a look at the tour guide below:

(ellipsis)

2. Look at the expressions below, taken from the leaflet:
   - the most important events
   - the best bars and nightclubs
   - the oldest buildings
   - the most majestic views

3. Answer the following questions.

   [Questions]

   a) Circle the nouns, as shown in the example: "the most important events"

   b) What words modify the word "events" in the given example?

   c) What words modify the word "views" in the example "the most majestic views"?

   d) How can we describe this pattern that modifies nouns?

   _____ + _____ + _____ + noun

   e) What is the difference in meaning between "majestic views" and "the most majestic views"?

   f) Why do you think we can find such structures in tour guides?

   g) Now, take a look at the example "the oldest buildings".
      Can you apply the same pattern to this case?

   h) If not, what is the pattern?

   _____ + _____ + noun

   i) Now, according to what you have answered, complete the rules in the chart:

Adjective	Rule	Example
(one syllable) old	the + adjective + _____	The oldest buildings.
(two or more syllables) important	the + _____ + adjective	The most important events.
(irregular) good	-	The best bars and nightclubs.

   ...

   T=teacher, S=student

Fill in the blank with the TWO most appropriate words.

The lesson plan above describes a(an) _____, a pedagogical activity where students are provided with grammar rules in a text and required to perform some operation with it. The purpose of this activity is to arrive at an explicit understanding of some linguistic properties of the target language.

Your Answer _____

10 Read the lesson procedure below and follow the directions.

---| **A** |---

T : Eyes on ME! Guys! Take out a piece of paper and a pen, plz! When you are quiet, I will tell you a story. Just listen to the story, not writing down anything. Ready? (*T tells the students the story.*)

> There was a boy. He was young. He was three years old. He went on a walk. He was attacked by bees. He was scared. He ran away. They followed him. He jumped into a lake. He stayed there until the sun set. The bees went away. He went home. I was eating eggs and bacon. I was happy to see my dog.

Activity Procedure

1. T tells Ss to work on their own and try to recreate the story to be as close to the original as possible. Then Ss hear and draw about the story two times. Ss are not expected to get it perfect. −2 mins.
(*After two minutes*)
2. T asks Ss to work with their partner in pairs to recreate the text based on their own drawing. −5 mins.
(*5 minutes later*)
3. Ss swap their answers with another pairs and T shows Ss the original text. Ss make corrections and the pair with the least mistakes gets bonus points.
4. T asks Ss what was wrong with this text. Ss say that there are missing transition words. (*Ss studied transition words last time.*)
5. T tells Ss to re-write the text with their partner to include at least
   • 1 relative clause
   • 1 cause and effect transition word
   • 1 contrast transition word
   • 1 addition transition word
6. T and Ss share all the different ways the sentences can be combined.
7. T asks Ss to vote for the best version and give some rewards.

T=teacher, Ss=students

Chapter

06

Referring to <A> complete the commentary in <B> with TWO or THREE words orderly.

| B |

The dictogloss procedure represents a modified version with 'DRAW and TELL'. Also, as a writing activity students were involved in (1) _____ activity by recreating the text with several transition words they learned the other day. Also, they paid attention to forms, transition words, in context, which is called (2) _____ approach in grammar teaching.

Your Answer (1) _____

(2) _____

11 Read the conversation and follow the directions.

Mr. Park, who is the English teacher of a middle school, is about to teach superlative.

T   : Look at these examples for forming superlative adjectives.
(*Write on the board, cute → the cutest, grand → the grandest.*)
Now make superlatives out of 'beautiful, outrageous, expensive.'
OK, now, what have you written?

Minjee : Beautifulest, outrageousest, expensivest.

T   : No, for these words, the superlative forms are 'the most beautiful, the most outrageous, and the most expensive,' Now, I want you to get into groups and figure out the rule.
(*after a few minutes*)

T   : Who thinks they have the answer? Junmin's group?

Jeemin : It's about how big the word is. If it is a big word, you use 'most'.

T   : Big. How do we measure the size of words?

Junhee : The number of syllables.

T   : OK. How many syllables do 'beautiful, outrageous, and expensive' have?

Jeemin : Three.

T   : Three. OK. so who can state the rule?

Junmin : Adjective with three syllables forms the superlative with 'most.'

T   : Very good.

T=teacher

Complete the comments by filling in the blanks using ONE word each.

Mr. Park is using the (1) _____ technique in teaching the superlatives. With this technique, the teacher gives students information about a structure without giving them the full picture. Then they are asked to infer the full rule from the partial information. This makes the students overgeneralize and leads them into errors, such as 'beautifulest,' 'outrageousest,' and 'expensivest.' They are given disconfirming evidence and then have to modify their hypothesis. The reason for giving students only a partial explanation is that they are more likely to learn the exceptions than if they are given a long list of exceptions to the rule to memorize in advance. It is based on (2) _____ learning, which leads students to discover the general rules at the end.

Your Answer   (1) _____

(2) _____

12   Read the activity procedure and follow the directions.

> *Ms. Park, who is the English teacher in a middle school, is just about to have an activity with her students. She has already explained how to construct the form of the present progressive and the present single at the beginning of the lesson.*
>
> Activity Procedure
>
> Step 1   Have students watch a short video clip and talk about it.
>
> Step 2   Have students listen to the teacher's instruction about the activity and have the activity slip.
>
> Step 3   Have students do this task A while watching the video clip again.
>
> > A. Write the numbers for the following sentences in order in which they appear in the video clip.
> >
> > _____ Dooly and Douner are dancing.
> > _____ Douner is looking for Dooly.
> > _____ Douner is singing.
> > _____ Dooly and Douner are watching television.
> > _____ Dooly is listening to classical music.
> > _____ Douner is talking on the phone.
> > _____ Dooly and Douner are swimming.
> > _____ Dooly is introduced her cat, Mimi.
> > _____ Dooly and Douner are playing in the park.
> > _____ Dooly is kissing Heedoing.
>
> Step 4   Have students check the answers in pairs talking about what they have watched, and then give the answers in a whole class.

Step 5   Have students do the task B in pairs.

> B. Yes or no?   Yes   No
>
>   1. Dooly and Douner play at the park often.   ☐   ☐
>   2. Dooly finds Douner.   ☐   ☐
>   3. Dooly likes to read.   ☐   ☐
>   4. Dooly loves the Teletubbies.   ☐   ☐
>   5. Douner has a cat.   ☐   ☐

Step 6   The teacher checks the answers with the students and review the form with usages.

Complete the comments by filling in each blank with ONE word.

Ms. Park gave her students the (1) _____ input activity which is manipulated in particular ways to push learners to become dependent on form and structure to get meaning. For example, in this activity, the students are exposed to 10 present progressive sentences at first while matching with the actions in the video clip. Then, they are exposed to 5 present simple sentences while finding out the general information about the characters. It is considered that Ms. Park tried to use the (2) _____ relationship while the students match the given forms with the given situation. In other words, the students have an opportunity to connect the form and the meaning, and finally construct the rules about the tenses on their own during this activity.

Your Answer   (1) _____

(2) _____

MEMO

서술형

01 Read the teacher's note in <A> and feedback types in <B> and follow the directions.

A

Mr. Park's Teaching Note

I am teaching English to 3rd-grade students in a middle school. When giving them feedback for their writing works, I usually correct their errors directly. Since they are low-intermediate level students, I thought that correcting the errors by themselves would be impossible. After several writing lessons, however, I got unexpected feedback from students. They thought that the direct correction is only useful to notice their grammatical errors but not so helpful to improve their writing proficiency. Thus, they wanted to get more detailed information on their performance rather than simple error correction. In other words, they asked me to give some advice on how to write better: they wanted to get some feedback on not only form but content as well. Based on their comments, I decided to give them detailed information about both grammar and idea levels. Particularly, by giving some practical solutions to writing weaknesses, I will show them how to improve their writing. Anyway, for the next writing lessons, instead of simply correcting their errors, I will provide summative feedback on their writings as I decided.

B

Feedback 1

[A student's writing]

What is is your favorite season of the year? Summer is my favorite season. The weather during this season was very hot. July and August is the hottest months of the year. People uses coolers, ACs, etc. to keep the surroundings cooler. The atmosphere in the evening is ideal for outdoor activities like playing, cycling, and etc. People tends to wear comfortable, light-coloured cotton clothes as cotton is a good absorber of water. *(ellipsis)*

[Teacher's Comment]

Great job! Using an attractive question is an effective way to start your paragraph. It is a good organizational skill. However, you should have described your favorite season in more detail. By doing so, you can help the readers visualize your favorite season, Summer. Also, there are some grammatical errors in verb usage such as tense and subject-verb agreement. *(ellipsis)*

Feedback 2

[A student's writing]

What is is your favorite season of the year? Summer is my favorite season. The weather during this season was very hot. July and

August is the hottest months of the year. People uses coolers, ACs,
                                          T   Agr

etc. to keep the surroundings cooler. The atmosphere in the evening is ideal for outdoor activities like playing, cycling, and etc. People tends to wear comfortable, light-coloured cotton clothes as cotton
Agr

is a good absorber of water.

(ellipsis)

T=verb tense, Agr=Agreement

Considering information in <A> and <B>, choose ONE feedback appropriate for Mr. Park and then support your choice with evidence from the passages.

Your Answer

_____

_____

_____

_____

02 Read the passage and follow the directions.

Below is part of a lesson plan using a/an _____ to teach the difference between 'used to' and 'would' for past habits.

Step 1

T sets the theme by introducing the topic of the summer holidays. T explains what to be taught as follows: "Today, we are going to learn about how to express our past habits. First, I am going to tell you about how I spent my summer holidays as a child in Australia, two times. You do listen carefully and also write down any keywords while listening. Let me start."

[Text]

When I was a child we used to go camping every summer. We'd choose a different place each year, and we'd drive around until we found a beach we liked. Then, we'd pitch our tent, as near as possible to the beach. We'd usually spend most of the time on the beach or exploring the country round about. We never went to the same beach twice.

Step 2

Ss individually listen to the story over two times and write down some words from the story. After grouping students, T asks them to reconstruct what they have noted down. Students are required to reconstruct the text, focusing on the past habits.

[One example of the reconstructed texts]

When I was a child we used to go to camping in the summer. We chose a different place each year. We drove until we found a beach which we liked. Then we pitched a tent, as near to the beach as possible. We used to spend most of the time on the beach or exploring the country around. We never went to the same beach twice.

Step 3

When Ss are done, T shows the original text through the screen. T asks Ss to find out any differences between their own text and the original text in terms of content and form.

They reconstruct the text with 'used to' but do not catch the contracted forms of 'would'. So, T writes down 'We'd choose', 'We'd drive', and 'We used to go camping.' on the board and asks Ss to guess when and how we use 'would' or 'used to'. After listening to Ss' guessing, T briefly explains the different usage of 'would' and 'used to' to express past habits.

Step 4

Ss write down their own texts, of a similar length and style, about their own childhood holidays.

Fill in the blank with ONE word. Then, choose TWO steps that facilitate a strong 'focus on form' approach and provide the reason for your each choice.

Your Answer

_____

_____

_____

_____

03 Read the passages and follow the directions.

┤ **A** ├

Perhaps no other aspect of language learning has been as controversial as teaching grammar. For many years, researchers and teachers have argued over whether we should even teach grammar. Despite the long-standing grammar debate, the fact remains that we do not use language without grammar. Perhaps, then, the problem is not grammar itself, but the ways that grammar has been taught and learned.

Early approaches to foreign language instruction often taught grammar separate from the larger contexts in which language is used. While these approaches were often effective for developing a receptive (reading) knowledge of a language, they sometimes failed to provide students with the ability to use language communicatively in speaking and writing. As a result, several approaches to language instruction have focused on developing communicative competence. Communicative competence does not mean an absence of grammar instruction but rather grammar instruction that leads to the ability to communicate effectively.

So, what does teaching grammar communicatively mean? It means designing grammar lessons to include a communicative task or activity. A communicative grammar lesson might start in very much the same way as a traditional approach with the presentation of a grammar item and examples, followed by communicative exercises to practice the grammar item.

Chapter

06

B

Activity A

Combine the clauses into one complete sentence using a relative pronoun. Check your answers with your partner and explain to your partner the grammatical rules you applied.

1. **Sentence 1:** There was a poor widow.
   Sentence 2: She had an only son named Jack and a cow named Milky-White.
   → _____ .

2. **Sentence 1:** All they had to live on was the milk.
   Sentence 2: They carried the milk to the market and sold it every day.
   → _____ .

3. **Sentence 1:** One morning they could not get the milk.
   Sentence 2: They got milk from the cow every day.
   → _____ .

Activity B

1. In pairs, read the following folk tale extracts, focusing on the parts in bold. What is the difference between the parts? When would you use one form or the other? Share your thoughts with your partner.

> *Once upon a time, there was a poor widow **who** had an only son named Jack, and a cow named Milky-white. And all they had to live on was the milk that the cow gave every morning, which they carried to the market and sold. But one morning Milky-white gave no milk, and they didn't know **what** to do.*
> *"**What** shall we do, **what** shall we do?" said the widow, wringing her hands.*
> *"Cheer up, mother, I'll go and get work somewhere," said Jack.*
> *"We've tried that before, and nobody would take you," said his mother; "we must sell Milky-white and with the money start a shop, or something." (ellipsis)*

2. After reading the folk tale, share your thoughts with your partner. Use more than three relative pronouns.

In <B>, choose the ONE activity that exemplifies the grammar teaching approach described in <A> and support your choice with concrete evidence from the data.

Your Answer _____

_____

_____

_____

_____

04 Read the passages and follow the directions.

┤ **A** ├

Ms. Choi's Teaching Log

I think that language should be studied, taught, and evaluated as a whole, putting a strong emphasis on its meaning, and this has been done in the following ways. First, I do my best to place the target language in a discourse level. This teaching strategy is beneficial in that students can understand the language in meaningful contexts. In addition, in terms of assessment, I do not separate one form of knowledge from others because many types of knowledge such as contextual, grammatical, and vocabulary knowledge are interconnected with each other. Keeping these ideas in mind, I will pick one of the fill-in-the-blank exercises from the list below.

┤ **B** ├

Task A

※ Read the sentences below and fill in the blanks with the words from the list.

1. Could you _____ me an email with details?
2. Dams are used to _____ water and control its flow.
3. From the Great Chef, _____ the opportunity to taste their specially designed menu.
4. Singapore _____ a small country.
5. The aeroplane _____ safely at the airport.

> • is   • landed   • send   • enjoy   • store

Task B

※ Read the passage and fill in the blanks with appropriate words considering the whole context. Use the words in the Word Bank.

I have the ability to do _____ different things. I _____ hike, cook, play sports, and read well. On Saturday, I chose to take a hike. The sun was shining and I had a positive _____. I felt really great about the day. I knew the hike would be special. I tried to convince my _____ to join me on the hike, but _____ did not want. He _____ the hike would not be fun.

[Word Bank]
- a lot of
- can
- attitude
- brother
- say
- he
- thought
- severe
- will

Based on <A>, choose the ONE task from <B> appropriate for Ms. Choi and write TWO reasons of your choice with evidence. Do NOT copy more than FOUR consecutive words from the passages.

Your Answer _____

_____

_____

_____

_____

Chapter

06

05 Review the passages below and follow the directions.

---| **A** |---

In L2 grammar teaching, there are many grammar activities to practice target structures from limited production exercises such as fill-in-the-blank, error correction, and sentence construction; as well as free-production exercises, such as role-plays or essays. However, researchers suggest that what matters in grammar activities is not the quantity, but the quality of them. In other words, they argue that these activities, above all, should be meaningful, engaging, and focused to help students acquire target forms. One of the researchers says that students will best acquire the structures or patterns when they are put into situations that require them to use structures and patterns for a communicative purpose other than decontextualized or mechanistic practice. Indeed, a neurological perspective suggests that the kind of language practice in meaningless drills is unavailable for use beyond the classroom.

---| **B** |---

Activity 1

The teacher reads one of the following sentences in the left column. Then, students choose the appropriate response from the right column.

• I'm bored.	• How about watching TV shows?
• I'm sleepy.	• How about going to bed?
• I'm thirsty.	• How about having something to drink?
• I'm tired.	• How about finishing work early today?

Example

T: I'm sleepy.
S: How about going to bed?
T: I'm thirsty.
S: How about having something to drink?

Activity 2

The teacher asks one question on the list. Then, students answer the question using the given forms.

[Questions]
- What time do you go to school?
- Do you eat breakfast?
- What do you usually have for breakfast?

[Answers]
- I go to school at _____.
- I had _____.

Example

T: Eunjin, what time do you go to school?
S: I go to school at 8 o'clock.
T: Do you eat breakfast?
S: Yes, I eat breakfast every day.
T: What do you usually have for breakfast?
S: I eat fried rice or French toast.

T=Teacher, S=Student

Based on <A>, choose ONE activity in <B> that is more helpful for students to internalize the target structures and provide the reason of your choice with evidence.

Your Answer

_____

_____

_____

_____

_____

Chapter
06

06 Read the passages, and follow the directions.

---| **A** |---

Ms. Lee's Teaching Note

Undoubtedly, discovery learning in teaching grammar has proved its efficiency as a means of motivating students to learn target forms. Therefore, I am planning to prepare a grammar lesson where students can notice how target grammar rules work in context without direct rule explanation. First, I prepare an authentic text, in which I do highlight the target forms. Students, then, are expected to understand meaning differences between the target forms while reading the whole text and then, figure out how each rule works in context. Compared to directly providing an explanation on grammar rules, I make sure that they will internalize the rules better while finding out the target rules in context by themselves. I think they should play an active role in their learning process by discovering the rule.

---| **B** |---

Activity 1

1. T writes down 'walk, cook, listen, stay, and learn' on the board and asks Ss to make them past tense.
2. T writes down the answers on the board.

> [On the board]
> walk → walked
> cook → cooked
> listen → listened
> stay → stayed
> learn → learned

3. T writes down 'go, eat, know, break, and drink' on the board and asks Ss to make them past tense again. Ss write down 'goed, eated, knowned, breaked, and drinked' on their notes.

4. T asks Ss to present their answers and writes down the answers on the board.

On the board	
change → changedt	go → **went**
borrow → borrowed	eat → **ate**
dress → dressed	know → **knew**
finish → finished	break → **broke**
call → called	drink → **drank**

5. Ss check their incorrect answers. Then, T puts Ss in groups of four and asks them to think about the difference between regular verbs and irregular verbs.

6. T makes Ss present their hypothesis and adds an explanation if needed.

Activity 2

1. T puts Ss in groups of three and introduces the Amazon website.

2. T introduces fifteen products from the Amazon and shows their customer reviews.

[Example] Customer Review
By Cassie.

I didn't know what I was missing until **I replaced** my 15 year old projection TV. This TV is the best **I have had** so far! **I have used** this T.V. for a few months now, and it is perfect. **I have had** no problems with picture and sound. It **was** very easy to set up, even for a 19-year-old female. This T.V. is a great size for any room!

3. Ss in groups read the reviews paying attention to the target forms in bold.

4. Ss discuss the differences the forms and answer the following questions.
   - What is the meaning of the present perfect tense?
   - What is the difference between 'I have had' and 'I had' in terms of meaning?
   - When do you use the present perfect tense or the past tense?

T=Teacher, Ss=Students

Based on <A>, choose ONE activity in <B> that is more appropriate for Ms. Lee and explain how the chosen activity corresponds with her lesson purposes.

Your Answer

_____

_____

_____

_____

07 **Read the passages and follow the directions.**

---| **A** |---

To maximize the number of vocabulary which they can teach per class, teachers should consider teaching a/an _____ instead of individual word forms. This is a set of words that includes a base word plus its inflections and/or derivations. For purposes of teaching, especially, it makes more sense to view sets of talk, talked, talking, and talks as members of a closely related 'family', not as four single words, and to help students recognize them as such.

---| **B** |---

Activity 1

※ Below are some example sentences of the word 'habitat'. Read them and guess the meaning of 'habitat' in pairs.

1. The hominoid groups move from their earlier forest HABITAT into open country to eat fresh flesh for survival.
2. Their clothes must fit their HABITAT, changing in response to external change.
3. Evolutionarily successful species are likely to populate its HABITAT fully and individuals are likely to be forced into peripheral regions with greater environmental variance.
4. There are instances of change in diet related to HABITAT: tawny owls living in wooded areas eat more moles and fewer birds, whereas in more open areas they eat more voles and birds.

Chapter

06

Activity 2

※ Read the text and underline the words closely related to each other.

[Do you know producer goods?]

Producer goods refer to the types of products used by producers in their production processes. They include capital goods (such as machinery, parts, and equipment), semi-finished products, and raw materials used by producers to produce consumer goods. Consumer goods refer to the final products used by consumers. Some goods can be categorized as producer goods or consumer goods. Cars, for instance, both consumers and producers, buy them. Likewise, fuel and computers, both can be used not only personally but also commercially.

Fill in the blank in <A> with the TWO most appropriate words from the passages. Then, choose ONE activity in <B> exemplifying the technique for teaching vocabulary described in <A> and write the reason of your choice with evidence from the passages.

Your Answer

_____

_____

_____

_____

08   Read the passages and follow the directions.

---| **A** |---

Ms. Park's Teaching Log

For beginner and low-intermediate students, I used to take the pattern practice where I directly provide students with the target grammar rules and practices. However, for not only upper intermediate-level but even beginner and low-intermediate students, such lessons seem to be less effective in that mechanical memorization of grammar rules does not stimulate their learning needs. Thus, I decided to use two new grammar teaching techniques in which the target forms are provided within context. First, I will provide students with a text including ample examples of the target form, instead of giving only a few isolated example sentences. By doing so, I will help students pay attention to target forms because of the frequency of exposure to target forms within the text. Also, I will highlight some of the target forms within the text in bold type. This will also make students easily notice the salient target forms and consequently help them internalize the forms into long-term memory. Based on these two techniques, I hope I can provide grammar lessons that are helpful to all students of different proficiency levels.

─┤ **B** ├─

The following is the lesson procedure to teach grammar in context for middle school students.

Lesson procedure

1. T shows a short video clip of different types of landforms such as hills, mountains, canyons, and valleys.
2. The class talks about landforms they have been to. T uses target forms, the comparative and the superlative while interacting with students.
3. T first provides students with a reading text including lots of examples of the comparative and the superlative. Only for the last three paragraphs, T highligts the target forms. T has students read the text about landforms in America.

American Landforms

Rocky Mountains

The Rocky Mountains fall to the farthest West of the Great Plains and make up an entire region. The mountain range extends from the highest point to the lowest point of the country, from Mexico to Canada. While the Appalachians look smoother after centuries of erosion, the Rockies are younger and much sharper.

The West

West of the Rocky Mountains, the land is more uneven and unpredictable than any other landforms. Deserts, beaches, forests and mountain ranges live side by side. The Great Basin, the lower, flatter area surrounded by higher ground, makes up much of Nevada and some of the states around it. Death Valley in California is the lowest point on the continent, more than 280 feet below sea level.

Coastal Plain

The Coastal Plain is one of the largest landform regions in the U.S. It's made up of low, flat land and extends from the Atlantic Ocean to the Gulf of Mexico.

Appalachians

West of the Coastal Plain lies the Appalachian mountains. **The oldest** mountains in North America, they are smooth and round, having been worn down over centuries of erosion. The mountains and the areas around them are covered in trees, and **the highest** peaks in the range are around 6,700 feet high!

Interior Plains

The Interior Plains are **the biggest** region, stretching across the middle of the country and covering many states. The Interior Plains are mostly flat, with forests to the east and grasslands to the west.

4. T provides comprehension questions and puts students in pairs to find the answers of the questions.
5. T checks students' answers for the comprehension questions.
6. T puts students in groups of four and asks them to talk about the target forms they noticed in the text.

(ellipsis)

Considering information in <A> and <B>, explain TWO new grammar teaching techniques Ms. Park decides to use for her students of different proficiency levels.

Your Answer

09   Read the passage and follow the directions.

<table>
<tr><td colspan="2" align="center">**Teaching Procedure**</td></tr>
<tr>
<td>Step 1</td>
<td>The teacher asks students what the best present is they have received from friends or parents. Then, the teacher writes down the following sentences on the board and explains the terms "double-object verbs" and "single-object verbs" using the two sentences.

1. She gave her father a book.
2. She explained the law to Mary.</td>
</tr>
<tr>
<td>Step 2</td>
<td>The teacher extracts some example sentences of the target forms 'double-object verbs' and 'single-object verbs' from one story. The teacher asks students to check the sentences carefully and finds out the number of object(s) in each sentence.

1. Santa must give me a present.
2. Mom buys you the gift.
3. He said something to me.
4. She cooks us a delicious meal.
5. I explain why I was a good girl this year to her.</td>
</tr>
</table>

	• The teacher puts students in pairs and provides a worksheet. Students in pairs discriminate between grammatical and ungrammatical sentences.

[Worksheet]
※ Indicate whether the following sentences are grammatical or ungrammatical.
(1) She gave a book to her father. (O / X)
(2) She gave her father a book. (O / X)
(3) The policeman explained Mary the law. (O / X)
(4) The policeman explained the law to Mary. (O / X)
(5) Mom buys you the gift. (O / X)
(6) Mom buys the gift for you. (O / X)
(7) She cooks us a delicious meal. (O / X)
(8) She cooks a delicious meal for us. (O / X)
(9) They reported the police the accident. (O / X)
(10) They reported the accident to the police. (O / X)

Step 3

• The teacher checks the answers with the whole class. Then, the teacher gives students ten minutes and asks them to work out a rule for verbs like 'give' and 'explain' using the following questions.

1. List the verbs in the [Worksheet] that are like 'give' and those that are like 'explain', respectively.
2. What is the difference between the verbs in the two lists?

• 10 minutes later, the teacher points out several pairs of students to present their findings for the rule of 'double-object verbs' and 'single-object verbs'.

Identify the name of grammar teaching technique used in the lesson procedure. Then, explain how students explicitly learn the target rule through steps 2 and 3.

Your Answer

_____

_____

_____

_____

_____

10 Read the passages and follow the directions.

A

Ms. Choi's Teaching Log

Most of my students think that learning grammar rules mechanically is boring and ineffective. Thus, I prepared a new type of activity considering two points. First, instead of teaching them grammar rules in a decontextualized way, I will provide a reading text including many examples of target grammar rules so that they can focus on form within the context. Besides, as an exercise for accuracy, they will figure out some errors of the target rules they just have learned. By doing so, I would like to teach my students grammar forms within the context and also how to use them accurately.

B

Lesson Procedure

1. T provides a reading text, Text 1, including third-person singular '-s', and plural forms.

> [Text 1]
> My dad is fifty years old. His name is Paul. He is tall and thin. He has got short blond hair and green eyes. He wears glasses. He is very intelligent and funny. He is an architect.
> His favorite hobbies are running, reading, and going fishing. He loves listening to music. He doesn't like rainy days.
> He usually gets up at half past seven. He has a shower and gets dressed. Then, he has breakfast with my mom and me. He usually has toast and orange juice. At half past eight, he goes to the office by train.

2. T asks Ss to underline verbs ended with '-s', and nouns of plural forms.
3. T checks the verbs and nouns Ss has underlined and talks about how to use them with the whole class. T introduces some nouns from Text 1 which are unable to use in plural forms or have different meanings in plural forms (i.e., toast, orange juice, breakfast/breakfasts, lunch/lunches)

4. T puts Ss in groups of three and asks them to read Text 2 to find errors of third-person singular '-s' or plural forms.

> [Text 2]
> My dad is fifty year old. His name is Paul. He is tall and thin. He
>   → years
> have short blond hair and green eye. He wear glasses. He is very
> → has   → eyes → wears
> intelligent and funny. He is an architect.
>   His favorite hobby are running, reading, and going fishing. He love listening to music. He doesn't like rainy day.
>   He usually get up at half past seven. He has a shower and gets dressed. Then, he has breakfast with my mom and me. He usually has toasts and orange juices. At half past eight, he goes to the office by train.

5. Ss in groups find the errors in the text and revise the paragraph.
6. T checks the answers with the whole class.
7. T ends the lesson by emphasizing the importance of not making errors of the target forms, especially, in writing.

Referring to <A>, write TWO teaching purposes of Ms. Choi in the grammar lesson and explain how each purpose has been achieved with evidence from <B>.

Your Answer

_____

_____

_____

_____

_____

11 Read the passages and follow the directions.

Ms. Song's Teaching Note

For teaching vocabulary, many teachers suggest that students should learn vocabulary by being exposed to language repeatedly, for example, through extensive reading. However, I believe, my students who frequently make mistakes in using appropriate words, need to learn vocabulary more explicitly. Thus, I prepared the following lesson procedure where they can learn vocabulary through authentic examples in diverse contexts. Besides, through the examples, they also can see how words are woven together. Below is part of the lesson procedure I prepared for my students.

Lesson procedure

Below is an excerpt from the online discussion posting where people freely write about their answers to the given question.

> Q. Why do people seek temporary happiness instead of permanent bliss?
>
> by Edward Green (answered 2 days ago)
>
> All types of happiness are only temporary. There is nothing like permanent happiness. Can you imagine someone having permanent health? There is no human being who does not have to suffer an illness, old age, and death; which are all painful. Just like every human being falls ill once in a while, every person suffers unhappiness once in a while. You can reduce the frequency and duration of illness, but you can never avoid it because your illness is often a result of external circumstances, which are beyond your control. Thus, seeking temporary happiness is a complete waste of your time, energy, and money.

Step 1 T asks Ss to skim the text individually and underline the words they don't know the meaning of.

Step 2 T makes Ss read the text one more time and find the main idea.

Step 3 T introduces a new vocabulary learning activity using a concordance program. T asks Ss to call out the words they have underlined and writes them down on the board. Then, T models how to use the program.

Step 4 T puts Ss in pairs and makes them search for the example sentences including the words from the real language data.

1. Many of them were TEMPORARY workers, you know support staff, people who cleaned, and cooked.

2. Employment? – All TEMPORARY jobs, answered Claire. 'dishwasher, building janitor...' the payment of the portion provided parents only with a TEMPORARY position of authority. Mostly, the father's payment was 'not a long affair continuing the financial link between parents and children.

3. This improvement in the use of fixed assets could be a long-term trend rather than a TEMPORARY performance because several effective strategies had been adopted in fixed asset management.

...

Step 5 Ss in pairs talk about the meaning of the target word, 'temporary' and diverse contexts when and how it is used.

Step 6 T asks Ss to write down the noun phrases including the target word. While writing down the phrases, Ss raise their awareness of the words that co-occur with the target word, 'temporary'.

Phrase 1	temporary workers
Phrase 2	temporary jobs
Phrase 3	temporary position
Phrase 4	temporary performance

<u>Step 7</u> Ss make their own _____ lines by writing out the sentences, or parts of sentences, that include the word 'temporary', and by aligning them accordingly.

> • We will meet them soon at our temporary home.
> • Consider a transition to a temporary job that's less stressful and has better hours.
> • We are finding the next CEO, and a temporary position is also open.

Fill in the blank with the ONE word from the passage. Then, based on Ms. Song's TWO teaching purposes, explain how students can acquire the word 'temporary' in the presented lesson procedure.

Your Answer

_____

_____

_____

_____

_____

12 Read <A> and <B>, and follow the directions.

A

In terms of expanding the vocabulary knowledge of students, three guessing strategies can be suggested as follows:

1. **Using semantic context**: when students encounter a difficult word in the text, they can infer the meaning by figuring out the overall meaning of a clause, a sentence, or even a paragraph in which the word is included.

2. **Using grammatical context**: students can analyze the surrounding conjunctions that show grammatical relations of the words within the sentence such as *and, but,* and *however.*

3. **Vocabulary analysis**: the word meaning can be inferred based on their existing knowledge of prefixes, suffixes, and roots.

B

As a pre-reading activity, Mr. Kim asks students to guess the contents of a news article based on the title 'Meet the illiterate orphan who molded his way to success'. Then, Mina asks the teacher the meaning of unfamiliar word, illiterate and he helps her to figure out its meaning.

Mina : What does it mean by the word *illiterate?*

Mr. Kim : Hmm . . . Do you remember what we learned last time?

Mina : Yes. We've learned about some morphemes, which help us to identify the meaning of words.

Mr. Kim : That's correct! So, Let's look at the word, *illiterate*. How many morphemes are there?

Mina : . . . *(Looking confused)*

Mr. Kim : Anybody knows?

Jisu : Two morphemes, *il* and *literate*.

Mr. Kim : So, what does it mean by the word *literate?*

Jinsu : People who can read?

Mr. Kim : Or write! *Literate* means 'being able to read or write'. And, now, look at *il-* at the beginning. What does it mean? We learned it last time. *(Nobody volunteers to answer.)*

Mr. Kim : Remember we talked about *Il-legal?* What was the meaning of *il-*, added at the beginning of the word, *legal?*

Mina : *(Raising her hand)* Opposite!

Mr. Kim : Exactly! Then, what does *illiterate* mean, Mina?

Mina : Can't read or write.

Mr. Kim : Good job! That's how you learn a new word.

Based on the information in <A>, identify the vocabulary teaching method Mr. Kim chooses in <B>. Then, explain how Mr. Kim leads students to figure out the unknown word 'illiterate' in class with evidence from the above data.

Your Answer

_____

_____

_____

_____

_____

13 Read the passage in <A> and the conversation in <B>, and follow the directions.

─┤ **A** ├─

Word formation occurs when we compound, clip, or blend existing words to create new words. Also, there are some other ways to form new words. The table below covers the definition of the processes and gives you some examples of each.

Processing	Example
Compounding words are formed when two or more lexemes combine into a single new word.	• stir + fry → stir-fry • high + light → highlight
Clipping is the word formation process in which a word is reduced or shortened without changing the meaning of the word.	• examination – exam • gasoline – gas
Blending is the word formation process in which parts of two or more words combine to create a new word whose meaning is often a combination of the original words.	• biographical + picture → biopic • breakfast + lunch → brunch
Derivation is the word formation process in which a derivational affix attaches to the base form of a word to create a new word.	• avail + able → available • teach + er → teacher
Loanwords are the word formation process in which a word from one language is borrowed directly into another language.	• algebra – Arabic • bagel – Yiddish

Chapter

06

─┤ **B** ├─

S1 : Ms. Song. What does "ad" mean? Is it the right word or a typo?

T : Oh, Sun-mi! 'Ad' means an 'advertisement'! People frequently use "ad" because "advertisement" is a bit long to speak and write.

S1 : I see. That's interesting. Then, can we use 'ad' instead of 'advertisement' in all situations?

T : That's a good question. In general, people use the shortened word in a casual conversation but not in a formal situation. In the formal situation, people use 'advertisement' rather than 'ad'.

S1 : Oh, okay. I should be careful about using it.

S2 : Ms. Song. I have another question. What is the meaning of 'sweeten'?

T : 'Sweeten'. Okay, let's make a guess. Is there any word coming to your mind when you read the word, 'sweeten'?

S2 : Hmm, sweet?

T : That's right! Adding '-en' to 'sweet' creates the word, 'sweeten'. The suffix '-en' means 'cause to be' here. Then, can you guess the meaning?

S2 : Making something sweet?

T : Very good!

T=teacher, S=student

Based on <A>, identify TWO types of word formation exemplified in <B>. Then, explain each identified type with evidence from <B>.

Your Answer

14 Read the passages and follow the directions.

┤ **A** ├

Strategies for Teaching Vocabulary

- **Cognate awareness:** to give learners an idea of the word's cognates whose linguistic origins are of the same: battle (English) vs. batalla (Spanish).

- **Contextual analysis:** to infer the word's meaning from the contextual use.

- **Word family and collocations:** to give learners an idea of the word family, groups of words that have a common feature and collocations, words that usually go together.

- **Morpheme analysis:** to perform an analysis of the word's morphemes, which helps learners to know better about the word.

─────── **B** ───────

Below is an excerpt from the conversation between the teacher and students during a vocabulary lesson.

Lesson Procedure

T : Okay, guys! Does anyone know what *active* means?

S1 : You move around...?

S2 : You are lively!

T : Right. Pretty close. Then, can you guys know when and how it is used?

Ss : *(silent)*

T : Cool. Don't worry. We will figure it out from now on. Let's check some examples.

(T shows example sentences through a screen.)

> • He has been a highly active participant in the discussion.
> • She has been very active in local politics for some years.
> • I like films with plenty of *action*.
> • Alcohol acts quickly on the brain.

T : Can you tell what adverbs come with *active*?

S3 : *Very active!*

S4 : *Highly active!*

T : Cool! Then, what is the verb form of *active*?

S5 : *Act.*

T : Nice! Then, how about a noun?

S6 : *Action.*

(ellipsis)

According to the information in <A>, identify the vocabulary teaching strategy used in the lesson procedure in <B>. Then, provide the evidence.

Your Answer

_____

_____

_____

_____

_____

15 Read the passage in <A> and the lesson procedure in <B>, and follow the directions.

───┤ **A** ├───

Form-focused instruction (FFI) refers to a range of instructional methods that direct learners' attention to language items. One of the main issues in FFI is the amount of attention that is given to language items. Consequently, FFI is generally divided into two main categories: *focus on forms* and *focus on form*. The former consists of instruction that is primarily oriented towards language items, with explicit instructional methods. In this approach, instructional activities have their primary goal as the teaching of specific aspects of the language, generally by systematically presenting discrete grammatical rules. In contrast, the latter refers to brief and spontaneous attention to language items provided in context while performing meaning-oriented L2 classroom activities. In other words, there is a primary focus on meaning, but there is also deliberate, albeit generally brief, attention to language form.

───┤ **B** ├───

Lesson Procedure

1. T asks Ss what their favorite books are and introduces the lesson topic, their favorite books.
2. T shows Ss a model text of an essay for introducing a book, including 'V-ed' and 'V-ing' forms.

[Paragraph from a Native English Speaker]

My favorite book is written by a Korean author, *The Vegetarian*, translated into English. There are two reasons why I like the book: first, I agree with the writer's point of view described in the text. I think the story describing the life of Yeong-hye, a home-maker who suddenly decides to stop eating meat can happen among our neighbors. Also, it helps me try to understand people thinking differently from me.

(ellipsis)

3. T puts Ss in pairs and asks them to tell their partners about their favorite books and the reasons.

4. Ss individually write a short essay to introduce their favorite books using the expressions from the text.

5. T points out some students to present their writings. While Ss present their writing, T makes notes of some errors of active participles and passive participles.

6. T writes down the sentences with errors and asks Ss in groups to figure out how to correct them and how 'active participles' and 'passive participles' differ in usage.

T=teacher, Ss=students

Referring to terms in <A>, identify how the students in <B> acquire the target forms. Also, support your choice with evidence from <B>. Do NOT copy more than FOUR consecutive words from the passages.

Your Answer

_____

_____

_____

_____

_____

16   **Read the passage and follow the directions.**

> *Below is an excerpt from the email sent by Ms. Oh, a new English teacher to Mr. Nam, a senior English teacher.*

Dear Mr. Nam

   I am writing this email to ask for your advice on teaching vocabulary. In my class, I have different levels of students. Some are high-level, but the others are low-level students. So, it is hard to decide which level of vocabulary I should focus on. This week, I provided 100 new words to memorize for the high-level students and 50 words for the beginner level students. However, even the advanced level of students only memorized the meaning of vocabulary but could not use it appropriately. Besides, beginner level students did not finish memorizing even half of the amount. For the next lesson, I want to find effective ways to teach vocabulary for each level of students. Can you give me any advice to help them?

Sincerely,
Seung-ah Oh

- -

Dear Ms. Oh

   Regarding the problem for your vocabulary lessons, I recommend that you teach the vocabulary based on a meaningful context rather than considering it as a discrete element. For your students who have different proficiency levels, you need to provide different vocabulary activities. For example, using realia, pictures, and gestures would be an effective way to teach vocabulary for the beginner level of students. On the other hand, simply learning vocabulary itself is not enough for the advanced level students. Hence, an activity using a corpus based on various and authentic data will be useful for them. Through this activity, the students can check words in authentic contexts and naturally internalize them. Also, they can learn not only the meanings but their collocations and usages. Try to follow my suggestion, and let me know if you still have a problem.

Best regards,
Ki-hoon Nam

Considering the information from the passage, identify the ONE main teaching principle that Mr. Nam believes most important for teaching vocabulary. Then, explain the vocabulary activity suggested for the advanced level students.

Your Answer

17   Read the passage and follow the directions.

Lesson Procedure

1. T puts Ss in groups of four.
2. T hands out the worksheet below to each group.

[Worksheet]

A. For each of the italic verbs, decide if the form is Past Simple Tense or Present Perfect Tense. Write PST or PPT under the verb.

(1) Annie *moved* to England with her parents in 2007.
(2) She *has lived* in England for six years now.
(3) She *has made* a lot of friends.
(4) I *have known* Annie since last year.
(5) We *became* friends when my family moved to her street.

B. The form of the verb depends on whether it refers to a finished time in the past or the time that is still continuing at the present. Decide what kind of time the expressions below refer to:

	Finished time	The time which continues at the present
In 2007		
For six years		
Since last year		
When my family moved to her street		

C. Sentence number 3 above does not show or mention any time. Do you think it refers to a finished time or a time that continues now?

D. Now complete the following rule:

Past Simple Tense is used to talk about events at _____ .
Present Perfect Tense is used to talk about events at _____ .

E. Now write some sentences about yourself or your friends.

(1) _____ in 2014.

(2) _____ years ago.

(3) _____ since _____ .

(4) _____ when _____ .

(5) _____ .

3. T asks each group to work with their group members to read through the Worksheet.

4. T asks each group to fill in the blanks on the Worksheet through Step A to E to find out the rules of the past simple tense and present perfect tense.

5. T tells each group to share the sentences they make on Step E with their group members.

T=teacher, Ss=students

Identify TWO characteristics of the grammar teaching lesson above differing from the traditional grammar teaching.

Your Answer _____

_____

_____

_____

_____

Build Up New

박현수 영어교육론 IV

Assessment

기입형

서술형

Assessment

🔒 정답 및 모범 답안 p. 29

☑️ 기입형

01 Read the passages and follow the directions.

┤ **A** ├

Ms. Choi's Teaching Log

Last week, I conducted a listening test to check my students' listening proficiency. I provided a 5 minute-long listening script and students chose the correct answer for 10 questions while listening to the script. The test results were given to each student today. I recorded their scores and ranks out of 30 students on the result sheet. By figuring out their current listening levels compared to the others, I thought it would help my students to maximize motivation for learning English. Some of my students looked disappointed with their test results. However, I believe that they will overcome the depressed feeling soon and study hard to improve their listening skills.

B

Hye-rim's Learning Log

According to the listening test results, I ranked only 20 out of 30 students in my class. After seeing my scores and ranks, I was so discouraged by the test results. What I expected from the test was not knowing how poor my English skill is comparing to the others. Instead, what does matter is whether I can pass the listening test or not. Thus, I hope my teacher uses (1) _____ testing to examine my own ability according to the predetermined learning criteria, not influenced by other students' performances. Instead of receiving the results only in a number score, I want to get some comments from the teacher on my test results. If the teacher tells me what I am good at and poor at, I will enhance my strengths and improve my weak points in listening skills. In other words, with the teacher's comment, the test can have positive (2) _____ since it makes me take the study more seriously.

Referring to the passages, fill in each blank with the ONE most appropriate word.

Your Answer (1) _____

(2) _____

02 Read the conversation between two English teachers and fill in each blank with the ONE most appropriate word.

> Mr. Choi : Hello, Ms. Shin. Do you have a minute?
>
> Ms. Shin : Yes, how may I help you?
>
> Mr. Choi : It's about the grammar test results of my students.
>
> Ms. Shin : Grammar test results?
>
> Mr. Choi : Yes, I checked my students' grammar skills using a cartoon strip story.
>
> Ms. Shin : A cartoon strip! How did you test your students with that?
>
> Mr. Choi : They wrote stories about 'People 100 years ago' and created their own cartoon strip stories. Through what they wrote, I could check whether they used past tenses correctly or not. Then, I gave them feedback, including strong and weak points of their grammar skills.
>
> Ms. Shin : Nice work! Your students must have benefited from the test!
>
> Mr. Choi : Yes. By giving students diagnostic information, I wanted to ensure the positive (1) _____ effects of the test.
>
> Ms. Shin : Then, what's going on their weak points?
>
> Mr. Choi : That's the point! Do you have any good idea?
>
> Ms. Shin : Well, in my case, first, I figure out the grammar mistakes my students make in common. Then, I provide them with a follow-up worksheet to practice the common error.
>
> Mr. Choi : Ah-ha! A follow-up activity. That sounds great!
>
> Ms. Shin : There is one more thing. After the practice, I retest my students.
>
> Mr. Choi : Wow! Test again?
>
> Ms. Shin : Right, usually I retest my students with a/an (2) _____ test. In this test, each item tests only one grammatical element, so it is very reliable to check if my students learn certain grammatical features.
>
> Mr. Choi : I see! Can you explain little more how to use the test?

Ms. Shin : Sure. As an example, last week, I gave my students a multiple-choice task to check if they learned how to use prepositions properly or not. Not only the multiple-choice task, but there are many different types of grammar tasks you can use, such as error-recognition and rearrangement items.

Mr. Choi : Thank you for the great idea, Ms. Shin. I will try to use the follow-up activity and retest my students as well.

Your Answer (1) _____

(2) _____

03 Read the passage and fill in each blank with a suitable term in ONE word.

A

Item Analysis Summary

- Score: Midterm 1
- The number of questions: 30
- Reliability: 0.71
- Standard of error measurement: 4.98

[Table 1]

Questions			
(X) ___(1)___ / (Y) ___(2)___	Poor (<0.1)	Fair (0.1-0.3)	Good (>0.3)
Hard (0-50%)	30		18, 22
Medium (51-85%)	9, 15, 24, 25, 27, 28, 29	17, 21	3, 4, 12
Easy (86-100%)	19, 20, 23, 26		1, 2, 5, 6, 7, 8, 10, 11, 13, 14, 16

| **B** |

Ms. Jang's Teaching Log

Today, I conducted an item analysis for 30 multiple-choice questions in this midterm and recorded the results on Table 1. From the table, X-axis shows the data of item (1) _____ which is to determine how well an item is able to distinguish between good and poor students. I calculated the data by comparing item responses to total test scores with high and low scoring groups of students. On the other hand, Y-axis shows item (2) _____ which is the percentage of students who answered the item correctly. To express the data on the table, I divided questions into three levels, Hard (0-50%), Medium (51-85%), and Easy (86-100%). The higher the value, the easier the question. According to the item analysis summary, overall 12 questions show negative item (1) _____, meaning that low scorers answered the questions correctly more than high scorers did. So, I need to review the problem of each question more closely later. Regarding (2) _____, most of the questions are on Medium and Easy levels as I intended except for 3 items. Hence, this midterm was successfully designed in terms of item (2) _____, but it is not ideal for (1) _____.

Your Answer (1) _____

(2) _____

04 **Read the passage and follow the directions.**

> *Ms. Jung designed the following cloze test and administered it to her students last week. In the test, the students were asked to choose the words that had been removed.*
>
> ### A Vocational Vacation
>
> From farms in Australia to snowboard lodges in Canada, many young people are enjoying working holidays.
>
> Once many students finish high school or college, they have the uncanny desire to travel as far away from home as possible. Visiting new places and seeing exotic locales around the world ___1___ can be a great learning experience, but there is one big problem that these young travelers face—a lack of money. Most countries nowadays are ___2___ young globetrotters by offering a six- to twelve-month working holiday for anyone between the ages of 18 and 30. ___3___ , they will be able to experience new cultures while making enough money to survive.
>
> In Australia, the working holiday program has been a phenomenal success. In its first year of existence, 1975, 2,000 working visas were ___4___ . By 2006, this number had increased to 113,000, which is estimated to have added US$1.3 billion to Australia's economy in that year. Many of the positions ___5___ are in the hospitality industry or harvest work, but some travelers are getting jobs in finance, health care, and education.
>
> · · ·

1. ⓐ on leave
   ⓑ in person
   ⓒ off record
   ⓓ by surprise

2. ⓐ applying to
   ⓑ leading to
   ⓒ occurring to
   ⓓ catering to

3. ⓐ As yet
   ⓑ On the contrary
   ⓒ This way
   ⓓ By all means

4. ⓐ squeezed
   ⓑ issued
   ⓒ featured
   ⓓ inspired

5. ⓐ available
   ⓑ vacant
   ⓒ inclusive
   ⓓ essential

Complete the following by filling in the blanks with ONE or TWO words.

Ms. Jung developed and used a/an (1) _____ cloze test to measure her students' discourse level comprehension as well as sentence level comprehension. Different with fixed-ratio cloze test, this type of cloze test allows the teacher to avoid deleting words that would be difficult to predict from the context. In the case of the test above, deleting discourse/sentence level words serves as a measure of relational understanding—namely, grasping (2) _____ relations between clauses.

Your Answer (1) _____

(2) _____

05 Read the dialogue and identify the test type in TWO words.

Student–Teacher Meeting

T : Welcome, Come on in. Sun-ho, how are you today?

S : Hello, Mr. Choi. I am good. Thank you.

T : Take a seat. Everything is alright? How was the test?

S : Yes, it is all good. But I think there was something I could not understand during the test. The questions that I answered were different with my classmates'.

T : Oh, yes, Sun-ho. It could be. It would be a new test type for you. During the test, the computer checked your answers and chose the questions fit to your English proficiency. In short, it selects the questions just for you. So this test is also called as a tailored testing. That's why your questions were different with the others'.

S : A computer chose questions? I didn't know that. That's interesting.

T : One more fact about the test, you cannot review or change the answers to questions that you have already answered.

S : You're right. I wanted to review my answers but I couldn't. Then, where can I see my test results?

T : Do you remember the website that I showed you after the test? Log in that website, and you can find your test results.

S : Great. You've solved my doubts about this test! Thank you, Mr. Choi.

T : I am glad you said that. Okay then. Have a good afternoon.

T=teacher, S=student

Your Answer _____

06 Read the passage below and fill in each blank with an appropriate term.

The following is part of testing items of the midterm drafted by Mr. Lee.

1. Choose the correct answer to complete the given sentence.
   Q. He may not come, but we'll get ready in case he _____.
   ① will   ② does   ③ is   ④ may

2. Choose the correct answer to complete the given sentence.
   Q. Then we _____ the loudest thunder you have ever heard!
   ① heard   ② did hear   ③ hear   ④ hearing

Examples like these are known as (1) _____ test which is to measure one aspect of language at a time. These multiple-choice examples are decontextualized: each item consists of a single-sentence format with no other context provided, either within the item itself or in the previous parts of the text. In terms of testing principles, as one of objective test formats, multiple choice items have high reliability and practicality. However, these show low (2) _____ about overall proficiency unlike open-ended items.

Your Answer   (1) _____

(2) _____

07 Read the passages and fill in the blanks with suitable words.

| A |

The following is the item discrimination table from the listening test result.

Item	1	2	3	4	5
High scorers with correct answer	3	4	1	3	2
Low scorers with correct answer	1	2	2	0	1
(1) _____ (TWO words)	0.5	0.5	-0.25	0.75	0.25

| B |

Ms. Park and Ms. Song reviewed the listening test result and analyzed it as follows.

The table in <A> shows how many high scores and low scores get a particular item correct. Generally, students who get any one question correct also have a relatively high score on the overall exam. However, according to this table, one item indicates that either the students who performed poorly on the test overall got the question correct or that the students with high overall test performance did not get the item correct. It is the case of Item 3. That is, Item 3 deteriorates the (2) _____ (TWO words) of the test as more low scorers find the correct answer than high scorers. Thus, this item might contain one of the following problems.

- There is a mistake on the scoring key.
- Poorly prepared students are guessing correctly.
- Well-prepared students are somehow justifying the wrong answer.

In all cases, action must be taken! So, since this item shows negative item difficulty, it should be revised or eliminated. Be certain that there is only one possible answer, that the question is written clearly, and that your answer key is correct.

Your Answer (1) _____

(2) _____

08 Read <A> and fill in the blank in <B> with ONE word.

---| **A** |---

Teacher A: I think assessment is not all about testing. Students should have an opportunity throughout the class to be informally assessed. For example, as for listening, one important aspect of informal assessment is giving credit for the listening done in class or as homework. Listening takes practice, and it makes sense to assess the practice rather than putting complete emphasis on tests. Samples of a student's work contain the followings:

- a statement from the student that introduces this and tells why its contents were selected
- samples of classwork. This can be work specifically on listening or other work that includes listening.
- a sample of outside-of-class work. In addition to expected "academic homework" assignments, this may include summaries of non-academic listening experiences such as watching movies or TV or listening to a conversation in English.
- a reflection on learning: self-evaluation of strengths and weaknesses

---| **B** |---

The mentioned lists presented in <A> might mean collecting examples of completed listening tasks, as part of a/an _____ of work that is turned in at midterms and finals, through which students reflect on their progress.

Your Answer _____

09   **Read the dialogue and follow the directions.**

Two teachers are talking about their achievement test to be administered the following week.

Mr. Joe : I have one concern about the achievement test that we will administer next week.

Ms. Lee : What is it? I hope it isn't a big problem because I don't want to make a whole new test again.

Mr. Joe : Well . . . I just thought about our idea of assessing students in comparison to the performance of other examinees, using the bell-shaped curve. I concluded that it isn't a good idea.

Ms. Lee : But last time we both agreed that it will give us further information about each student's percentile rank in class.

Mr. Joe : But it's their achievements that we want to find out. Not their ranks in the class. What if all students have studied well and understand the class materials? Then, shouldn't all of them receive good scores regardless of other examinees' performances?

Ms. Lee : Hmm. I got your point. So, you have a better idea?

Mr. Joe : Yes. What about grading them in terms of a preset standard for acceptable achievement? Then, student achievement can be reported for the individual's skill and the performances of other examinee become irrelevant.

Ms. Lee : That makes sense. Let's begin developing the standard. We have little time left.

Complete the Comments by filling in each blank with the ONE most appropriate word.

Before the conversation demonstrated above, the two teachers developed a/an (1) _____ test which ranks each student with respect to the achievement of others, discriminating between high and low achievers in class. However, after the discussion, they concluded that such type of a test is inappropriate for their purpose. Then, they decided to change the (1) _____ test to a/an (2) _____ test to be able to assess the individual's achievement.

Your Answer (1) _____

(2) _____

10 Read the passage in <A> and the conversation between a teacher and a student in <B>, and follow the directions.

┤ **A** ├

Imagine being a teacher in a new classroom. You begin teaching a lesson only to be met with stares of confusion from your students. When you ask the students if they understand what you are teaching, they reply that they have no idea what you're talking about. Now imagine teaching the same class after conducting a pretest to determine what the students already know about the topic. Which scenario sounds preferable? Which would result in a better experience for both the teacher and the students? Of course, the latter would have a better result. The pretest in the latter case is a/an _____ that allows a teacher to determine students' individual strengths, weaknesses, knowledge, and skills before instruction. It is primarily used to identify students' difficulties and to guide lessons and curriculum planning.

┤ **B** ├

The following is part of the individual conference that Ms. Kim had about the test results with one of her students, Hye-mi.

T : So, Hye-mi. How was the test?

S : It was good! Not too hard, not too easy.

T : That's great Did you check the results?

S : Yes, I did and... I did not know that my writing skill is lower than average.

T : Oh, well. That's why we take the _____. You can check your current language skills. Should we see the results closer then?

T : Yes.

T : Okay, for reading, you are at the top 3%. Great job!

S : Thank you. I guess it's because I have more vocabulary knowledge than usual students. I really like learning new vocabulary. It's very interesting.

T : I see! That's the secret! Then, let's see listening... it's top 5%, which is good and speaking is top 10% which is still good. But, writing! I think writing skill is something that you need to focus on for this semester.

S : I know. Writing has been so difficult area for me since the first grade.

T : Hmm... How about joining an English newspaper club? This semester I am going to take a charge of the club. I will let each student will write one news article every week. It can be a great practice for writing with lots of fun!

S : That's a great idea! Thank you, Ms. Kim. I think I finally find the way to improve my writing skills. I did not expect that the test results can be useful this much!

T : You're very right! That's the benefit of this test. It gives you ideas on which skills you need to focus on your future learning.

T=teacher, S=student

Based on the information in <A> and <B>, fill in the blanks in <A> and <B> with the TWO most appropriate words. Use the SAME words in both blanks.

Your Answer

_____

11 Read the conversation between two teachers and follow the directions.

T1 : Hi, Mr. Park. What are you doing?

T2 : Hi, Ms. Kim. I am reviewing my students' writing works. There are so many grammar mistakes. That's a big problem.

T1 : Didn't you have a multiple-choice grammar test last week? How was it?

T2 : Oh, most of them did great on that test. But maybe, it was not enough to check their grammar knowledge. They know the rules but obviously don't know how to apply them in writing.

T1 : Hmm... What about preparing for another test?

T2 : Another one? Do you have any good ideas?

T1 : For example, a dictation-based writing test. You read aloud a story two or three times, and then ask students to rewrite it. Through this test you can see if they understand the rules and use them properly. Furthermore, you can evaluate their listening & writing skills and vocabulary knowledge.

T2 : Feeding two birds with one scone! But... that could be an overwhelming activity for low-intermediate level students.

T1 : Don't worry. You can give some keywords so that they can listen and write the text within their proficiency level.

T2 : That sounds cool. Hmm, what do you think about the beginners? It could still be enough for them?

T1 : Well, for beginning level students, you can also add picture-cues to help them comprehend and remember the storyline.

T2 : Keywords and picture-cues! I guess that will be enough to support my students. Thank you, Mr. Park. I will try the new test and let you know how it works.

T1 : Cool!

T=teacher

Complete the comments by filling in the blank with the ONE most appropriate word.

In the above dialogue, the two teachers are talking about testing students' grammar knowledge using a dictation-based writing test. The test described by the teachers here is a kind of _____ testing which requires a test taker to use several language skills at the same time such as listening and writing as well as grammatical knowledge.

Your Answer _____

01   Read the passage below and follow the directions.

Mr. Shin, a middle school English teacher, is teaching low intermediate level students. Recently, he conducted a proficiency test to assess students' overall proficiency. The test results showed that their listening ability is relatively lower than the other skills. Accordingly, he tried to figure out where and how students' understanding broke down through group conferencing. After talking with students, however, he realized that the conducted listening test format had some problems rather than students' listening ability itself. In terms of the test format, some of the questions were too long and complicated, so students had to spend lots of time reading these questions, which led to an extra burden. The other listening questions, also, asked students to write long answers. Thus, they could not clearly answer these questions even though they had very good listening skills. In short, the listening items of the proficiency test seemed to measure reading and writing skills rather than listening itself. In other words, the listening test format did not measure exactly what it was supposed to measure. So, Mr. Shin decided to give students an opportunity to take a make-up test. Following the preparation process, he designed a new listening test as below.

T's Preparation

1. T searches a few accommodation ads from the online newspaper.
2. T chooses an article coming with an interview video between two people discussing:
   • information from the various ads and personal preferences regarding this information.
   • a ranking of the accommodations in terms of preference.
3. T prepares a table as shown below.

[Listen and Fill in the Blanks]

Location / Information	Noryangjin area	Yeouido	Gangnam	Shin-chon	Samcheong-dong
Number of bedrooms					
Rent cost					
Date available					
Features					
Person A's rank					
Person B's rank					

Among the five major assessment principles, identify the ONE that is the greatest drawback shown in Mr. Shin's listening test and explain why the test violates the identified principle with some evidence from the passage.

Your Answer

_____

_____

_____

_____

_____

Chapter

07

02 Read the passages and follow the directions.

┤ **A** ├

Ms. Park's Teaching Note

For this semester, I will teach English to 1st-grade students in a middle school. Before starting my lesson, I conducted the following grammar/vocabulary test to diagnose their current language level.

Item 1

I don't know how we are going to get to the airport. We will have to _____ for a taxi to come.

a. plan   b. arrange   c. book   d. hire

Item 2

If you don't like the soup, why don't you _____ to the waiter and he can bring you another one.

a. complain   b. protest   c. criticize   d. insult

Item 3

Hunmin Chong-um which meant "the proper sounds for teaching people." was created under King _____ during the Choson Dynasty.

a. Taejo   b. Sejong   c. Jeongjo   d. Danjong

Item 4

Because of her behavior, she now has _____ friends than before.

a. less   b. fewer   c. little   d. few

Item 5

Yesterday, I watched an _____ movie produced by Steven Spielberg in the late 1980s.

a. boring   b. disappointing   c. amazing   d. scary

| B |

After 20 students have answered the five multiple-choice items, I got the test results as below.

[Response Frequency Distribution]

Items	High / low groups	a	b	c	d
Item 1	High group (n=10)	7*	1	1	1
	Low group (n=10)	6*	1	2	1
Item 2	High group (n=10)	7*	1	1	1
	Low group (n=10)	5*	1	3	1
Item 3	High group (n=10)	2	5*	2	1
	Low group (n=10)	1	7*	1	1
Item 4	High group (n=10)	5*	4	0	1
	Low group (n=10)	4*	3	2	1
Item 5	High group (n=10)	0	0	10*	0
	Low group (n=10)	0	0	10*	0

* = Key answer

Considering <A> and <B>, identify TWO problematic items and explain why each identified item is problematic in terms of the construction of multiple-choice items and then, the test results.

Your Answer

_____

_____

_____

_____

_____

03 **Read the passages and follow the directions.**

┤ **A** ├

Ms. Song's Teaching Log

This semester, I have conducted a formative test to evaluate my students' language skills every week. I designed a test based on one target skill once per week and thus, in four weeks, I could test all four language skills such as listening, reading, speaking, and writing. Then, I provided the test scores in percentage so that each student could compare his or her own performance with the others. Usually, I thought a competitive atmosphere among students motivates and stimulate them to study harder. However, after several times of tests, my students complained that the test was not closely related to the lessons they participated in. According to them, they had four skills integrated lessons but the test covered only one single target skill. Besides, they added that the current test type was not helpful for them because simply score ranking neither motivates them nor gives enough information about their own performance. Hence, I decided to plan the other type of formative tests based on their needs. I changed not only how to evaluate them but what to evaluate. This week, I provided my students with a new formative test and received positive comments from them.

+ **B** +

Below is the part of the test task and results that Ms. Song has designed based on her students' comments. She wants to test students' speaking skills using the role-play practiced in her lessons. Students who get over 12 out of 20 will pass the test.

Test Task Directions

[Situation]

Two of your closest friends are having an argument. One friend is blaming the other saying that he is not punctual. The other one is trying to justify being late. You want to stop the fight between them. What would you do? Write a role-play script within 20 sentences.

1. Seat in groups of four.
2. Read the given situation and write a role-play script including your group answer.
3. Practice the role-play for 20 minutes.
4. Present the role-play you have prepared to the whole class.

[Evaluation Form]
- Group: A
- Student: Kim Min-su.

Criteria	Your performance	Standard grade
Content/Idea	4	5
Fluency	2	5
Intelligibility	2	5
Participation	4	5

- Total: 16 out of 20
- Grade: Pass
- Comment: Min-su! Overall, you did a great job! You actively participated in making the script with your group members! Besides, your group idea was well expressed during the role-play. *(ellipsis)*

Identify the new type of formative test that Ms. Song conducts in <B>. Then, explain how the identified test satisfies students' needs mentioned in <A> with evidence from <B>.

Your Answer

04 **Read the passages and follow the directions.**

A

Ms. Kim, English teacher, teaches 2nd graders in a middle school. In her writing class, students wrote persuasive writing. After writing the second draft, students were asked to evaluate their own writing based on the checklist below. Ms. Kim also evaluated students' writing using the checklist. Below are the checklists done by the student, Dana, and Ms. Kim.

Evaluation (by Dana)	Y	N
Introduction with a clear thesis statement	✓	
Engage the reader	✓	
Vary beginnings of each paragraph	✓	
Sufficient supporting ideas	✓	
Text in three paragraphs	✓	
Persuasive language		✓
Linking words	✓	
A recapping conclusion	✓	

Name: Dana Park / Signed: Dana / Date: 2022.05.01

Evaluation (by Ms. Kim)	Y	N
Introduction with a clear thesis statement	✓	
Engage the reader	✓	
Vary beginnings of each paragraph		✓
Sufficient supporting ideas		✓
Text in three paragraphs	✓	
Persuasive language		✓
Linking words		✓
A recapping conclusion	✓	

Name: Dana Park / Date: 2022.05.01

Chapter

07

B

Ms. Kim's Teaching Note

For my intermediate-level students, I usually provide them with written feedback for their writing drafts. However, giving written comments to each of them takes me too much time. Hence, in today's class, instead of written feedback, I provided students with a checklist to self-evaluate their drafts. After they wrote the second draft, I asked them to evaluate their writing individually using the eight criteria from the checklist. Since it was the first time for them to evaluate their own writings, the results were not included in part of the evaluation grade but were only used for references. Thus, after class, I also evaluated their writings using the same checklist. According to the evaluation results, most students wrote the thesis statements clearly but showed lots of weak points in their writings. Nevertheless, most of them did not accurately reflect on what they did good or bad. Thus, there are big differences between students' evaluation and my evaluation (teacher evaluation). Some of them evaluated their writing too positively, and the others evaluated their writing too negatively. For example, in Dana's case, she overestimated her writing and checked 'yes' to 7 out of 8 criteria. However, when I read her writing, there were many weak points. Especially, the number of supporting ideas was insufficient. I asked them to write at least four supporting details but there were only two in her essays. In persuasive writings, sufficient supporting details are more important than anything else but she missed the point. Consequently, although there was a clear thesis statement in her writing, she failed to persuade readers. Mostly, students' evaluations, like Dana's case, tend to be too subjective and thus unreliable. To prevent such problems, I decided to prepare a training session for self-evaluation. By giving them chances to understand each criterion clearly, I will make them assess their writings in more objective and reliable ways.

Among the eight criteria in the checklist in <A>, choose ONE strong point and ONE weak point of Dana's writing described in <B>. Then, provide the major reason that makes a big difference between the teacher's and the students' evaluation results and write Ms. Kim's solution briefly.

Your Answer

_____

_____

_____

_____

_____

05 **Read the passages and follow the directions.**

┤ **A** ├

Mr. Park attended a workshop for English teachers where he could get useful information about how to make a test as authentic as possible. Based on the information below, Mr. Park decided to use Test 1 for his students rather than Test 2.

※ Evaluate the extent to which the given test task has the
_____ based on the following criteria:

Criterion 1 The language in the test is as natural as possible.
Criterion 2 The items are as contextualized as possible rather than isolated.
Criterion 3 Topics and situations are interesting, enjoyable, and humorous.
Criterion 4 The test task represents or closely approximates tasks that might occur in the real world.

B

Test 1	Test 2

"Going to"
 1. What ─────── this weekend?
   a. you are going to do
   b. are you going to do
   c. your gonna do
	1. There are three countries I would like to visit. One is Italy.
	   a. The other is New Zealand and the other is Nepal.
	   b. The others are New Zealand and Nepal.
	   c. Others are New Zealand and Nepal.

2. I am not sure. ─────── anything special?
   a. Are you going to do
   b. You are going to do
   c. Is going to do
	2. When I was twelve years old, I used ─────── every day.
	   a. swimming
	   b. to swimming
	   c. to swim

3. My friend Jieun and I ─────── a party. Would you like to come?
   a. am going to
   b. are going to go to
   c. go to
	3. When Mr. Brown designs a website, he always creates it ───────.
	   a. artistically
	   b. artistic
	   c. artist

4. I'd love to! ───────.
   a. What's it going to be?
   b. Who's going to be?
   c. Where's going to be?
	4. Since the beginning of the year, I ─────── at Millennium Industries.
	   a. am working
	   b. had been working
	   c. have been working

5. It is ─────── to be at Ruth's house.
   a. go
   b. going
   c. gonna
	5. When Mona broke her leg, she asked her husband ─────── her to work.
	   a. to drive
	   b. driving
	   c. drive

Chapter

07

Fill in the blank in <A> with ONE word. Then, from <A>, identify the ONE most appropriate criterion that makes Mr. Park decide to choose Test 1 instead of Test 2 and provide the reason of your choice based on its characteristic from <B>.

Your Answer

_____

_____

_____

_____

_____

06 Read the conversation below, and follow the directions.

Mr. Park, a new English teacher, has visited the office of Ms. Lee, a senior teacher, to ask for advice about the speaking test that he has prepared for 2nd-grade students. Below is an excerpt from the conversation between two English teachers.

Mr. Park : Hi, Ms. Lee. Do you have a minute?

Ms. Lee : Mr. Park. Come on in. How's your speaking test going?

Mr. Park : It's almost done. But I want you to check the test before finalizing it.

Ms. Lee : No problem. Can you show me the test?

(Mr. Park shows Ms. Lee the test he has designed. Below is the part of the test specification.)

[Test Specification]

No.	Types	# of students	Time	Score
1	Interview	1	5 mins	20
2	Picture description I	1	5 mins	20
3	Picture description II	1	5 mins	20
4	Role-play	3	10 mins	20
5	Discussion	3	10 mins	20

Ms. Lee : How many students do you have?

Mr. Park : 40. All intermediate level.

Ms. Lee : I have a question. Did you calculate the time you need to test all of your students?

Mr. Park : No.... Not yet.

Ms. Lee : Let me do it just for the first one. For the interview, you need 200 minutes without considering the intervals. That's more than 3 hours! Also, you have four more speaking tests!

Mr. Park : You mean, there are too many different types of tests?

Ms. Lee : Exactly! It does not seem practical. How about choosing only 2 types of tests?

Mr. Park : That's better. Then, I will arrange the picture description and discussion only.

Ms. Lee : Okay. So, how will you evaluate your students?

Mr. Park : I will ask Mr. Kim to be another evaluator. First, while recording students' performances, I will evaluate them on a real-time basis. After the test, Mr. Kim will watch the recording and evaluate them once again. The average between the two scores will become my student's final score.

Ms. Lee : One more thing. Did you conduct a pilot test?

Mr. Park : Yes, I did. Here are the test results. Three students from Mr. Kim's class have taken the tests.

   (*Below is the part of the test results.*)

[Test results]

No.	Types	Student	Score from Mr. Park	Score from Mr. Kim
1	Interview	A	18	10
		B	9	17
		C	11	20
2	Picture description	A	7	16
		B	18	10
		C	12	19
	...			

Ms. Lee : Hmm... The test results seem to have another problem.

Mr. Park : Can you clarify the problem?

Ms. Lee : The test results are inconsistent. There must be some misunderstanding about the scoring criteria between you and Mr. Kim.

Mr. Park : Well... Could be. Then, I should ask another person for the evaluation?

Ms. Lee : It's not the problem of Mr. Kim. When there are two or more scorers, it is better to have a training session about the scoring criteria before evaluation. It will help you to avoid such a huge gap between scores.

Mr. Park : You're right. We had not talked about the criteria yet. I need to take some time to deeply talk about the scoring criteria with Mr. Kim. Thank you, Ms. Lee.

Identify TWO problematic principles of assessment that Ms. Lee points out about Mr. Park's speaking test. Then, write the reasons for your choice with evidence.

Your Answer

_____

_____

_____

_____

_____

07 **Read the passages and follow the directions.**

┤ **A** ├

  Ms. Lee will conduct a standardized test to make new program eligibility decisions. Based on the test results, she will select the top 10% of students and start a new English program as an after-school activity. With this in mind, she looked over the test manual for a standardized test. The following is an excerpt from the manual:

Speaking section: This section measures the student's ability to speak in English. It is not related to any particular textbook of a specific course of study. The speaking section evaluates the ability to express one's own ideas and opinions. This section consists of (1) introducing yourself (2) describing your favorite memory and (3) choosing the pros/con of a given topic with supporting ideas.

┤ **B** ├

  Below are the examples of two testing types showing the test results of a standardized test.

[Type A]

Skills	Score	Passing mark
Listening	- /100	70/100
Reading	- /100	70/100
Speaking	- /100	60/100
Writing	- /100	60/100

[Type B]

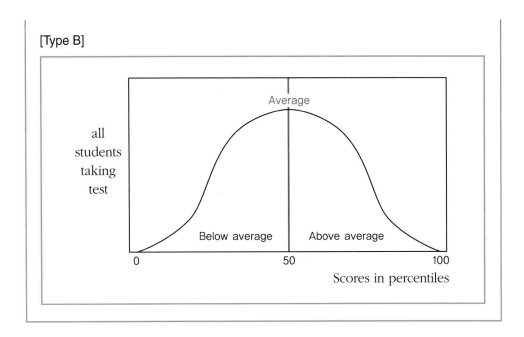

Based on <A>, choose the ONE appropriate type of testing in <B> for Ms. Lee to address her testing purpose. Then, write the name of the chosen testing type and support your choice with evidence from the passages.

Your Answer

_____

_____

_____

_____

_____

08   **Read the passage and follow the directions.**

> *Below is the conversation between two English teachers talking about the new type of assessment for mixed-level students.*
>
> T1 : Mr. Park. Do you have a minute?
>
> T2 : Of course, Ms. Kim. How can I help you?
>
> T1 : I need your advice for evaluating my students' reading proficiency. I conducted several types of reading tests but they were not effective and unhelpful for my mixed-level students. How can I test their reading skills effectively?
>
> T2 : Oh, well. First, let me ask you one question. What are the purposes of your test?
>
> T1 : I want to check up on what students have achieved during the lesson and, then, help them get some diagnostic information for further study.
>
> T2 : Hmm, if so, how about evaluating what has been done in class rather than using tests?
>
> T1 : You mean assessing what students already performed during lessons?
>
> T2 : You're right. I usually assess students' outcomes of diverse activities they have performed in class. It works very well!
>
> T1 : Can you explain more about it?
>
> T2 : For example, I ask my students to collect all completed tasks conducted during lessons. Then, I make them hand in the best examples of completed reading tasks during the whole semester.
>
> T1 : Then, it's not a paper and pencil test.
>
> T2 : Nope. It's not. Actually, according to proficiency levels, reading skills have been practiced during lessons, haven't they? So, I believe, it totally makes sense to assess the outcomes of the practice.
>
> T1 : That's true. Then, the assessment will represent the classroom content very well! That's all for the evaluation?

T2 : Hmm, one more thing I include for the evaluation is their own journals. I ask them to write journals after each lesson so that they can actively engage in their own learning process by self-evaluating their own strengths and weaknesses. By doing so, they can reinforce their strengths and improve their weaknesses in further reading lessons.

T1 : What a great effect! Cool! I should try the same ways to assess my mixed-level students' reading skills! Thank you, Mr. Park!

T=Teacher

Based on the conversation, explain the new type of assessment that Mr. Park suggests using the TWO ways to assess students' reading skills. Then, write TWO key principles of assessment that the identified type of assessment strongly reflects.

Your Answer

09 Read the passages and follow the directions.

---| **A** |---

Ms. Park's Teaching Note

Today, I participated in a teacher seminar regarding how to design multiple-choice items properly. Since many new teachers joined the seminar, they carefully listened to lots of useful information about multiple-choice items some experienced teachers provided. Below are parts of the material from the seminar.

> [Reading Material] What is A Multiple Choice Item?
>
> A multiple choice item consists of a problem, known as the (1) _____ and a list of suggested solutions, known as alternatives. The alternatives consist of one correct or best alternative, which is the answer, and incorrect or inferior alternatives, known as (2) _____.

The following are guidelines for constructing multiple-choice items to assess students' reading comprehension:

1. Use plausible distractors.
2. Use a question format rather than incomplete statements.
3. Keep option lengths similar.
4. Avoid clues to the correct answer.
5. Use only one correct option.

B

Below are some examples of multi-choice items that are intended to measure students' ability to make inferences:

[Reading Text]

The sun shone brightly, warming the cool earth. Tiny worms poked their heads from the dirt, and one tiny yellow crocus opened its petals. All around, dew sparkled, so that the grass resembled a vast field of diamonds. The budding trees rustled gently in the light breeze, and birds sang cheerfully high in their branches. A lone bee hummed lazily around the patch of lavender where Winston had carelessly left his shoes the day before. *(ellipsis)*

1. What time of day is it?
   a. dawn   b. morning   c. afternoon   d. night

2. What season is it?
   a. winter   b. spring   c. summer   d. lovely and warm fall

3. What is a crocus?
   a. a bicycle   b. a flower   c. a ball   d. a tree

4. Who is Winston?
   a. a dog   b. a bee   c. a child   d. a boy

Fill in each blank in <A> with the ONE most appropriate word. Among the items in <B>, choose TWO problematic items which do not follow all guidelines for constructing multiple-choice items from <A>. Then, explain the reasons for your choice with evidence.

Chapter

07

Your Answer

10 Read <A> and <B> and follow the directions.

┤ **A** ├

Mr. Song's Teaching Log

Today, I administered a speaking test using a picture description activity. Then, I asked two of my colleagues (Mr. Park and Ms. Joe) to score the 20 students' speaking performances using a/an _____ rubric based on four criteria. The results of the scoring are presented below.

[Mr. Park's rubric]

	S1	S2	S3	S4	
Content	2	3	3	2	
Fluency	4	4	4	5	...
Accuracy	4	2	2	4	
Pronunciation	5	2	4	4	

[Ms. Joe's rubric]

	S1	S2	S3	S4	
Content	5	4	4	3	
Fluency	2	1	1	2	...
Accuracy	2	4	4	2	
Pronunciation	1	5	2	2	

Score 1-5=1 is the lowest score and 5 is the highest score.

B

Mr. Park's Note

I think the speaking ability of Mr. Song's students overall was pretty high. For instance, when I score their fluency, I counted the number of pauses observed during their performance. Since most students had few pauses, which did not interrupt the flow of speaking, I gave them good scores. As for the pronunciation, I observed how well I could understand them. In other words, I checked their intelligibility. Thus, I gave a high score as long as the pronunciation was not hindering me to understand the content.

Ms. Joe's Note

Overall, the students' performances were not so impressive. In speaking, I think fluency is a matter of speed in delivering the speech. However, not even a single student could speak fast enough. Thus, in fluency, none of them got over 4 points. Besides, I used the pronunciation of native speakers of English as a standard to evaluate their pronunciation skills. However, there were only a few students who have pronunciation close to that of native speakers. Therefore, I could not help giving most of them low scores for pronunciation.

Fill in the blank in <A> with the ONE most appropriate word. Then, write the testing principle that is mainly violated in Mr. Song's test and provide the rationales of your choice with evidence from <B>.

Your Answer

11 Read the passages and follow the directions.

┤ **A** ├

Ms. Kim's Teaching Note

I am planning to test my students' grammar and vocabulary knowledge with a new testing method. Normally, I used to choose a multiple-choice test that requires test-takers to read some questions and then choose one correct answer among the given options. However, after having a conference with students, I realized that it does not precisely measure students' actual knowledge of vocabulary/grammar because of the decontextualized testing method. That is, a multiple-choice item test focuses on an isolated target word or a form without context. Accordingly, that kind of test does not closely related to lesson contents since they practiced the communicative use of target words or grammatical items within context during lessons. Thus, based on their needs, I decided to prepare a new test. First, the new test will examine students' abilities to use many skills simultaneously. Specifically, when students take a new test, they need to find out the answers based on a calculated guess, using linguistic expectancies and background knowledge. Thus, they should use not only reading ability but also other language abilities like writing because the test is an integrative measure. Second, the new testing items will be closely related to what students have learned during the lesson. This week, for example, I taught different kinds of transition words and verb tenses. Accordingly, I will intentionally delete these target items within the reading text so that students can focus on them by filling in the blanks with words or forms appropriate for the context.

B

Test 1

Jamal and his dad went camping in the mountains. There they built a campfire and cooked hot dogs and marshmallows. Then, they went to sleep in a tent. During the night, Jamal woke up three times. At midnight, he woke up because he heard his dad snoring. At 3 a.m., he woke up again because he felt an insect crawling on his face. One hour later, he woke up again because he got thirsty.

※ Read the story and answer the questions.

1. Jamal and his dad go camping in the desert. (T/F)
2. Jamal and his dad cook hamburgers. (T/F)
3. Jamal woke up three times during the night. (T/F)

Test 2

※ Read the story and fill in the blanks.

Jamal and his dad (1) _____ camping in the mountains. There, they built a campfire and (2) _____ hot dogs and marshmallows. (3) _____, they went to sleep in a tent. During the night, Jamal woke up three times. At midnight, he woke up (4) _____ he heard his dad snoring. At 3 a.m., he (5) _____ up again (6) _____ he felt an insect crawling on his face. One hour later, he woke up again because he got thirsty.

The scoring method is the acceptable word method.

Test 3

※ Read the story and fill in the blanks.

> Jamal and his dad we_____ camping in the mountains. There they bu_____ a campfire and cooked hot dogs and marsh_____. Then, they went to sle_____ in a tent. During the night, Jamal wo_____ up three times. At mid_____, he woke up because he heard his dad snor_____. At 3 a.m., he woke up again be_____ he felt a_____ insect crawling on his fa_____. One hour later, he woke up again because he got thir_____.
>
> ** The scoring method is the exact word method.*

Of three different types of tests in <B>, choose ONE most appropriate test for Ms. Kim and explain how the identified test corresponds with her TWO testing purposes, adding its two measuring elements as evidence.

Your Answer

_____

_____

_____

_____

_____

12 Read the passages and follow the directions.

---| **A** |---

Test specification

Category	Description
Grade	1st grade in a high school
Purpose	assess students' strong and weak points in oral skills on the first day of classes in the new semester
Task type	presentation (listen to the spoken file and present the summary orally: an integrative test)
Scoring method	analytic scoring a. **Criteria**: content, fluency, accuracy, pronunciation b. Content is worth 4 points, and the other criteria are 2 points. The score for this task is added up to 10.
Scoring procedure	a. Two evaluators (Ms. Song/Ms. Park) b. If there is a gap between two evaluators' scores of more than 2 points in total, the evaluators discuss and arrive at a rating that they agree upon.

B

Sujin's Learning Log

Last Monday was my first day in high school. I was so excited to meet new friends and teachers. On that day, it was Ms. Song's English class, in which we took a speaking test. Take a test on the first day of high school! Most classmates including me were very embarrassed. However, we could understand her intention. She said that she simply wanted to check our overall English proficiency and divided us into different levels. Thus, she added that she wanted to reduce our learning gaps through level-differentiated instruction. That's why we took a test at the beginning of the lesson. During the test, she played a listening file of a short story and asked us to make a summary for one minute. While listening to the story, I took notes for a summary. Thanks to the notes, I was able to summarize the story quite well. After the test, she explained that this test actually would be evaluated not only by her but by Ms. Park, a senior English teacher. Thus, she recorded what we just did and then would share the files with Ms. Park later. For the evaluation, anyway, Ms. Park and Ms. Song were supposed to score our presentations according to four different criteria. Also, Ms. Song emphasized that, for this test, the key criterion is the content of the summary. At that time, one of my friends asked a question, "what if there is a big difference between two teachers' evaluation results?". She said with a big smile, "If so, they will apply the average score". Tomorrow, I will get the results of the English test. Hopefully, I can get a good score and make a good impression on her.

Identify TWO categories from the test specifications in <A> that the actual test in <B> does not follow. Then, support your answers with evidence from <B>.

Your Answer

_____

_____

_____

_____

13 Read the passage and follow the directions.

There are some concepts to determine the extent each multiple-choice item serves the testing aims. These are (1) _____, (2) _____ and distractor efficiency. The first concept is defined as the extent to which an item is easy or difficult for a determined group of test takers. If an item is too easy or difficult for a group of test takers, it means that it doesn't make a distinction between a high-ability and low-ability group of test takers. This value can be calculated by using the formula stated below.

$$(1) \text{\underline{\hspace{2cm}}} = \frac{\text{\# of Ss answering the item correctly}}{\text{Total \# of Ss responding to that item}}$$

An appropriate multiple-choice item usually has (1) _____ that ranges between 0.15 and 0.85. Another concept about the efficiency of multiple-choice items is (2) _____. This concept refers to the extent to which an item differentiates between high and low-ability test takers. If an item gets correct answers from most of the high-ability group of test takers and incorrect answers from most of the low-ability test takers, this means that this item discriminated between the low and high-ability groups of test takers. This value can be calculated by using the formula below:

$$(2) \text{\underline{\hspace{2cm}}} = \frac{\text{high group \# correct} - \text{low group \# correct}}{1/2 * \text{total of your comparison groups}}$$

Items with high (2) _____ have a value close to 1.0 and the items with low (2) _____ have a value closer to zero.

The final term distractor efficiency is about how the responses are distributed to the distractors. If a distractor is not chosen as the correct answer by any of the low ability group members, this means it is not an efficient distractor. There isn't a specific formula to find this value, but it is possible to make a conclusion by looking at the frequency table showing the distribution of the responses. An example of response frequency distribution is seen below:

[Response Frequency Distribution]

	Options	A	B*	C	D	E
Item 1	High-ability students (10)	2	4	0	3	1
	Low-ability students (10)	1	4	0	2	3

* is the correct answer.

Fill in each blank with the TWO most appropriate words, respectively. Write the answers in order. Then, write TWO reasons why Item 1 is problematic with evidence from the table of <Response Frequency Distribution>.

Your Answer

_____

_____

_____

_____

_____

14   Read the passages and follow the directions.

A

Below is part of a speaking test that 2nd-graders in a middle school took yesterday.

Directions: Traditions are the beliefs and ways of doing things that are passed down from parents to children. Some traditions have been around for a long time, but sometimes people decide to start new traditions! Talk about one tradition of your family using the questions below. You will have 5 minutes for preparation. Answer each question for 30 seconds to 1 minute. Use the expression box, if needed.

Questions
1. What are some traditions your family celebrates in the fall?
2. Who is/are included?
3. What do you wear?
4. What do you eat?

[Expression Box]
- Eat dinner as a family.
- Do the dishes together.
- Have the same meal on the same day each week.
- Have a family movie night.
- My family celebrates ~.
- My family tradition is ~.
- Usually, (list of family members) gathered in (place) at/on (time).
- My mother/father/sister/brother/family likes/dislikes to ~.

[Scoring rubric]

Criteria	Poor	Okay	Good	Very good
Pronunciation				
Content				
Grammar				

┤ **B** ├

Minsu's Learning Log

Yesterday, I took a speaking test and my test result was not good. What a disappointing result! I thought my speaking skills are pretty good but, in a conference after the test, my teacher commented that my speaking skills are lower than the other students. Thus, she recommends practicing speaking skills a lot. I could not accept that my speaking skills are lower than those of other students, so I checked the test result once again. Then, I found that the scoring rubric includes only three criteria to evaluate my speaking skills. That's why my speaking skills are evaluated as not good. Before the test, my teacher talked about how to improve speaking skills and emphasized various aspects of speaking skills such as fluency, appropriateness, diversity of vocabulary, etc. However, such aspects were not reflected in the scoring rubric, which ought to be included. Moreover, I found another problem. Since this test could not measure my speaking skills accurately, it did not provide me with sufficient diagnostic information, either. Actually, the test results we got consisted of only a scoring rubric without any comments. Then, how could I improve my speaking skills? My teacher gave 'poor' in my pronunciation. If she evaluated so, at least she should have given me some comments on what the problems are and how to solve them.

[Minsu's Speaking Test Result]

Criteria	Poor	Okay	Good	Very good
Pronunciation	✓			
Content			✓	
Grammar		✓		

Based on <A> and <B>, write TWO testing principles that are poorly applied in the given speaking test. Then, explain your answers with evidence from <B>.

Your Answer ▸

15 Read the passage and follow the directions.

Ms. Kim designs a new proficiency test and wants to measure the extent of the agreement between the new test and an existing validated test. The scatter chart shows the test scores of sample students who have taken both the new test and the existing validated test, TOEFL Junior.

[Scatter chart]

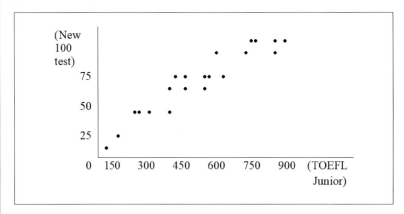

Ms. Kim's Teaching Note

Last week, I recruited some students who have taken TOEFL Junior this year. Since they already had the score from the validated proficiency test, they were perfect sample students to show the correlation between TOEFL Junior and my new proficiency test. After taking my new test, their test results showed that it is valid enough. For example, Student A who has the highest TOEFL score among sample students received the highest score in my new proficiency test. Besides, Student E who has the lowest TOEFL score got the lowest test score on my test. Thanks to the results, I could finalize my new proficiency test.

Identify the ONE type of criterion-related validity that Ms. Kim tries to measure and write how to prove the correlation between her new test and the validated test, TOEFL Junior, based on evidence from the passage.

Your Answer

_____

_____

_____

_____

_____

16 Read the passages and follow the directions.

─┤ **A** ├─

Below is part of Soomin's writing collection from March 1st, 2021 to June 30th, 2021.

My Writing Performance
(2021.03.01.~2021.06.30.)

March 30th, 2021

I remember when I was in an amusement park and that it was so fun that the bumper cars but hurts sometimes because we hit other bumper cars hard... *(ellipsis)*

...

April 10th, 2021

In 2020, I travelled to Germany. I chose this country because my grandmother was from German and in my childhood, she talking every time in German. *(ellipsis)*

...

June 7th, 2021

When I was five years, I hated to go to see the doctor. One day, my mom had taken an appointment for the dentist. While my mom was talking with the secretary, I started to cry.

(ellipsis)

B

Soomin's Log

Since the starting week of this semester, my teacher has asked us to collect my writing pieces from the classes. At first, I felt that collecting writings was a bit burden. However, while reviewing the collection, I realized this is actually very useful for improving my writing skills. First of all, I could check my writing progress through the collection. Thus, I became to have ownership of my next writing lesson. Besides, through the teacher's feedback at the end of the semester, I could figure out that I am poor at the correct usage of grammar. So, for the next semester, I will focus on improving my grammatical knowledge. Anyway, this writing collection was greatly helpful for me. If I did not collect my writings, I would not be able to decide the next goal to improve my writing skills. She noticed that the accumulated collection would be reflected as part of the writing assessment to evaluate my writing skills.

Identify the name of the performance assessment exemplified in <A>. Then, referring to <B>, write TWO benefits of the identified assessment from the student's standpoint.

Your Answer

_____

_____

_____

_____

17 Read the two students' logs and follow the directions.

Min-jae's Log

Today was the last day for my English writing course. So, I had a writing test to assess what I had learned through the coursework. In the test, I needed to write a descriptive paragraph introducing my classroom using a list of vocabulary given from the test. The vocabulary list consists of the words that I learned throughout the writing course. Writing a descriptive paragraph, also, was what I practiced several times during the course. Since both the assessment task and its contents were already covered in the coursework, I could finish the test within the given time limit without any problem.

Eun-bi's Log

Today, my teacher had us take a writing test. Since we had had no test so far, I asked the teacher why she decided to give a test. She answered that it was to check whether we achieved the course objective or not. Also, she added that each course has a specific objective, which focuses on students' knowledge and skills acquired during the course. This was why she gave us the writing test this time. Anyway, all the test questions were related to the course contents and so familiar to us. It seemed like reviewing what I learned through the course work.

Fill in the blank with the ONE most appropriate word. Then, write the testing purpose and the main characteristic of the test that two students have taken. Do NOT copy more than FOUR consecutive words from the passage.

> The test type that Min-jae and Eun-bi have taken is a/an _____ test conducted at the end of the course.

Your Answer

_____

_____

_____

_____

_____

18   Read the passage and follow the directions.

Lesson Plan

- Grade : 1st year of a high school
- Level : Intermediate
- Skills : Listening & Speaking
- Topic : School rules
- Lesson Objectives : Students will be able to

1) _____

2) _____

Lesson Procedure

1. As a warm-up, T asks Ss to call out any school rules they can think of.
   (e.g.) Arrive on time, Put on the school uniform neatly.
2. T shows a video about school rules. While watching the video, Ss identify any school rules they have already mentioned in the warm-up activity.
3. T puts Ss in pairs and provides each pair of Ss with a copy of the script. Ss watch the video for the second time, checking on the script and highlighting the words related to school rules.
4. T asks several pairs to present the words they have highlighted on the script.
5. Then, T elicits the target language form, must/mustn't, from Ss and asks them to infer the rule.
6. Ss in pairs read the script again and discover the rule for must/mustn't for themselves.
7. T asks Ss to present the rule they have found and briefly summarizes the language item.
   (e.g.) T: As you discover, we use "must" to talk about obligations and we use "mustn't" to say that something is not permitted or allowed, that is, for prohibition. And we add "must/mustn't" before the imperative form.

8. T puts Ss in groups of four and provides a copy of worksheet for each group. In the worksheet, there is a sample writing, "student contract" and a blank for "teacher contract". T and Ss read the "student contract" together and T explains the use of the modal verb of obligation, "must" and of prohibition "mustn't" in the contract.

[Worksheet]

Student Contract

Behaviour
Students must come to class prepared to learn.
Students mustn't sleep in class.

...

Class times
Students must arrive to class on time.
Students mustn't go to the toilet with their friends.

...

I agree to respect the rules and obligations above.

Signature _____

- -

Teacher Contract

[blank]

---

9. Ss in groups write an imaginative "teacher contract" that includes all the rules and regulations they think a teacher should follow. T encourages Ss to use must/mustn't as much as they can. The contract should not be too serious but an amusing or imaginative set of rules.
10. When they are done, each group presents their teacher contract to the class. The other groups write down the rule(s) they like the most. When all groups have presented their contracts, Ss pick the class's favorite rules.

Fill in the blanks with the TWO major lesson objectives. Do NOT copy more than FOUR consecutive words from the passage.

Your Answer _____

_____

_____

_____

_____

19 Read the passage in <A> and the lesson procedure in <B>, and follow the directions.

┤ **A** ├

Ms. Kim, a high school English teacher, tries to help her students improve their reading fluency based on strategy-based instruction. Thus, she sets a group of lesson objectives for her reading lessons of this semester as seen below.

Lesson Objectives

Students will be able to
- ask questions of individual experience to activate their schematic knowledge.
- skim the text for the gist.
- distinguish between literal and implied meanings.
- guess the meaning of unknown words using contextual clues.
- detect culturally specific references and interpret them in the context of the appropriate cultural schemata.
- analyze the language from the text to better understand the characters.

B

Teaching Procedure

Ms. Kim prepared a reading lesson for her 1st-year students based on two of the lesson objectives that she sets out to accomplish this semester.

The Story of An Hour

- Kate Chopin

   Knowing that Mrs. Mallard was afflicted with heart trouble, great care was taken to break to her as gently as possible the news of her husband's death. It was her sister Josephine who told her, in broken sentences; veiled hints that revealed in half concealing. Her husband's friend Richards was there, too, near her. It was he who had been in the newspaper office when intelligence of the railroad disaster was received, with Brently Mallard's name leading the list of "killed". He had only taken the time to assure himself of its truth by a second telegram, and had hastened to forestall any less careful, less tender friend in bearing the sad message ... *(ellipsis)* ...

---

1. T introduces a reading text titled "The Story of an Hour" written by Kate Chopin. Then, T asks students to check the image on the right which is the cover of the story and think about what this story is about.

2. T provides some preset questions and asks Ss to find out the answers while reading the text.

> • What is the actual meaning of Mrs. Mallard's saying, "free, free, free"?
> • Surface level: _____
> • Deep level: _____
> • What would be the intended meaning of Josephine's saying, "Maria"?
> • Surfac level: _____
> • Deep level: _____
>
> *(ellipsis)*

3. T makes Ss share the answers to the questions they have found in pairs. Then, T checks the answers with the whole class.

4. T puts Ss in groups of four and provides them with the chart seen below. Ss fill in the character sketch chart in groups.

> ※ Think about the words that have been used to describe Mrs. Mallard and Mr. Mallard. Work with your group members to write these words in the chart below.
>
> [Character Sketch Chart]
>
> | Mrs. Mallard | Mr. Mallard |
> |---|---|
> | • • • • | • • • • |

5. T introduces some descriptive words and models how to write a character description paragraph. Then, T asks Ss to write a descriptive paragraph in groups.

6. T asks Ss to post their group writings on the class blog and share feedback about each group's writing piece.

T=teacher, Ss=students

Identify TWO lesson objectives from <A> that the lesson procedure in <B> focuses on. Then, explain how each objective is achieved with evidence from <B>.

Your Answer

_____

_____

_____

_____

20 Read the teacher's reflection and follow the directions.

Teacher's Reflection

Usually, for midterm evaluation, I write about how well they have achieved diverse objectives of the course including a letter grade, their strong and weak points. Definitely, this narrative evaluation provides positive washback for students' further study. However, such a lengthy explanation is too time-consuming for me: it takes 50 minutes to write about a single student. Also, some students argue that the narrative evaluation heavily relies on not explicit criteria but the evaluator's overall impression, so it can be less reliable. To solve these problems of narrative evaluation, thus, I decided to use a new evaluation form as a mid-term evaluation for my high-intermediate level students who were undertaking the listening-speaking course. The new form is as seen below.

[Midterm Evaluation Form]

• Instructor: Ms. Song   • Student: Minsu PARK   • Grade: B+

Checklist

	Excellent progress	Satisfactory progress	Needs improvement	Unsatisfactory progress
Listening skills		✓		
Note–taking skills		✓		
Public speaking skills	✓			
Class participation effort		✓		

Brief comments: _____

_____

_____

_____

After evaluating students' midterms, I thought that the new evaluation form has a high (1) _____ because the evaluating process was so simple and time-saving. I only ticked off each criterion and added short comments. By doing this, I can save my time and energy for evaluation. In addition, it has good reliability and maintains (2) _____ that narrative evaluation can provide. Since uniform measures based on clear criteria are applied across all students, the evaluation result is more reliable. Besides, some short comments about students' strong and weak points can provide them with diagnostic information. Thanks to this new evaluation form, I could compensate for some disadvantages of the narrative evaluation.

Fill in the blank (1) and (2) with the ONE most appropriate word, respectively. Then, explain how the new midterm evaluation form solves the problems of narrative evaluation in terms of TWO described assessment principles. Do NOT copy more than FOUR consecutive words from the passage.

Your Answer _____

_____

_____

_____

_____

21 Read the passages and follow the directions.

A

Teacher's Note

Last week, I attended a teacher training on how to design a multiple-choice item. A multiple-choice question consists of a problem, known as the stem and a list of suggested solutions, known as (1) _____. They include one correct answer and the other incorrect options, known as (2) _____. Below are the principles from the workshop.

Designing an Effective Stem

Rule 1
The stem should be meaningful by itself and should present a definite problem.

Rule 2
The stem should not include irrelevant information in the stem, which can decrease the reliability and the validity of the test scores.

Rule 3
The stem should be negatively stated only when significant learning outcomes require it.

Rule 4
The stem should be a question or a partial sentence, instead of being constructed with an interior blank.

| B |

The following are some of the multiple-choice items that Ms. Jung designed to assess her students' comprehension after reading a text about a hedgehog, Henri.

※ Choose the best answer for the following questions.

Q1. Which of the following is a true statement?
    (a) Henri likes to eat fish and chips.
    (b) Henri likes to eat sandwiches and crisps.
    (c) Henri likes to eat beetles and earthworms.
    (d) Henri likes to eat peas and carrots.

Q2. Hedgehogs have a really short _____ period: it's only around 35 days from conception to birth.
    (a) juvenile
    (b) gestation
    (c) marriage
    (d) hibernation

Fill in each blank in <A> using ONE word. Write the answers in order. Then, referring to the rules from <A>, explain each reason why the two testing items in <B> are problematic.

Your Answer

_____

_____

_____

_____

_____

22 **Read the passages and follow the directions.**

┤ **A** ├

Analyzing the reliability, difficulty level, and discrimination of your multiple-choice questions requires only a few simple calculations and can help you determine the effectiveness of your assessment, whether it is a quiz, exam, or in-class question.

- **Reliability:** coefficient alpha — a measure of the internal consistency of the exam. This statistic ranges from 0 to 1.00, and the higher the value the better.

- **Item difficulty:** the percentage of students answering the question correctly. It can range between 0.0 and 1.0, with a higher value indicating that a greater proportion of examinees have responded to the item correctly, and it is, thus, an easier item.

- **Item discrimination:** the ability of an item to differentiate among students based on how well they know the material being tested. The possible range of the discrimination index is - 1.0 to 1.0; however, if an item has discrimination below 0.2, it suggests a problem.

┤ **B** ├

Below is part of the results of the multiple-choice test taken by 2nd graders in a middle school.

Option	Upper Group (%)				Lower Group (%)			
Item	a	b	c	d	a	b	c	d
1	21	26	23	30*	22	25	24	30*
2	13	10	70*	7	25	27	28*	20

*denotes the answer.

Between Item 1 and Item 2 in <B>, choose ONE problematic item and identify the major cause of problem in <A>. Then, explain why it is problematic with evidence from <B>.

Your Answer

_____

_____

_____

_____

_____

23 Reading passages <A> and <B> and follow the directions.

| A |

Rubric 1

• Your writing score is *Credit*.

Rating	Criteria
High Distinction (4)	The audience is able to easily identify the focus of the work and is engaged by its clear focus and relevant details. Information is presented logically and naturally. Mechanical errors or misspelled words do not distract the reader.
Distinction (3)	The audience is easily able to identify the focus of the student work which is supported by relevant ideas and supporting details. Information is presented in a logical manner that is easily followed. Minimal interruption to the work due to misspellings and/or mechanical errors.
Credit (2)	The audience can identify the central purpose of the student work without little difficulty and supporting ideas are present and clear. The information is presented in an orderly fashion that can be followed with little difficulty. There are some misspellings and/or mechanical errors, but they do not seriously distract from the work.
Pass (1)	The audience cannot clearly or easily identify the central ideas or purpose of the student work. Information is presented in a disorganized fashion causing the audience to have difficulty following the author's ideas. There are many misspellings and/or mechanical errors that negatively affect the audience's ability to read the work.

Rubric 2

	Pass (1)	Credit (2)	Distinction (3)	High Distinction (4)
Content (Relevant ideas and supporting details)			✓	
Organization (Sequencing of elements)				✓
Mechanics (Correctness of grammar and spelling)		✓		

B

Mr. Lee's Teaching Log

I am preparing a writing test for my students. The first aim of this test is not to check the overview of the student's achievement but diagnose each student's strengths and weaknesses for writing skills. I believe that such concrete information can motivate the students intrinsically. Another purpose is to use the test results as data in preparing diverse writing practices which help my students improve their weak points. Hence, I need a proper scoring rubric based on major writing elements in order to achieve the purposes.

Considering the information in <A> and <B>, identify each scoring method that Rubric 1 and Rubric 2 demonstrate, respectively. Then, choose ONE Rubric in <A> for Mr. Lee and provide TWO reasons for your choice considering Mr. Lee's purposes for the test. Do NOT copy more than FOUR consecutive words from the passages.

Your Answer

24   Read passages <A> and <B>, and follow the directions.

| A |

Topic: Writing Character Descriptions

Lesson Objectives:
- Students will be able to describe their favorite cartoon character.
- Students will be able to self-evaluate their writing piece and revise it.

Writing Activity:
- Show a picture of cartoon characters in front of the students.
- Explain the proper format of descriptive writing and provide a writing sample.
- Ask students to choose their favorite character and do a brainstorming about the features of the character.
- When done, ask students to write their description in proper format.

Assessment:
- Give a clear direction on how to evaluate based on the criteria of the checklist.
- Ask students to evaluate their own writing work.

Checklist	YES	NO
1. Does your paragraph have a topic sentence?		
2. Is your writing written in correct grammars? (Less than five errors=Yes, Five or more=No)		
3. Does your writing use diverse descriptive adjectives? (Five or more adjectives=Yes, Less than five=No)		
4. Does each sentence end with a punctuation mark?		

Revising work: Revise your draft based on the checklist, and post it on a class blog to get the teacher's feedback by next week.

B

Sunho's Reflection

Today, I wrote about Frodo, a dog character, from Kakao Friends. When I was done, my teacher gave me a special checklist with four criteria, and I evaluated my writing piece which was unusual work. My paragraph has a topic sentence, so I checked 'YES'. Also, I believe my grammar skill has no problem and I checked 'YES'. For the third criteria, I checked 'YES' because I tried to use many descriptive adjectives. For the fourth, of course, I checked 'YES' because I tried my best to write this paragraph. Since I did my best and I like my writing, so I checked YES for all criteria. However, when my teacher evaluated the writing, she gave me a C, an average grade. My evaluation result was very different from my teacher's and so were my classmates' results. Was I too generous to myself? By next week, I need to revise my writing and post it on the class blog. However, I think my writing is already good. I can't understand why my teacher gave me a C, not an A. On top of all that, there was no comment or feedback from my teacher after the lesson. Hence, I had no idea what to do to make my writing better. I hope I can have a face-to-face conversation with my teacher to get advice for revising my writing piece.

Identify the type of the alternative assessment that the teacher uses in <A>. Then, explain ONE problem of the identified assessment emerged in <B>, and provide a solution from Sunho's perspective.

Your Answer

_____

_____

_____

_____

_____

Chapter

07

25 **Read the passage and follow the directions.**

> *Below is the conversation between two English teachers talking about one type of performance assessment.*
>
> Ms. Lee : Mr. Go! Is everything alright?
>
> Mr. Go : Yes, except for one thing.
>
> Ms. Lee : One thing? What is it about?
>
> Mr. Go : It was about a/an _____ conducted during a group activity last week. I just got feedback from my students.
>
> Ms. Lee : Feedback? What did they say?
>
> Mr. Go : Some of them did not agree with the assessment results. They said they contributed a lot more than the others for the group task completion but received the same grade with the others who did not participate in actively. Besides, they said that some did a group activity only when I was watching them.
>
> Ms. Lee : Oh, that's a big problem.
>
> Mr. Go : It is. Do you have any suggestions to solve this?
>
> Ms. Lee : Well, let me think. First, which criteria and scales did you use for the assessment?
>
> Mr. Go : I used criteria such as preparation, concentration, collaboration, and task completion while observing their group work. Then, I graded them with three levels from A to C.
>
> Ms. Lee : A to C? Hmm . . . Rather than three levels, how about grading them with five different levels, A to E?
>
> Mr. Go : A to E? What's that for?
>
> Ms. Lee : Three levels are not enough to tell students' performance differences. Assessment with five levels has higher reliability.
>
> Mr. Go : Ah-ha! I see.
>
> Ms. Lee : Additionally, I agree with your students that one teacher alone cannot observe every moment of all students.
>
> Mr. Go : You're right. I have 35 students, so it was not easy to assess them by myself during a short group activity time.

Ms. Lee : In my case, I make my students evaluate each other's performance as well. Usually, they evaluate how much each member participates in the group work on a scale of 1 to 10.

Mr. Go : That's a great idea! Then, the assessment process can be more objective.

Ms. Lee : That's right!

Mr. Go : Thank you, Ms. Lee. That was great advice!

Ms. Lee : Any time.

Fill in the blank with ONE type of performance assessment that Mr. Go conducts. Then, write TWO solutions that Ms. Lee suggests Mr. Go should use to solve the problems of the identified assessment. Do NOT copy more than FOUR consecutive words from the passage.

Your Answer

_____

_____

_____

_____

_____

26 Read the passages and follow the directions.

---| **A** |---

Basic Steps of Lesson Procedure

Step 1 Warm-Up

A teacher "warms up" the students by activating the students' background knowledge and introducing new knowledge.

Step 2 Objective Discussion

The teacher is, either explicitly or implicitly, trying to help students learn WHY they are doing what they are doing, and HOW these objectives, if obtained, might help them.

Step 3 Present and Model

A teacher gives students new information they must know or new skills that they must acquire. The teacher here attempts to scaffold, explain, or otherwise break down information for students to grasp the new concepts. In addition to presenting or instructing, the teacher is encouraged to provide models (examples) for students to follow.

Step 4 Guided or Controlled Practice

Students are invited to practice their new skills and become familiar and comfortable with it. This practice is often very controlled, meaning that it is done with a lot of guidance from either the teacher or other experts.

Step 5 Less Guided Practice

Students are given practice that has fewer constraints and higher difficulty. For example, students might be required to do an activity in pairs or groups.

Step 6 Independent Practice

Students perform an independent activity. This means that the student will work alone to demonstrate the knowledge or skills that they have acquired.

Step 7   Assessment

Evaluating student work can happen at any stage of a lesson. _____ (TWO words) generally refers to the kind of assessment that is done during instruction and could include asking questions, giving informal quizzes, and eliciting student participation.

B

Below are excerpts from English lessons.

Activity 1

When teaching prepositions difficult to understand such as "in, on, and at," a teacher draws a graphic organizer on the board to show that there is a certain degree of specificity that each preposition has in regards to location and time.

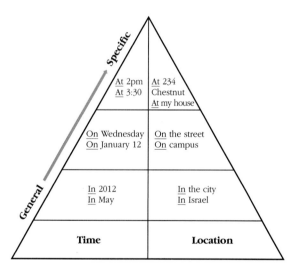

Activity 2

1. The teacher introduces an activity called Impromptu Speech.
2. The teacher gives some target phrases that students are required to use.
3. Students are asked to choose a topic related to the theme they have studied today.
4. Using the given phrases, students speak on that topic for 2 minutes per person.
5. Students vote for the best student and then the teacher gives him or her a reward sticker.

Fill in the blank with an appropriate term and then identify which Step(s) from <A> is exemplified in each activity from <B>. Additionally, write the evidence for each. Do Not copy more than FOUR consecutive words from the passages.

Your Answer

_____

_____

_____

_____

27 Read the passage below and follow the directions.

> Mr. Kim is an English teacher in a middle school. To measure his students' vocabulary knowledge, he developed a proficiency test with 30 multiple-choice items. However, since the test turned out to be ineffective for assessing the students after the administration, Mr. Kim felt the necessity of reviewing some of the test items, which are shown below.
>
> Vocabulary Test
>
> Item 1 There were _____ magazines in the convenience store.
>   ⓐ little   ⓑ no   ⓒ any
>
> Item 2 Would you please _____ me a cup of coffee?
>   ⓐ get   ⓑ delicious   ⓒ fabulous
>
> Item 3 He _____ me to go to the store and get some milk.
>   ⓐ told   ⓑ said   ⓒ spoke
>
> Item 4 Identical twins appear exactly _____.
>   ⓐ different   ⓑ alike   ⓒ ugly
>
> Item 5 The bird in front of the house is an _____.
>   ⓐ owl   ⓑ master   ⓒ decade

Choose TWO poor items in Mr. Kim's test and provide your rationales.

Your Answer _____

_____

_____

_____

_____

Chapter

07

28 **Read the passages and follow the directions.**

A

A/An (1) _____ item consists of a problem, known as the stem, and a list of suggested solutions, known as alternatives. The alternatives consist of one correct answer, and incorrect options, known as (2) _____.

Constructing Effective Alternatives

- All alternatives should be plausible answers, though only one of them should be correct.
- Alternatives should be stated clearly and concisely.
- Alternatives should be parallel in form.
- The alternatives "all of the above" and "none of the above" should not be used.
- Alternatives should be free from clues about which response is correct.

B

The following are some of the testing items which Mr. Choi designed to assess his students' understanding of a reading text, 'What is DNA?' they have read.

Q1. Who gathered the data that helped reveal the structure of DNA?
A. Francis Crick
B. James Watson
C. Rosalind Franklin
D. Shrek, the Monster

Q2. DNA can best be compared to a building:
A. Bricks
B. Blueprint
C. Pricey
D. Residents

Fill in each blank in <A> using ONE word in sequence. Then, referring to <A>, explain the reason why each testing item in <B> is problematic.

_____

_____

_____

_____

_____

29 Read the passages and follow the directions.

A

Ms. Jung's Teaching Log

My students loved today's writing lesson, where they created their own advertisement on commercial products. At first, from the beginning of the lesson, I grouped students with the same ability. According to the group level, also, I diversified the task complexity. For example, I provided a template, some examples of commercial advertisements, and language supports depending on group proficiencies. Hence, all groups successfully completed today's missions and showed great participation. However, still I am contemplating how to evaluate their products. Intensive writing lessons unfold during all the semester. Thus, I want to focus on students' ongoing writing skills and thereby evaluate their abilities based on the written products they have done in class. Besides, since I continue to manage level-differentiated writing lessons I am considering to evaluate students' accumulated works from the same ability groups. Moreover, I will provide students systematic periodic review and valuable feedback on each work so that they can reflect the information about their strength and weakness on the next writing lesson.

| B |

Ms. Jung's Writing Scheme in 2019

Period 1~2   Topic: Make Our Own Commercial Advertisement
Written product: An AD-Poster
Periodic Review

Period 3~4   Topic: Introduce Your Town
Written product: A town map
Periodic Review

Period 5~6   Topic: What are the symbols that represent you?
Written product: Five symbols representing yourself
Periodic Review

Period 7~8   Topic: Do you know online manners?
Written product: Netiquette guideline
Periodic Review

Period 9~10   Topic: Do you prefer to spend or save money?
Written product: Your money plan
Periodic Review

Considering the information in <A> and <B>, identify the type of assessment that Ms. Jung considers to evaluate students' writing skills. Then, explain TWO main testing principles applied to the identified assessment type. Do NOT copy more than FOUR consecutive words.

Your Answer

Build Up New

박현수 영어교육론 Ⅳ 문제은행

Guideline for Pre-service Teachers

초판인쇄 | 2023. 7. 20. **초판발행** | 2023. 7. 25. **공저자** | 박현수·송은우
발행인 | 박 용 **발행처** | (주)박문각출판 **표지디자인** | 박문각 디자인팀
등록 | 2015년 4월 29일 제2015-000104호
주소 | 06654 서울시 서초구 효령로 283 서경빌딩 **팩스** | (02)584-2927
전화 | 교재주문·학습문의 (02)6466-7202

저자와의
협의하에
인지생략

정가 38,000원
ISBN 979-11-6987-404-5

Guideline for Pre-service Teachers

Build Up New

박현수 영어교육론 Ⅳ 문제은행

박현수·송은우 공저

정답 및 모범 답안

Guideline for Pre-service Teachers

토픽별 문항정리
임용시험 최적화 훈련

Build Up New

박현수 영어교육론 Ⅳ 문제은행

2024 교원임용시험 전공영어 대비

Build Up New

박현수 영어교육론 Ⅳ 문제은행

박현수·송은우 공저

정답 및 모범 답안

Guideline for Pre-service Teachers

토픽별 문항정리
임용시험 최적화 훈련

01 Second Language Acquisition

📖 본책 p. 22

📝 기입형

문항번호	정답	
01	pushed output	
02	scaffolding	
03	u-shaped	
04	metacognitive	
05	(1) collocations	(2) interference
06	contextualized minimal pairs	
07	(1) repetition	(2) pushed output
08	uptake	
09	notice the gap	
10	fossilization	
11	(1) negative	(2) positive
12	(1) interference	(2) foreignizing (또는 foreignization)
13	(1) focus-on-form / focus on form	(2) dictogloss
14	(1) controlled	(2) automatic

본책 p. 46

01 In <B>, Juwan goes through 'fossilization' in that he keeps mispronouncing 'island' ['aɪlənd] into 'island' [áislənd], even following the teacher's repeated correct pronunciation of 'island' ['aɪlənd]. Also, Minju shows 'hypercorrection' in that she mispronounces even /l/ sound into /r/ sound caring too much for /r/ sound after the teacher's explicit correction on confusing sounds, /r/ and /l/.

02 The regulatory style that Mr. Kim's students think the most appropriate is 'identified regulation' in that they put a high value on studying English as known in Items 6 and 7. On the other hand, they think 'external regulation' the least appropriate, as shown in Items 1, 2, and 3, because they do not obey and comply with others' opinions to study English.

03 lexical. Minwoo makes collocation errors that are negatively influenced by his native language (interference). Therefore, the lesson in <B> can help Minwoo avoid making such errors by raising his awareness of the acceptable collocations (word combinations) in English.

04 Jaesuk has strong (high) interpersonal intelligence in that first he learns better in group works and also he is good at helping others and listening to their opinions as "people smart".

05 According to <A>, meaning-negotiation occurs to have a mutual understanding between interlocutors when there are communication breakdowns. In <B>, for example, Issac uses a clarification request by asking "Many human?" and a confirmation check saying "So, you mean, Koreans like Kimchi itself and also for cooking?". As for Minju, she uses a comprehension check saying "Understand?".

06 Ms. Park suggests that the errors are due to overgeneralization, whereas Ms. Kim thinks her students' errors are caused by interference (negative/interlingual transfer of L1). In the case of Ms. Kim, based on the contrastive analysis hypothesis, she believes if she teaches students all grammatical differences between English and Korean preemptively, their errors can be prevented.

07 In this conversation, Student 1 employs the strategy of keeping the floor, saying 'like, something like, I mean', which enables her to fill pauses and to gain time to think (to keep the turn to speak) during the conversation. On the other hand, Student 2 uses an approximation strategy saying an alternative term 'trees' instead of the target word 'maple trees'.

08 scaffold. Ms. Ahn helps his students to complete the writing task successfully in two ways: first, by arranging mixed-level grouping, she encourages the advanced and low-level students to collaboratively write down the ending of the story successfully. Also, walking around the classroom, she provides students with feedback, suggestions, or language help as needed.

09 As Topic clarification in <A>, Eric says "How so?" in <B>. With this utterance, he makes Mark provide detailed information about the topic, the uses of *salt*. Also, by saying "By the way, why are you so interested in salt usage?", as Topic shifting, he draws a new topic for conversation, *sugar*.

10 scaffolding. In <B>, the teacher uses a semantic map and a group work (group discussion) as scaffolding strategies. The semantic map shows the relation between new words and concepts. A group discussion, also, helps students to successfully understand difficult words and new concepts.

11 In <B>, the teacher says "I watch it with my sister?" as implicit and output-prompting feedback. Following his/her feedback utterance, the student self-corrects his incorrect form, *watch*, into correct form, *wached*, leading to the acquisition of past tense, *ed-ending*.

12 Between the two lessons, Lesson A leads students to notice the gaps between their utterances and correct forms. For example, the teacher in Lesson A makes students complete the given task, making a promotional poster, first. Then, she requires them to focus on their problematic utterances by giving corrective feedback with further explanation, not preselecting and presenting the grammatical points.

13 Graph (a) shows Soomin's case, while (b) is Jaewoo's. Regarding Soomin's case, she continues studying English hard even after the recovery stage with a comparable increase in cultural development. Differing from Soomin, Jaewoo adapts to the new culture without the benefit of an increase in language proficiency, resulting in the proficiency gap between Soomin and Jaewoo.

14 Soo-ah tends to be a field-independent learner who focuses on details too much. Thus, she needs to focus on the overall meaning and main idea through a summarizing activity. However, as a field-dependent learner, Ji-eun is easy to follow the whole content but frequently makes errors. Thus, she needs to do a proofreading activity, where she notices and self-corrects some errors.

15 Mr. Kim relies on the Natural Approach which puts emphasis on students' understanding of English. In class, above all, he maximizes students' exposure to the target language input in meaningful contexts. In addition, he wants to delay students' production of language until they have sufficient comprehension ability.

16 Ms. Kim uses a clarification request and a didactic recast as corrective feedback. Regarding the former, by saying that "Excuse me?", she prompts the student to provide a response. As for the latter, she reformulates the student's utterance minus the grammatical error, saying that "You left home at 7 a.m!".

17 ergative. A certain phase underlined in <A> indicates backsliding where students go through in the learning process. For example, in the beginning, they use the verb "broke" in transitive and ergative context. However, at the next step, they recognize the ergative construction, "The vase broke" as an error.

02 Classroom Context (1)

기입형

📖 본책 p. 84

문항번호	정답	
01	(1) blended	(2) dialogue journals
02	(1) referential questions	(2) clarification request
03	subject-integrated	
04	(1) recast	(2) uptake
05	Community Language Learning (대소문자 무관)	
06	uptake	
07	(1) comprehensible input	(2) comprehension check
08	(1) facilitator	(2) recast
09	advance organizers	
10	theme-based	
11	digital literacy	
12	Think-Aloud / Think-aloud	
13	reflective	
14	Blended Learning (대문자)	
15	readability (대소문자 무관)	

서술형

📖 본책 p. 110

01 minimal pairs. Ms. Kim's opinion is more appropriate to explain the teaching materials and technique for the following reason: the activities teach students pronunciation explicitly first by making them to discriminate (listening) minimal pairs such as sheep and ship or slip and sleep and then to imitate the pairs in isolation and in contrast.

02 Ms. Park takes theme-based instruction in that she organizes her lesson based on the real-world topic, social media. Through it, she wants to maximize students' motivation and encourage the use of four skills in a balanced way.

03 sociolinguistic. As a response to the compliment, Speaker B uses a self-praise avoidance strategy by downplaying the value of the hat.

04 **Version 1**
Ms. Kim does not apply two principles: 'challenge students for both higher and lower levels of ability' and 'be fair to all students'. In Step 5, the teacher does not provide the advanced level students with any extra activities but leaves them feeling bored and waiting for the others. Besides, in Step 6, when scoring students' work, the teacher does not take off points for advanced students' mistakes, which is unfair to the lower level students.
Version 2
Ms. Kim does not apply the two principles: 'challenge students for both higher and lower levels of ability' and 'be fair to all students'. In Step 5, despite the fact that the advanced level students finish Activity 2 early and feel bored, she does not provide any extra activities to challenge them. Besides, in Step 6, she gives a whole mark only for the advanced although they make minor slips, which is unfair to the lower levels.

05 **Version 1**

Textbook B is appropriate for Mr. Lee's students based on the following two reasons: first, since it provides new words through reading texts and gives chances to use a guessing strategy, they do not need to mechanically memorize them. Besides, it includes enough meaning-focused activities which enable them to practice actual communication without worrying about accuracy.

Version 2

Textbook B is appropriate for Mr. Lee's students for two reasons: presenting new words in reading text and then encouraging a guessing strategy, and including meaning-focused communicative activities. With Textbook B, that is, students do not have to mechanically memorize words as they desired. Also, they can be free to engage in actual communication without bothering about accuracy (making mistakes/using incorrect forms).

06 According to the evaluation results, the textbook uses real-world language excellently but does not facilitate level-differentiated learning. Thus, as a solution, Ms. Kim decides to prepare extra writing activities for the advanced and a list of new vocabulary for the beginners so that all students can be highly motivated in the lesson.

07 Activity 2 is the most appropriate for Mr. Kim with the following reasons: first, it facilitates students to build their comprehension ability through physical actions without forcing them to produce the target language. Besides, based on the meaningful context, 'Making Fondue', it provides them with the target language input.

08 Type C is the most appropriate for Mr. Kim's lesson with the following reasons: first, during the task cycle, students can maximize their talking time during communicative group activities. Besides, in the language focus, students can learn and practice language errors occurred during their task performance, not predetermined language items.

09 • Students will be able to generate example vocabulary including target word parts (prefix, suffix, and root).
   • Students will be able to figure out the meaning of nonsense words based on the analysis of word parts.

10   For Ms. Park, Syllabus 2, which is a task-based syllabus, is more appropriate in that her students can express their own ideas and opinions while performing the tasks related to their real lives and then learn related grammar and vocabulary based on their task performance, not pre-selected.

11   Conversation 1 shows a display question, "where was she?", commonly used to check students' learning. On the other hand, Conversation 2 exemplifies referential questions like "What is your favorite social media?" (or "Do you have any specific reason?"), which requires students' personal information.

12   Textbook A is appropriate for Ms. Song's lesson because it provides students with opportunities to create or explore personal/real-world content students want. Besides, sufficient problem-solving activities can help students explore new knowledge all by themselves.

13   The mentioned lesson has the strong point that it gives students a chance to perform a real-life task using the target form. On the other hand, it shows the weak point in that it does not use an inductive approach (or use a deductive approach) and confuses beginners by giving a direct rule explanation with metalanguages.

14   Example 2 satisfies Mr. Kim's two suggestions. First, the teacher asks the open-ended question(s), "have you ever had similar feelings as the writer?" (or "Really? When?"). Besides, he provides his real feeling/ thoughts as a response to the student's utterance, saying "You must've been so lonely!", not a simple evaluation.

15   affective filter. Ms. Kim follows three important teaching principles: maximize interaction between students, speak only English in the classroom and no interruption from a teacher during group works. However, her only English classroom seems to raise students' affective filter during the class in that they never use Korean in class. Also, owing to her 'no interruption' principle, they can not get any help during group work.

16 gambits. Ms. Song uses the lexical approach in that she directly teaches lexical chunks (or gambits) as seen in the lesson procedure. She believes that students can express their opinions/ideas more effectively or have a natural and fluent conversation by using lexical chunks (or gambits).

17 The teachers talk about mobile-assisted language learning. It facilitates collaborative learning through easier communication between students. Moreover, it promotes self-learning and personalized learning by giving students a greater degree of choice. However, it can be inconvenient for working at length such as reading or writing a long text.

18 According to the results of the coursebook evaluation, both teachers mark grammar items, language styles, and English language variety as 'poor'. Thus, as extra teaching materials, they need to prepare the authentic text including the target forms and some dialogues to show informal language styles and various English models used in different countries (World Englishes).

19 Ms. Shin applies methods (b), (d), and (e). First, she elaborates the original text by adding the sentence 'He looked like a crown'. Also, she rewrites the passive form, 'I won't be bought by anyone' into the active form 'Nobody will buy me', less complicatedly. Finally, she changes the more difficult word 'shattered' into a much easier one 'broken' in the modified version.

20 Ms. Kim wants to newly choose Syllabus B because it focuses on reading, speaking and writing skills in the process of the weekly lessons. Specifically, it deals with detailed skills and knowledge such as how to skim, attention getting and collecting information, etc. during each lesson.

21 Textbook B can be recommended for Ms. Kim. First, it has "activities based on real-life situations" so that students can use authentic language as Ms. Kim wishes. Also, it gives students "opportunities for peer evaluation" which enables them to learn from each other and take responsibility for their own learning.

22   The activity in <A> is an Audio-motor unit. According to the teaching log in <B>, Mr. Lee wants to raise students' awareness of Western culture which is immediately applicable in their real lives.

23   Ms. Park uses Think-aloud technique. Through this technique students can learn to monitor their thinking as they read, thereby improving their comprehension. Also, they can identify and solve their confusing points in the text.

24   Mr. Lee wants to personalize the textbook materials to meet his students' needs for easier reading sections and their interests in animals. Accordingly, he decides to use, first, number 6 'Simplifying' and number 4, 'Replacement'.

25   The student uses a phonological avoidance strategy saying 'I liked the wind' to avoid using the word 'breeze' which she cannot correctly pronounce. Besides, she uses a word coinage strategy to compensate her insufficient vocabulary knowledge by inventing a new word 'airballs' that two words 'air' and 'balls' combine together.

26   Ms. Song supplements the original activities by adding extra ones: watching a video clip and presenting their group essay.

27   advance organizer. An advance organizer helps students to activate their schematic knowledge and predict the story. Besides, it facilitates faster learning and longer retention by visualizing the link between their existing knowledge and new knowledge.

03 Classroom Context (2)

본책 p. 174

문항번호	정답	
01	(1) strategic	(2) circumlocution
02	ambiguity tolerance	
03	(1) personalization	(2) focus on form
04	(1) integrated	(2) scanning
05	(1) cohesive devices	(2) coherence
06	blended	
07	(1) peer scaffolding	(2) facilitative anxiety
08	block time class (또는 block scheduling)	
09	(1) impulsive	(2) top-down
10	affective filter	

📖 본책 p. 194

✏ 서술형

01 Suji goes through the first developmental stage, the declarative knowledge stage, in that she knows the rule of the third-person singular '-s' but is not able to use it correctly. Then, Ms. Kim gives direct correction to prevent Suji from permanently internalizing (fossilizing) the incorrect forms.

02 Students can practice a circumlocution strategy through the role-play activity in <B>. According to [Example], Student A does not know the exact target word, 'anniversary'. However, he prevents the communication breakdown by explaining (describing) the unknown word, like "it's a special day. Janny and I got married on the same date last year".

03 Activity 2 is more appropriate for Mi-jin in that she is expected to use speaking and writing skills as well as reading by sharing her preferences or opinions and then writing her anecdote. Also, it encourages her to develop an interpersonal and an affective strategy.

04 Ms. Song's students show ambiguity intolerance and excessive field independence. Thus, Textbook A can raise students' ambiguity tolerance by asking them to guess unfamiliar words from texts. Also, it can help students focus on the whole context while summarizing and sharing their own ideas about reading topics.

05 The new type of learning is experiential (language) learning. Through this, students can have a better understanding of the course material by actually experiencing it and then linking classroom learning with real-world events.

06 Jaemin shows intrinsic: achievement motivation in that he thinks just finishing a free talking course as a great achievement. On the other hand, Suhye has extrinsic: social motivation, because she wants to take the next reading course to keep good connections with three friends who sign up for the course with her this semester.

07 Textbook A is better for David while Textbook B is helpful to Sally. That is, Textbook A consists of an intermediate level of language and contains the topics about science and culture as David wants. Also, Textbook B helps Sally express her ideas/opinions through enough chances for real communication and various genres of model writing with related writing activities.

08 rapport. As seen in the note, the teacher focuses on the strategy, "Value and respect what students think and say."

09 As an instructional technique the teacher chooses (the) audio-motor unit(s) where following his verbal directions, students carry out a series of actions (physical actions) within a cultural routine, 'eating at a restaurant', with required props such as fork, spoon, and knife.

10 task-based. Syllabus A is more appropriate for Mr. Choi with the following two reasons. First, it helps students perform real world tasks with diverse skills. Also, it enables them to learn key expressions, language form, and skills in the process of the task in action.

11 The teaching approach mentioned in the conversation is flipped learning. It enables students to prepare the day's topic with enough time and at their own pace. Also, it can give them more time for collaborative works in class. Finally, it allows teachers to plan remedial lessons based students' learning difficulties observed.

12 The error Jisuk makes in (a) is classified into 'addition' and 'local error'. First, Jisuk adds an unnecessary element 'were' and, also, his error does not interfere with the meaning. Thus, Ms. Park chooses 'recast' as feedback on Jisuk's error because she wants to maintain communicative flow without interruption.

13 Ms. Song focuses on two teaching points: needs analysis and integrated skills lesson. According to needs analysis based on the survey, she brings the reading topic related to students' interest, habitat destruction. Moreover, through observation, she designs the lesson to use diverse skills like reading, speaking, and writing.

14 According to the textbook evaluation in <A> Ms. Park and Mr. Bae need to prepare the extra teaching materials as follows: authentic contents, some vocabulary works and suprasegmental practice.

15 culture shock. To overcome the conflict or discomfort (culture shock) caused by different cultures, students should realize what the differences are between Korean and other cultures. Thus, the culture capsule can be recommended, which is a brief description of some aspect of the target language culture.

04 Receptive Skills

 기입형   📖 본책 p. 234

문항번호	정답	
01	(1) Language Experience Approach (대소문자 무관) (2) personalization	
02	(1) extensive	(2) readability
03	graded readers	
04	(1) information transfer	(2) scanning
05	(1) extensive reading	(2) intensive reading
06	Summarizing (첫 글자 대문자)	
07	(1) top-down	(2) bottom-up
08	jigsaw	
09	metacognitive strategies / strategy	
10	graded readers	
11	interactive	

✎ 서술형

01 The original comprehension question given by T2 requires an inferential level in that students need to infer the implied information in the text. However, inferencing is too demanding for low intermediate students in T1's class. Accordingly, T1 suggests the literal comprehension questions (level) in that they can easily find the answers in the text.

02 The listening activity in Ms. Shin's class is selective listening which requires students to scan information from discourse-level listening texts. While listening to the interview for 3-4 minutes, students do not have to process all information but listen to specific information needed to fill in the table such as numbers of bedrooms, rent cost, and personal preferences.

03 Language Experience Approach (대소문자 무관). Language Experience Approach is appropriate for Ms. Lee's new class. First, since the reading text/topic is closely related to students' own experiences, it can highly motivate them. Besides, this reading technique facilitates various language skills in that it gives students a chance to share their experiences and then read their own text the teacher transcribes.

04 In Stage 1 and Stage 3, students are expected to use both levels of processing. In Stage 1, they elicit their prior knowledge and new information about the metaverse through a video clip. Also, they preview some words and phrases extracted from the text before reading. Also, in Stage 3, they should answer some questions of literal and inferential levels. That is, they find out information stated in the text and beyond the text.

05 Mr. Kim uses a think-aloud technique so that his students can improve their reading comprehension. By saying aloud their thoughts (reading process) based on the given questions students monitor (build) their comprehension.

06 The reading text that Mr. Choi chooses does not satisfy two criteria of exploitability and presentation for the following reasons. According to the evaluation results, it is not appropriate to teach target reading strategies. Moreover, its illustration does not appeal to students.

07 Ms. Park originally considers readability to choose a reading text but, after the conference, she newly takes into account suitability of content. Thus, she chooses a new text about 'How to write a text message' instead of writing poetry and gives them a chance to personalize the reading text by asking them to send an actual text message using the tips from the text.

08 The SQ3R technique is used in Ms. Choi's lesson. Based on its five steps, Jaemin can understand the text better and become an effective reader. Also, through the reciting/rewriting step, he can enrich his vocabulary (memorize new words more easily).

09 The lesson procedure follows objectives (3) and (6). In the lesson, students in groups skim the text quickly to find out the main idea. Also, they discuss how and why to divide the given text into two separate ones that make sense.

10 semantic mapping/map. In Step 2, the visual strategy helps students predict the upcoming reading text based on their prior (schematic) knowledge about the topic, mental health. Also, in Step 6, it enables them to integrate their existing knowledge on the topic with one newly obtained from the text so that they can better understand and remember what they read.

11 The activity exemplified in the lesson is an information transfer listening activity where students can focus on listening skills without being overwhelmed by the extra burden of using any other skills.

12 Activity 1 focuses on literal comprehension and Activity 2 requires interpretive comprehension. In Activity 1, the answers to whether the sentences indicate facts or opinions are explicitly written in the text. As for Activity 2, the two why questions make students infer the answers which are not directly stated in the story.

13 graded readers. Minjin points out two benefits after reading the graded reader(s) which are fit for her level. First, she can gain confidence ahead of fluently reading English books. Second, she can easily acquire new words because they are repeatedly exposed within context.

14 The listening tasks mentioned in <B> allow students to engage in predicting and inferential listening, respectively. In the first task, they are supposed to predict what they are going to hear based on the title and given visuals. During the second task, also, students are asked to infer the speaker's intention and feelings with their schematic knowledge, which are not explicitly stated in the text.

15 Exploitability. With highly marked exploitability and authenticity, Text B is the most appropriate for Ms. Song's lesson. First, it satisfies Ms. Song's reading purpose that she wants to improve students' reading skills through diverse reading strategies. Besides, it consists of authentic language which stimulates students' motivation.

16 According to the conversation in <B>, Jun-ho has difficulty in finding whether ideas of a text is properly organized or not, which is a matter of coherence. Hence, Worksheet A can be suggested for Jun-ho, which is to check the coherence of a text by asking to select one sentence irrelevant to the whole passage.

17 The alternative listening type is extensive listening, which has two characteristics: first, students can choose for themselves what they listen to based on their interests. Second, listening materials can be obtained from diverse up-to-date digital sources such as YouTube and TED Talks.

05 Productive Skills

 기입형   📖 본책 p. 300

문항번호	정답	
01	(1) rapport	(2) incidental / implicit
02	register	
03	(1) dicto-comp	(2) dialogue journals
04	reasoning-gap	
05	(1) adjacency	(2) suprasegmentals
06	cohesive devices	
07	dicto-comp	
08	(1) Error Correction Code	(2) inductive
09	(1) suprasegmental	(2) intelligibility
10	dictocomp / dicto-comp	
11	proofreading	
12	genre-based	
13	redundancy	

01 decision-making. Ms. Song uses the activity because it facilitates students' integrated skills and also enables them to be more responsible and independent learners. During the activity, students need to read a passage, write a paragraph, and share their ideas. Besides, they make the best decision among the five options for themselves.

02 intelligibility. Activity 1 focuses on suprasegmentals in that students can practice different types of intonation such as falling, rising, fall-rise, or rise-fall. On the other hand, Activity 2 focuses on segmental phonemes in that students discriminate individual sounds (vowels and consonants) of minimal pairs called out by the teacher.

03 Mr. Lee asks for Ms. Kim's advice about two problems with his English lesson, 'uneven turn-taking' and 'error reinforcement'. For even turn-taking, Ms. Kim suggests that Mr. Lee should prepare a classroom task like a jigsaw where all students take individual roles. Also, to prevent error reinforcement, she urges (invites) him to provide students with a follow-up activity as a treatment for their repeated errors.

04 In terms of two features, 'language formality' and 'performance effects', Text 1 consists of a spoken language, and Text 2 represents a written language. For example, Text 1 uses the relatively informal expression 'started' while Text 2 employs 'commenced' as a more formal expression for the same meaning. Besides, Text 1 shows the speaker's hesitation and pauses like 'um' and 'em' for two/three seconds, but Text 2 does not.

05 adjacency pairs. Activity 1 focuses on adjacency pairs mentioned in <A>, with which it teaches students how to appropriately respond to the other's utterance in terms of conversational skill development.

06 The text in <B> uses 'reference' and 'lexical cohesion' to join sentences together. For example, the word 'the sport' is referred to 'it' in the text. Also, 'the sport' is not only repeated but also used as the superordinate word of 'soccer' in the subsequent sentence.

07 Step 3 and Step 5 have the wrong description of the writing process. First, not process-oriented writing, but product-oriented writing is explicitly stated in Step 3 although students have the chance to revise their own writings. Also, in Step 5, students are asked to finalize their informational essay in terms of the style of the writer-based writing, whose purpose is to give the necessary information to the readers.

08 The non-native speaker in <B> lacks (a) grammatical(linguistic) competence and (b) sociolinguistic competence. As seen in conversation, she continues making errors of past tense by saying "go" and "is" instead of "went" and "was". Also, when the native speaker gives a compliment, she gives sociolinguistically inappropriate answer to it. That is, she says "No, it's not good at all." instead of "thank you".

09 dictocomp (dicto-comp, dicto-composition). Dictocomp satisfies Jaeho's needs in that it helps him to practice writing in the paragraph level after listening to a short story. Also, it helps him rewrite what he has listened to based on some language support like key words from the short story.

10 Lesson B is more appropriate for Ms. Song for the two following reasons: first, based on the dialogue and given questions, students notice the target forms underlined and discover the rule by themselves. Besides, through the writing activity, they can have the chance to express their own ideas while using the forms.

11 The teacher's written feedback is called Error Correction Code (ECC) based on two correction principles: first, Mr. Park indicates errors only related to the target grammar rules (i.e., articles and subject-verb agreement), which helps Saewha reduce her cognitive load. Plus, since he shows the types and the locations of errors without providing correction, Saewha can correct them by herself and learn the rules more clearly.

12 conference (conferencing). As shown in the conversation, the strong point of Eunji's writing lies in the introduction with a clear thesis statement (or main idea) and conclusion recapping key points. However, her writing lacks cohesion (clear relationship) between sentences. Thus, the teacher suggests using some linking words like 'moreover' to show the clear relationship between sentences.

13 formality. The lesson procedure in <A> shows a role-play activity with two advantages. Through it, students can learn appropriate English expressions related to "apology" in real (diverse) situations. Therefore, they can effectively internalize the target expressions by using them in diverse (meaningful) situations.

14 sociolinguistic. The activity in <B> focuses on the adjacency pairs. As two utterances given by two speakers, they represent that the second utterance is functionally dependent on the first. Through this activity, the teacher instructs students to appropriately respond to each other.

15 Two types of cohesion exemplified in the conversation are 'demonstrative reference' and 'clausal substitution'. Firstly, saying 'that', the student refers to 'I practice speaking a lot with my friends'. Also, he substitutes 'I use English in daily life occasionally' to 'so'. Such cohesive devices can help interlocutors better comprehend each other by connecting information between utterances.

16 The written conversation in <A> is a dialogue journal. Through it, Do-Joon can build a rapport with the teacher. Also, he can practice basic writing mechanics such as correct punctuation, capitalization, and spelling by writing regularly.

17 intelligibility. The lesson procedure in <A> deals with segmental and suprasegmental units (segmentals and suprasegmentals). At the beginning of the lesson, students use minimal pairs to distinguish the two segmental units of /r/ and /l/. In the latter part of the lesson, they do a role-play giving stress to content words in the given sentences.

18 According to Mr. Park's teaching log in <A>, he plans a jigsaw activity in <B> for his speaking class for the following two reasons. First, a jigsaw allows students to understand the material in depth while sharing and integrating information for peer-teaching as he pleases. Second, each student can develop self-efficacy while contributing to the group with their own expertise.

19 cohesive. The teaching technique the teacher uses is demonstration (modeling). That is, she demonstrates the entire writing process, from choosing proper words, to cohesively combining the information, to completing a coherent paragraph through Step 1 to Step 5.

20 Ms. Lee does not implement suggestions (d) and (e). As for (d), instead of teaching students subtleties of tone such as pitch, speed, and rhythm, she highlights that what they say is more important than how they say. Regarding (e), Ms. Lee only checks their efforts for preparing interview without considering voice volume and clear articulation.

Vocabulary & Grammar

☑ 기입형

📖 본책 p. 372

문항번호	정답	
01	frequency	
02	structured input	
03	concordancer	
04	(1) explicit	(2) word formation
05	input processing	
06	(1) unplanned	(2) guessing
07	(1) lexicogrammatical	(2) corpus
08	Frequency	
09	consciousness-raising task / CR task	
10	(1) sentence combining	(2) focus on form
11	(1) garden-path	(2) inductive
12	(1) structured	(2) form-meaning

📑 본책 p. 400

✎ 서술형

01 Feedback 1 is more appropriate for Mr. Park in that it provides detailed information (feedback) on both content and form (grammar and idea levels) by pointing out good organization skills, insufficient description and some grammatical errors such as tense and subject-verb agreement.

02 dictogloss. In the lesson procedure, Step 2 and Step 3 lead students to focus on form strongly. In Step 2, students are required to reconstruct the text they have listened to, focusing on 'would', and 'used to' related to the past habits. Then, in Step 3, by comparing reconstructed text with the original text, they find out when and how to use the target forms 'would', and 'used to' respectively.

03 Activity B exemplifies the grammar teaching approach mentioned in <A> in that the target forms are taught in a communicative activity or exercise. After presenting when and how to use 'relative pronouns' such as who, which, that, and what, in the short text, it makes students do a communicative exercise, sharing their thoughts using the target forms.

04 Task B is appropriate for Ms. Choi in that, first, its short story format provides language at the level of discourse and gives the meaningful context for students to understand the language as a whole. Besides, it can be used to evaluate students' knowledge related to context, grammar, and vocabulary simultaneously by leaving blanks for a lot of, can, attitude, etc.)

05 Activity 2 is more useful in that it requests students to use the target forms in communicative situations. For example, they provide their real information using the target forms as 'I go to school at 8 o'clock' and 'I eat fried rice or French toast.'

06 Activity 2 is more appropriate for Ms. Lee's lesson purposes in that students notice how the highlighted target forms work in an authentic context. Besides, they figure out (discover/discuss) the rules (when to use) of target forms based on the given questions.

07 word family. Activity 2 exemplifies teaching vocabulary based on word family in that the text introduces a set of words including a base form and its inflections/derivations, produce, producer, products, and production.

08 Ms. Park has used input flooding and input enhancement techniques. The former leads students to frequently be exposed to the target forms within context. The latter helps students easily notice the highlighted target forms in bold within the text.

09 The grammar teaching technique used in the lesson procedure is a consciousness-raising (CR) task. Through Step 2, students pay attention to the target forms, double-object and single-object verbs by figuring out the number of object(s) in each sentence. Then, in Step 3, they find out the difference between 'double-object verbs' and 'single-object verbs' by distinguishing between grammatical and ungrammatical sentences.

10 Ms. Choi has two teaching purposes in her grammar lesson: making students focus on form in context and teaching accurate uses of target forms. By providing example sentences of target forms in Text 1, she makes students focus on the target forms within context. Then, with chances to correct errors of target forms in Text 2, she encourages them to accurately use the target forms, the third-person singular '-s', and plural forms.

11 concordance. According to Ms. Song's two teaching purposes, students learn the word 'temporary' through authentic language examples in different contexts and its collocations.

12 With vocabulary analysis in <A>, Mr. Kim helps students to approach an unknown word '*illiterate*'. That is, he asks students to get the meaning of '*illiterate*' by guessing the meaning of two morphemes '*literate*' and '*il-*' as a root and a *prefix*, each.

13 In terms of word formation, the words 'ad' and 'sweeten' belong to clipping and derivation respectively. As an example of clipping, 'ad' has the same meaning but is a shortened form of 'advertisement'. Also, the new word 'sweeten' is created by adding the suffix '-en' to the word 'sweet' as the process of deviation.

14 The students in \<B\> are taught 'Word family and collocations' of the word 'active'. They pick up 'active', 'act', and 'action' as word family that has common features. Also, in terms of collocations, they figure out that the adjective 'active' comes with the adverbs 'very' and 'highly' from the example sentences.

15 Students acquire the target forms based on focus on form. In this approach, the target forms, 'V-ed' and 'V-ing', are provided in context and students are asked to use the forms in a meaning-focused activity, writing an essay.

16 Mr. Nam suggests that Ms. Oh teaches vocabulary in context. Based on this teaching principle, accordingly, he picks up a concordancer for the advanced level students. Through the activity, students can internalize the target words within an authentic context. Plus, they are equipped with collocations and correct usages of the vocabulary.

17 Unlike traditional approaches to teaching grammar, the grammar instruction assists students to derive grammatical rules from example sentences. Also, it includes steps where they personalize the target forms by applying the rules for their own situation.

07 Assessment

📖 본책 p. 444

문항번호	정답	
01	(1) criterion-referenced	(2) washback
02	(1) washback	(2) discrete-point / discrete-item
03	(1) discrimination	(2) difficulty / facility
04	(1) rational deletion	(2) semantic
05	computer-adaptive testing / test	
06	(1) discrete-point	(2) validity
07	(1) Item discrimination	(2) internal consistency
08	portfolio	
09	(1) norm-referenced	(2) criterion-referenced
10	diagnostic test	
11	integrative	

🗐 본책 p. 462

01 Mr. Shin's listening test has no validity in that it, actually, measures reading and writing skills rather than listening skill itself. That is, students have to read the lengthy and complicated comprehension questions and write long answers.

02 First, Item 3 is problematic in that it measures not students' vocabulary knowledge but their world knowledge about Korean history, which causes its negative item discrimination. Also, Item 5 is problematic because it provides an unintended clue, 'an', and thus all students choose the correct answer, leading to its zero item discrimination.

03 The new formative test in <B> Ms. Song planned is a form of criterion-referenced testing. Different from the existing formative test, it measures integrated language skills in that students write a role play script and do (practice) the role-play. Also, it provides students with the necessary information to be improved next based on the analytic scoring and comments.

04 Dana's essay shows the introduction with a clear thesis statement but insufficient supporting ideas. However, since she too subjectively evaluated her writing, there is a gap between her and Ms. Kim's evaluation results. Thus, Ms. Kim wants to have a training session so that students can evaluate their writings in more objective and reliable ways after understanding each criterion clearly.

05 authenticity. Mr. Park chooses Test 1 based on Criterion 2, whose all items are contextualized.

06 Ms. Lee points out that Mr. Park's speaking test has some problems with practicality and (inter-)rater reliability. First, conducting five types of speaking tests which take 5 or 10 minutes per test for 40 students does not seem practical timewise. Also, the evaluation results from two scorers are inconsistent. For example, in the interview, Student A gets score of 18 from Mr. Park but 10 from Mr. Kim.

07 Type B is more appropriate for Ms. Lee who wants to select the top 10% of students for a new after-school program. As norm-referenced testing, it helps her to make the comparison between students based on the scores in percentiles.

08 The new type of assessment Mr. Park suggests is portfolios which assess students' actual performance based on the best examples of reading tasks from the lessons and their own journals. With these two ways, students' portfolios show strong content validity and washback effect.

09 (1) stem, (2) distractors. Item 2 and Item 4 do not follow the guidelines, 'Keep option lengths similar' and 'use only one correct option', respectively. The former includes one longer option, d. lovely and warm fall, than the others, and the latter includes two possible options, c. a child and d. a boy.

10 analytic. The test violates inter-rater reliability in that, first, Mr. Park assesses fluency in terms of pauses, whereas Ms. Joe sees fluency as the speed of delivery in speaking. Besides, he considers intelligibility while scoring pronunciation, but she uses the pronunciation of native speakers of English as a standard to score the students' pronunciation. Thus, in the scoring results, some discrepancies have occurred between two raters.

11 Test 2 is appropriate for Ms. Kim. First, it integratively (simultaneously) measures many skills like linguistic expectancies, and reading and writing ability as Ms. Kim's testing purpose. Also, its testing items, transitional words and past tense verb forms, are what students have learned last week. Thus, it is closely related to lesson content.

12 The actual test does not match the purpose and scoring procedure presented in the test specifications. First, it measures students' overall proficiency to place them into different levels, not requiring diagnostic information about their strong and weak points. Also, if there is a gap between two evaluators, not the rating they agree on through a discussion but the average score is applied.

13 (1) item facility, (2) item discrimination (대소문자 무관, 순서대로 작성 시 정답처리). Item 1 shows no (zero) item discrimination between both groups because all students of high-ability and low-ability choose the same number of correct answers. Also, it has a nonfunctional Distractor C, which no one chooses.

14 Construct validity and washback are poorly applied in the speaking test. First, the scoring rubric only consists of three criteria, pronunciation, content, and grammar, minus fluency and appropriateness, which should be included. Also, the test result does not give students any diagnostic information on what problems are and how to solve them.

15 Ms. Kim tries to measure the concurrent validity of the new proficiency test. As seen in the scatter chart, the new proficiency test and the existing validated test, TOEFL Junior, are highly correlated. For example, Student A receives the highest score and Student E gets the lowest score on both the new test and TOEFL Junior.

16 The performance assessment exemplified in <A> is (writing) portfolios. Based on this collection, the student can see their periodical writing progress and, thus, have ownership. Moreover, with the teacher's feedback, she recognizes the weak points and sets the next goal to improve her writing skills.

17 achievement. This test is designed to determine how well students achieved the course objectives (or they acquired the knowledge and skills presented during the course work). Also, the test includes particular material/contents covered during the course.

18 Ms. Han focuses on content validity and washback (effect) on the test. First, she designs the test based on what students have learned in class. (or aligns exam questions with the course content). After the exam, by informing students of their strengths and weaknesses during the discussion, she helps them better prepare for further study. She, also, plans the next lesson based on linguistic area to be improved.

19 The reading lesson in <B> focuses on the following two objectives: "distinguish between literal and implied meanings". and "analyze the language from the text to better understand the characters". Firstly, with the preset questions, students figure out the surface and the implied meanings of "free, free, free", and "Maria". Then, they identify words describing Mr. and Mrs. Mallard and fill in the character sketch chart.

20 (1) practicality, (2) washback. In terms of practicality and reliability, the new evaluation form can solve the problems of the narrative evaluation which depends on the teacher's impression. That is, ticking off each skill on the checklist, the teacher can save time and energy for evaluation. Also, thanks to its explicit and clear criteria, she can make test results more reliable.

21 (1) alternatives, (2) distractors. The two items, Q1 and Q2, violate Rule 1 and Rule 4, respectively. First, the stem in Q1 is not meaningful in that it does not give a concrete problem. Next, in Q2, the stem is constructed with an interior blank, instead of a question or a partial sentence format.

22 Item 1 is problematic because the same percentage of students in each group choose option d, the correct answer. Thus, since it shows zero item discrimination between the upper and the lower groups. it should be revised.

23 Rubric 1 demonstrates a holistic scoring method, while Rubric 2 is for an analytic scoring method. Considering Mr. Lee's purposes, Rubric 2 can be suggested for two reasons. First, scoring different components of writing skills can give the students information on each individual's strong and weak points. Next, based on the diagnostic information, Mr. Lee can prepare remedial activities to improve students' weaknesses.

24 The alternative assessment in <A> is a self-assessment. As shown in Sunho's reflection, however, it lacks scoring objectivity. That is, the evaluation results are less reliable due to the subjectivity of students. As Sunho mentions, the teacher should provide conferencing, which is to give comments and feedback on students' writing works.

25   observation. Ms. Lee provides two solutions to Mr. Go: diversifying the performance levels from three to five levels and conducting peer assessment.

26   Formative assessment. Activity 1 exemplifies Step 3 while Activity 2 shows Step 6. In Activity 1, the teacher provides new information, prepositions, with a graphic organizer and explains how to use each preposition according to location and time. Activity 2, however, requires students to individually present Impromptu Speech about today's theme.

27   Items 2 and 5 in the test are problematic in that students can answer them much easier for the following reasons. Item 2 has a key answer (i.e., get) whose grammatical category is different from those of distractors (i.e., delicious, fabulous). Item 5 provides an unintended clue, the indefinite article 'an' in the stem, so the test-takers can immediately choose 'owl' that begins with a vowel.

28   (1) multiple-choice, (2) distractors. The two testing items in <B> violate 'Constructing Effective Alternatives' in <A> in terms of two aspects: first, Q1 includes an implausible alternative, 'D. Shrek, the Monster'. which does not serve as a functional distractor. Regarding Q2, one alternative 'C. pricey' is an adjective that is not parallel in form with the other alternatives, a noun.

29   Ms. Jung is likely to consider portfolios that have high content validity and positive washback. First, she wants to evaluate the works which students have done in class. Second, she likes to provide their strengths and weaknesses in written works through periodic feedback.

Build Up *New*

박현수 영어교육론 Ⅳ 문제은행

Guideline for Pre-service Teachers

정답 및 모범 답안

초판인쇄 | 2023. 7. 20.   **초판발행** | 2023. 7. 25.   **공저자** | 박현수·송은우

발행인 | 박 용   **발행처** | (주)박문각출판   **표지디자인** | 박문각 디자인팀

등록 | 2015년 4월 29일 제2015-000104호

주소 | 06654 서울시 서초구 효령로 283 서경빌딩   **팩스** | (02)584-2927

전화 | 교재주문·학습문의 (02)6466-7202

저자와의
협의하에
인지생략

ISBN 979-11-6987-404-5

New Build Up

박현수 영어교육론 시리즈

(I)

BASIC KEY Concepts
for Classroom Teaching

(II)

Authentic Data
for Classroom Teaching

(III)

2011~2023학년도
기출문항 분석

(IV)

Topic별 문항 정리
-임용시험 최적화 훈련

Build Up New

박현수 영어교육론 ⅣV 문제은행

2023 고객선호브랜드지수 1위
교육(교육서비스)부문 1위

2022 한국 브랜드 만족지수 1위
교육(교육서비스)부문 1위

2021 조선일보 국가브랜드 대상
에듀테크 부문 수상

2021 대한민국 소비자 선호도 1위
교육부문 1위

2020 한국 산업의 1등
브랜드 대상 수상

2019 한국 우수브랜드
평가대상 수상

2018 대한민국 교육산업 대상
교육서비스 부문 수상

2017 대한민국 고객만족
브랜드 대상 수상

브랜드스탁 BSTI
브랜드 가치평가 1위

9 791169 874045
13

ISBN 979-11-6987-4

www.pmg.co.kr 학원 문의 02-816-2030 동영상강의 문의 02-6466-7201